ROUTLEDGE LIBRARY EDITIONS:
SOCIOLOGY OF EDUCATION

Volume

I0129569

CLASS, IDEOLOGY AND COMMUNITY EDUCATION

CLASS, IDEOLOGY AND COMMUNITY EDUCATION

WILL COWBURN

R Routledge
Taylor & Francis Group

LONDON AND NEW YORK

First published in 1986 by Croom Helm Ltd

This edition first published in 2017
by Routledge
2 Park Square, Milton Park, Abingdon, Oxon OX14 4RN

and by Routledge
711 Third Avenue, New York, NY 10017

Routledge is an imprint of the Taylor & Francis Group, an informa business

British Library Cataloguing in Publication Data
A catalogue record for this book is available from the British Library

ISBN: 978-0-415-78834-2 (Set)
ISBN: 978-1-315-20949-4 (Set) (ebk)
ISBN: 978-1-138-22527-5 (Volume 14) (hbk)
ISBN: 978-1-138-22529-9 (Volume 14) (pbk)

Publisher's Note
The publisher has gone to great lengths to ensure the quality of this reprint but points out that some imperfections in the original copies may be apparent.

Disclaimer
The publisher has made every effort to trace copyright holders and would welcome correspondence from those they have been unable to trace.

Class, Ideology and Community Education

WILL COWBURN

CROOM HELM
London • Sydney • Wolfeboro, New Hampshire

© 1986 Will Cowburn
Croom Helm Ltd, Provident House, Burrell Row,
Beckenham, Kent, BR3 1AT
Croom Helm Australia Pty Ltd, Suite 4, 6th Floor,
64-76 Kippax Street, Surry Hills, NSW 2010, Australia

British Library Cataloguing in Publication Data
Cowburn, Will
    Class, ideology and community education.
    1. Community schools — Great Britain
    2. Education — Great Britain
    I. Title
    370.19'4'0941   LB2820

    ISBN 0-7099-3497-1
    ISBN 0-7099-4830-1 Pbk

Croom Helm, 27 South Main Street,
Wolfeboro, New Hampshire 03894-2069, USA

Library of Congress Cataloging-in-Publication Data

Cowburn, Will
    Class, ideology and community education.

    Based on the author's thesis — University of
Sheffield, 1985.
    1. Community education — Great Britain. 2. Labor
and laboring classes — Education — Great Britain.
3. Community schools — Great Britain. 4. Adult
education — Great Britain. I. Title.
LC1036.G7C68   1986   370.19'3   86-16771
ISBN 0-7099-3797-1
ISBN 0-7099-4830-1 (pbk.)

Printed and bound in Great Britain by
Biddles Ltd, Guildford and King's Lynn

CONTENTS

Contents

Appendices

"The great are not great.
The great only appear great
because we are on our knees.
Let us arise."

Jim Larkin

ACKNOWLEDGEMENTS

'Class, Ideology and Community Education' takes its title from and is based upon a thesis completed at Sheffield University in 1985. Thanks are offered to Bill Hampton, my supervisor, for his calm, considered and most useful advice: also to officers in various departments of Sheffield City Council for their assistance. I must also thank all the members and users of Open Door, Chapel Green, Sheffield Pensioners Action Group and the Community Work Apprenticeship Scheme; and the staff of Northern College, in particular Bob Fryer, its Principal, for the access and time so willingly given.
     Though I had to give the community school a fictitious name and location, the staff know who they are and to them a special thanks has to be given for the open welcome they provided and the freedom with which they spoke about community education and their school. A special thanks to the Head and Community Tutor who gave their time and made sure mine wasn't wasted. The advice given by Simon Frith and Bob Burgess of Warwick University helped to make the transition from thesis to book so much less daunting than expected. A debt is also owed to John Rex, who in 1971, when I asked him an important question, answered 'Yes'. And finally I must offer thanks to the Gods for the mortality of the human race, the razor sharp realisation of which is the real author of what follows.

          Will Cowburn.

Chapter One

AN ELABORATE FACADE

"Altruism is cutting off a dog's tail, eating the meat and giving the bones to the dog" Gerald Kersch, 'The Angel and The Cuckoo'.

Ursula felt her heart faint inside her. Why must she grasp all this, why must she force learning on fifty-five reluctant children, having all the time an ugly, rude jealousy behind her, ready to throw her to the mercy of the herd of children, who would like to rend her as a weaker representative of authority. A great dread of her task possessed her. She saw Mr. Brunt, Miss Harby, Miss Schofield, all the schoolteachers drudging unwillingly at the graceless task of compelling many children into one disciplined, mechanical set, reducing the whole set to an automatic state of obedience and attention, and then of commanding their acceptance of various pieces of knowledge. The first great task was to reduce sixty children to one state of mind or being. This state must be produced automatically, through the will of the teacher, and the will of the whole school authority, imposed upon the will of the children. The point was that the headmaster and the teachers should have one will in authority, which should bring the will of the children into accord.1

Ursula Brangwen and her teacher colleagues in Lawrence's Rainbow had a hard time teaching at Brinsley Street School, and the harshness of their experience was not softened by any understanding of why schools and education were as they were. For them, their school was simply one in which a particular way of teaching had to be pursued: it expected and demanded of them that they operate a pedagogy of oppression and none of them really asked why this should be so. Their fatalistic, unquestioning acceptance of their situation stands as the antithesis to an educated response, where education is concerned with trying to understand the world, with trying to make sense of it. In <u>The Rainbow</u> the teachers show us how necessary it is for them to behave as they do, within the setting of the school: they do not give us any explanation as to why the school should provide the setting it does. And it is this point which is crucial if we wish to understand education in fiction and fact: the actors' accounts for their actions can only tell us part of the story, can only present some of the picture. To make sense of the way in which Ursula and her colleagues had to teach we have to go beyond their explanations and beyond Brinsley Street School.

Seventy years after our fictional characters were doing their duty the question of understanding education and how it is practiced is as important as ever; and again, if we are to understand it we have to go beyond the accounts given to us by the principal actors. This poses certain problems for our principal actors are teachers and education-alists and they tend to be reluctant to accept that their accounts of the practice of education may be at odds with its reality. To clarify what is meant here we can think of football supporters, who, when arrested for violent behaviour, explain that they simply hate the supporters of the opposing team. Serious students of 'soccer hooliganism' may well give an account of the violent behaviour which talks of working class culture, of locality, of masculinity; one which, in short, has a higher level of adequacy to it. With regard to teachers and educationalists, we have to ask whether there is any valid reason as to why their accounts should be accepted as adequate explanations of education's practice. For it is the case, whether we are dealing with 'hooligans' or teachers, we are deal-ing with people, actors in a social world. If soccer violence can be addressed by social scient-ists, so too can education. In both areas social scientists can seek to go beyond the reasons given by the interested parties in order to try to ex-plain what is really going on. If the point we are making is disturbing and upsetting, if there is resentment at having teachers bracketed with soccer hooligans, then it is important to ask why there should be such a reaction. Is it assumed that the 'educated' are exempt from sociological analysis. Are they 'special' people whose thoughts as to what is going on correspond with that which is going on? The demand we are making here, provocative or not, is simply that we avoid making the mistake of treating what teachers and educationalists say about education, as the only material to be subjected to analysis. Their accounts are important, but they are only accounts, which may or may not come near to explaining the way in which, and to what purpose, the education system operates. For, of course, the subject of our work is the education system, not the teachers and educationalists, as individuals, working within it. It was the school, as an expression of the education system, which demanded that Ursula and her colleagues 'chose' to teach as they did. How similar today's system is to that of Ursula's time is not at issue; rather, what is at issue is an education system, the 'function' of which may be hidden from and misunderstood by many who work within it.

We will be concerned to illuminate that which is hidden and to facilitate understanding, and with specific reference to an aspect of the education system, that is, community education. Throughout this work 'community education' will be used to refer to and describe those mainstream educational changes being organised around community schools and community colleges. It will not be used to include the radical adult educational writing and work of Lovett et al for such approaches to education will be utilised as critical aids in the debate with community education. They will be seen, in many ways, as community education's opposites. The task then is to offer a way in which community education can be located and understood.

Broadly there are two methods of inquiry which we describe as the mechanical and the theoretical. The mechanical would examine the explanations of, and claims made for, community education by its practitioners and advocates: it would be concerned with evaluating the chances of success for the aims and objectives of community education. Depending upon the country in which the inquiry was to be made questions would be asked concerning the origins and roots of community education and, in the main, the answers would be accepted at face value. For example, in Britain Henry Morris might well be identified as the founding father of community education owing to the key role he played in establishing the first community college in Cambridgeshire.2 Whilst in the United States of America,

3

Charles Stewart Mott and the C. S. Mott Foundation
might well be similarly identified for the role
played in founding the first community school in
Flint.3 Having received these explanations for
community education's becoming, the mechanical
inquiry would then concern itself with the changes
which had taken place since and would be interested
to discover to what extent community education was
succeeding. The theoretical method of enquiry,
however, would pursue a different path. With
regard to the origins of community education, the
mechanical method seeks to discover how it came
into existence, whose idea was it: the theoretical
method is more concerned with explaining why community education arrives on stage, and who owns the
theatre. With regard to the practice of community
education, the mechanical method seeks to find out
whether community education is achieving some of
its declared aims, improving the quality of life,
for example: the theoretical method is more concerned with explaining why and how community education comes to be the thing having the aims it has.
The theoretical inquiry treats the claims to objectives and aims as the problematic to be addressed, not something to be taken for granted.

For us the theoretical method is a more valuable one because it aims to tell us why things
happen, as opposed to how they happen. The theoretical method does not over-rely upon the accounts
and explanations offered by the actors; there is no
necessary correspondence between what community
education is doing and what its practioners believe
it is doing. Adopting the theoretical approach
means we are not tied to a particular aspect of our
subject; we can go behind the aims and objectives,
the words of our actors in order to discover the
meaning of the script to which they work. As we
unravel the various threads of community education
we will discover important factors common to
community education in different countries; factors
deeper in meaning that the similarities between the
claims made for community education by its
advocates in the different countries. These deeper
common factors will show to us community education
in a most interesting and rewarding light.

The mechanical method of enquiry was, in many
ways, the mode of operation for the sociology of
education until the early 1970's. It accepted as
non-problematic its overall subject area and tended
to enquire whether x or y was working or not
according to its stated purpose. It saw no need to

4

challenge and demand that stated purposes explain themselves. This mechanical way of studying and researching education was seen as the only valid method, according to Plowden.

Because education is an applied discipline, the relation between research and practice is and should be reciprocal. From studies of what individual teachers are doing, useful pointers can be obtained to fruitful directions for experiment and research: research in education or such ancillary sciences as child development, social psychology or learning theory will throw up ideas with which the innovating teacher can experiment.4

Plowden accorded a value to research only if it directly contributed to the work of the teacher in the classroom, and was openly sceptical of all educational research until "the value of research to classroom practice is demonstrated".5 Research and inquiry, constrained in such a manner, cannot treat certain aspects of school and education as problematic; consequently it is unable to deepen its understanding and this cannot help but lessen its value, despite the insistence from Plowden that these constraints actually gave it its value. By the early 1970's educational research had begun to break free of this methodological straightjacket and had begun to adopt a theoretical approach and enter hitherto restricted areas. It started to go behind the mechanical 'how' of education to its theoretical 'why'. It began to abandon an approach wherein the demands of school and classroom were treated as given and non-problematic. This new approach to research came primarily from the sociologists and it sought to practice as independently as possible; to carry out its work no longer as a supplier to a customer. The new research saw the Plowden, mechanical type, having as its fault, the very element which Plowden praised so highly, the close functional relation to education's practitioners, the teachers in their schools.

This new approach to research would make problematic the areas and things previously accepted at face value. It would aim to "examine, to question, to raise doubts about, to criticise the assumptions on which current policy, current theory and current practice are based".6

This will be our approach: not simply to argue with community education's theories, but to

challenge the assumptions upon which such theories
are based. As we address education and community
education we will be asking questions about real
purposes, not only those purposes which have been
articulated by teachers and educationalists. As we
address and begin to answer theoretical questions
we cannot but help answer the more mechanical ones
for once we comprehend why a phenomenon occurs, we
are well placed to understand whether it can work
or not. And our assessment will be a more valid
and sophisticated one for it will not have confused
the objective purpose of community education and
education overall with the purpose as stated by
interested parties. Reality will not be confused
with rhetoric.

Before we begin to deal with the realities of
education and community education it is necessary
to put forward the analytical tools to be used in
the work. In order to comprehend education it is
essential to step outside it in order to understand
the society of which it is a part and in which it
plays a role. Consequently we must have concepts
appropriate to the facilitation of a social understanding. We need to be able to characterise the
society if we are to understand fully the role of
education in it, and for this we must use the
concepts which have been proved valuable in explaining the social world. Education is, of
course, about educating individuals, but it is
about much more and this cannot be grasped unless
conceptual tools of social analysis are used. Individuals were educated in the age of the coach and
four as they are in the age of the space shuttle
but it is apparent that the ways in which these
individuals were and are being educated are not the
same. The way of educating is different as is the
society in which it takes place. Without the conceptual tools of a social analysis we cannot explain the changes which have taken place both in
the educating and in the society. To understand
the education of our individuals we have to understand the setting in which it takes place; we have
to have an explanation of the social. This social
explanation will never account for every individual, but, of course, social explanations have
never claimed to do so.

Though the education system might claim to be
concerned only with individuals, individuals, per
se, will not be our concern: we will be concerned
with individuals as members of classes and the
individual/class dialectic will be present through-

out our work. In the work we will show how the
strong emphasis given to the individual within
education is part of a process which aims to deny
the significance of class and indeed how it can be
seen as a way in which a class constructed education is represented as being class free, as being
concerned with individuals regardless of class. We
will explore the argument that knowledge is more
usefully related to class interest in the world
than it is to individual ability.

> But the child's consciousness is not something
> 'individual' (still less individuated), it
> reflects the sector of civil society in which
> the child participates, and the social rela-
> tions which are formed within his family, his
> neighbourhood, his village etc. The individ-
> ual consciousness of the overwhelming majority
> of children reflects social and cultural rela-
> tions which are different from and antagon-
> istic to those which are represented in the
> school curricula.7

The validity of what will be our class approach to
the analysis of education will be proven as we
explore our subject areas, and what we mean by
class will best be seen as we use the concept in
our practice of theoretical analysis. However, it
is necessary to give something of an outline of the
concept so as to avoid confusion. Categories of
social classes, such as the Registrar General's in
Britain, do have their uses, though they will not
be used by us: we do not see class as a way in
which societies are stratified, that is, wholes
which are arranged hierarchically according to
occupation; instead we see class in a conflictual
light. Here it is not a whole which is stratified,
rather it is opposites constituted whole by their
opposing. Though class does relate to occupation,
it is not as rungs of a ladder, each nearer to the
top, but all still parts of the same ladder.
For the purposes of clarity we need briefly to
follow Marx here. "All production is an appropria-
tion of nature on the part of an individual within
and through a specific form of society."8 For Marx
this first historic act, production, is the
starting point. Man in whatever society must
reproduce himself and those means which facilitate
self-reproduction. Marx abstracts production in
general in order to place and comprehend it, and
having done so his concern is then with the speci-

7

fic forms of society with their specific modes of production. For Marx and for us, "human beings never produce simply as individuals but only as members of a definite form of society".[9] The society may be feudal, agricultural, capitalist or socialist; whatever form it takes, it is fundamentally a social arrangement which is more than the total of all individuals within it. All societies then, have been and are engaged in production and classes are aspects of the relations of production; they are the outcome of how production is arranged and undertaken. Within a capitalistic society this model of class is basically a dichotomous one with a dominant and dominated class. The dominant class is the one which owns, effectively if not juridically, the means of production; the dominated class owns only its capacity to labour. Marx, naturally, was aware that the position in the real world was not so simple for classes derive from sets of relations of production, one of which may be in the ascendant or the descendant; thus we have a dominant class structure reflecting a dominant, rather than a single set of relations of production. In other words, in a capitalist society there are 'leftover' modes of production from the preceding society and hence 'leftover' aspects of the class system of that society. For Marx and for us it is only necessary to look out of the window at the world in which we live to see that classes are not inert homogeneities without internal contradictions and fractions. For Marx the two major and opposing classes of capitalist society are the bourgeoisie and proletariat and it is how they stand in relation to the means of production that is the most crucial factor in giving them their identities. The critical point to Marx's concept of class is the one of classes opposing each other for it is only in the opposing, the struggle, that they become truly visible. And for Marx, it was this opposing, this struggle, which was the primary motive force producing societal change. As a concept it explains the motive force of change and is the key to any understanding of the specific conjuncture.

Though it is production and the economics of production which give us our classes, classes are not simply about production. And the struggle of the classes does not take place only in the economic arena. If we attempted to locate groups of people in classes purely according to the role they play in the production of surplus value then we

would be guilty of producing a 'marxist' alternative to the classificatory schema of the Registrar General. This would be totally at odds with
the analytical method of Marx for it would be to
define class in stasis, whereas the correct arena
for its analysis is that of class struggle. If
class is about struggle as a way of comprehending
how the world moves then we cannot attempt to stop
the world moving in order to understand class and
the world.

> Class is not this or that part of a machine,
> but the way the machine works once it is set
> in motion - not this and that interest, but
> the friction of interests - the movement
> itself, the heat, the thundering noise. Class
> is a social and cultural formation (often
> finding institutional expression) which cannot
> be identified abstractly, or in isolation, but
> only in terms of relationship with other
> classes; and, ultimately, the definition can
> only be made in the medium of time - that is,
> action and reaction, change and conflict.
> When we speak of a class we are thinking of a
> very loosely defined body of people who share
> the same congeries of interests, social
> experiences, traditions and value-system, who
> have a disposition to behave as a class, to
> define themselves in their actions and in
> their consciousness in relation to other
> groups of people in class ways. But class
> itself is not a thing, it is a happening.[10]

Our working class and bourgeoisie then will
not be defined; rather they will come to define
themselves as we analyse the arena in which they
conduct their educational struggle. We will be
concerned with the relation between education and
the day to day reproduction of capitalist/class
society. We will be concerned with how classes
perceive themselves and others and how they are
perceived and treated by others. And in this day
to day perceiving and reproducing of classes, we
identify class struggle for the perceiving and
reproducing do not simply take place, they are
struggled for.

Closely linked to class, as an explanatory
concept for understanding the world, is ideology.
An ideology is an account for the world or a facet
of it which is at odds with the thing it describes.
Ideologies arise from reality, though a partial

reality, which they then refract and distort in a manner suited to the interests of the ruling group or class of the society in which they occur. A simple example from British History would be that ideology which insisted that the monarch was divinely appointed and was God's chosen representative: this ideology aimed for the consent to government, of those to be governed. Ideologies do not claim to represent the ruling individuals, groups or classes whom they serve; rather they lay claim to universality. Ruling groups and classes do not rule by force alone, nor simply as the result of conscious popular support. Ideologies have to be seen for the assistance they give to the rule of groups and classes; they minimise their need to resort to the use of force and repression in order to continue to rule. "It is the role of ideologies to secure the assent of the oppressed and exploited."11 Ruling groups and classes do not simply manufacture ideologies; ideologies do come from the real world and in various ways are as likely to be subscribed to by their beneficiaries as by those whose assent they seek.

> Class ideologies create three images of the class that is struggling for dominance: an image for itself; an image of itself for other classes, which exalts it; an image of itself for other classes, which devalues them in their own eyes, drags them down, tries to defeat them, without a shot being fired.12

From this point of Lefebvre's we can see that ideologies have to struggle towards achieving their goals. If it were the case that they simply succeeded in a straightforward functional manner then we would hardly be likely or capable of appreciating their existence. As long as we are able to identify an ideology then, it is the case that we have not totally subscribed to it, for then it would no longer be an ideology, but would be the 'truth'. As with our concept of class we do not seek to define it purely as an abstract concept, but to introduce it as a concept so that we might better appreciate it when we witness it in action. Throughout our investigation of class, ideology and community education we will be concerned with the ideological struggle within and over education to ensure its continued service to the bourgeoisie.

> It is necessary that the inferior classes

should continue to be taught to know their position, and to conduct themselves properly. So far I approve of schools.[13]

With the concepts of class and ideology crucially relevant to our way of analysing the educational world, what exactly is the task before us? In a phrase, it is to provide an aetiological account and critique of community education, and it is to do this because such an account and critique are long overdue. As our work progresses we will achieve a clearer understanding of what is meant by community education for the work itself will bring it into a sharper focus. At present community education is something which shimmers in a haze; it has no clear outline and can mean all things to all people. Such a situation protects community education from a certain amount of criticism, for it cannot be criticised as a thing, a coherent whole. Criticisms have to focus on it, a definition at a time, and it can ignore such criticisms by changing its definition of itself, as an educational chameleon. Community education can mean whatever the user of the term wishes it to mean. It is used to describe a variety of educational phenomena and a plethora of approaches to education. It can no longer be allowed to escape the attention of critics by being all things to all people. By the end of our discussion we will have provided an explanatory account as to why a multiplicity of educational practices and philosophies from as far apart as The Philippines, Britain and Japan should seek to present themselves under a title of community education. This will be achieved, not by studying each country with a community education service (an impossible task) but by a careful investigation of WHY community education came to exist in the capitalist country of Britain. As we answer this question we will be locating the key factors which have relevance to all capitalist countries pursuing community education; and the way in which we answer it will act as something of a guide to those who would wish to explain the detailed becoming of community education in other countries. The analytical approach we adopt will produce its rewards regarding community education in the U.S.A. or in Singapore. Why does community education come to exist; what role does it play vis-à-vis class relations and class struggle: these are the significant questions to be posed in countries where class relations are those of dichotomous struggle and conflict.

To explain the arrival of community education we do not need any special tools or ways of explaining, ones which explain only in terms of community education: rather we need a way of accounting for educational change in general, which can then be seen as relevant to the aetiological explanation of community education in particular. Throughout our discussion a certain way of accounting for educational change will be ever present and this way of accounting will produce six specific themes which we will need to be kept at hand as we deal with education in general and community education as our special area of interest. The themes are present throughout the work and in their presence they inform it.

Educational Change

The question as to whether the lower orders in Britain should be educated was raised in a particular period with its own distinctive economic, social and political structure. The way in which the question was posed and the attitudes and possible answers to it depended, to a great extent, upon class position and class interest. Indeed the very question itself was posed as one possible strategy for reproducing a society in which there would continue to be lower orders. As a consequence, the state assisted and eventually state provided education system has to be understood as a way of dealing with the social, economic and political issues held to be problematic to the reproduction of class society. As Chapter Four will demonstrate, education, as a provided system of instruction, enters history's stage, first and foremost, as a weapon of one class to be used against another. Provided education was to teach the working class to know its place and not to oppose its betters. From the very earliest days of the state assisted education system, education was discussed in the light of the service it could give to the economic and political ordering of society. Given education's early anchoring to the bedrock of a fiercely class conscious society, and the role it was to play as a servant to such a society; then the question of educational change can be seen to be a complex and difficult one. When change does take place, how does it happen, and whose interest is it to serve; how does it relate to the economy with its classes of owners and workers, and just how real is it? Is

12

education changed or is its appearance changed?

It is our argument that the economic struggle between the classes of the dominant class relationship of capitalist society, that is, the bourgeoisie and working class, is paralleled by an educational struggle between the same two classes. For the bourgeoisie, its interest lies in ensuring education continues to be a weapon in its hands, whilst the interest of the working class is the utilisation of this weapon against those who wield it. In the early days of state assisted education this struggle was located easily and the clear links between education, economics and politics were there for all to see. However, as capitalism developed and its attendant ideologies grew in sophistication, these links ceased to be glaringly obvious. The difficulty here, of course, is that far too many teachers and educationalists have assumed a thing to be no longer present if its presence is no longer obvious. Consequently they ignore the reality of these links and the struggle of education, and in so doing they further camouflage the class struggle in a provided education system. In effect they recognise the history of provided education and the relevance of class to it (how could they not?) but then they proceed to forget it, for they assume class to be no longer relevant, without having any valid base for such an assumption. They believe change has been so significant as to remove class from education's structure without having constructed any account for such meaningful change. Change seems to be something which happens, in a manner and to a direction which requires no explanation.

For us educational change is primarily the result of class struggle in the educational arena and it is so because of the model of analysis we bring to the arena, and the educational material therein which demands of us that we account for it in such a manner.

Throughout history, patterns of privilege have been justified by elaborate facades. Dominant classes seeking a stable social order have consistently nurtured and underwritten these ideological facades and, insofar as their power permitted, blocked the emergence of alternatives.[14]

How this struggle over education, as an ideological facade, takes place is crucial for an un-

13

derstanding of educational change. This struggle is a part of and an informer to our six themes which themselves will inform much of our discussion.

Liberation and Social Control

In the early and mid nineteenth century Britain the lower orders were striving for an education which would hopefully give them the knowledge they believed they needed to liberate themselves from the conditions in which they were forced to live, work and reproduce themselves. They wished to understand the world so as to change it.

> Only by understanding himself could the working man understand the world in which he lived, and conversely, true self-knowledge was impossible without a comprehension of the structure and historical identity of the section of society in which the personality was formed. The search for such knowledge was both a pre-condition and a result of the growth of class consciousness.[15]

They wanted an education which they believed would enable them to transform the political, social and economic ordering of society. At the same time their masters wanted to provide them with an education which would convince them that the ordering of society was as it should be; wanted to provide them with an education which would, if not negate, then at least considerably weaken any growth in understanding and class consciousness. They believed that "a body of efficient schoolmasters is kept up at a much less expense than a body of police or soldiery".[16]

The outcome of this early and mid nineteenth century struggle was something of a victory for the bourgeoisie, symbolised by the Education Act of 1870 which introduced compulsory schooling. However, the victory, important as it was, in no sense was a final one, nor one without its contradictions; nor could it be for as long as the economic and political system which gave rise to it remained basically intact. The struggle continued but upon a new battlefield. Education pre and post 1870 has to be seen in the light of this struggle. Whether sections of the bourgeoisie and working class are conscious of it or not, it is the case that the bourgeoisie has to continue to struggle to try to

14

achieve a social control education in order that it can reproduce the economic and political structure of society which gives it its privileges and power. We will later see how this struggle provides the key to understanding, for example, the elementary/ secondary education distinction, the notion of a given educable capacity, the concept of an individual intelligence, and the aetiology of community education. In a crude form of shorthand, we can say that a social control education seeks to explain why the world must be as it is; whilst a liberation education seeks to understand the world so as to discover whether it need be as it is. These notions of education relate to classes with interests in conserving the world and with changing it.

Education's Constant Problem: The Working Class

For the bourgeoisie, with its interest in conserving the world and reproducing it as it is, the actual existence of the working class, from which it extracts surplus value, is a constant problem. It is as much a problem now as it was a century past. For the working class to be a class from which surplus value can be extracted, it has to be identifiable as a class: the contradiction, naturally, is that if it is identifiable in the eyes of the bourgeoisie, it must be potentially identifiable to itself. A class with an identity for itself as a class, can oppose as a class. Education, then, has to be understood as a way of attempting to reproduce the working class, as a class in the economic sense, but not to reproduce it as a class in the cultural sense, not as a class with identity for itself. Education is to serve the interests of the bougeoisie by its never ending attempt to resolve the contradictions of this situation. It is a part of the struggle of the bourgeoisie to convince the working class of its own non-existence as a class. Thus it has to denigrate the class and find it lacking whilst claiming to be doing no such thing. Or, in the language of our characterisation of ideology, it deals with class matters but claims to be dealing with universals unconnected to class. In capitalism's formative years it could talk of the ineducability of the working class; could stress how unsuited it was to anything other than the most elementary forms of educational provision. In those early days there was little need for a sophisticated argument and

15

ideology to explain the education/class relationship. This is no longer the case, nor has it been for many years. The bourgeoisie still has a similar task to that of Hannah Moore's time* but it cannot be seen to be attempting to carry it out in a similar manner and offering similar justifications. The talk of lower orders and labouring classes has had to become talk of the disadvantaged and under-privileged. The working class of Hannah Moore's time was viewed as a dangerous threat to the economic and political order of society and education was to be provided for it to counter such a threat. We have to see education today as having a similar role. The crucial difference between Moore's time and ours, is that in hers the working class, as a whole, was quite openly attacked as a class; whereas in ours it is not so attacked, as a class, but is assaulted as a collection of individuals whom it is claimed need to be assisted out of their disadvantage.

As we progress we will see how the existence of the working class, in a cultural, social and political sense, has been education's constant problematic since the class was first provided education. The cultural, social and political existence of the bourgeoisie has, we note, never been a problem for provided education. For those who are tempted to dispute our class analysis, at this early stage, this point alone should at least postpone that temptation. If an identifiable class has been the constant problem for something claiming to be above class, then that claim has to be suspected of being false, of being one which does not reflect the situation as it exists in the real world.

Reformism

As it has been the working class which has been education's constant problematic, and as it has been a major role for education to struggle against the cultural existence of the class, then we have to ask how education has managed to conduct this struggle for over a century without exploding out of its educational arena. The reasons given by Moore and her compatriots for the problematic nature of the working class' existence could not be given today; they have had to change. Yet the

* We will encounter Hannah Moore and her contribution to education in Chapter Four.

16

bourgeoisie is still here, as is the working class, and it still poses a problem for the bourgeoisie. What part has reformism played in the phrasing of the questions of the bourgeoisie as to the problematic existence of the working class: are the old class insults still with us, clad now in the language of disinterested concern?

It is often argued that the state has produced reforms in response to campaigning pressure. This is too simple in the extreme. Reforms have to be understood as much for what they preserve as for that which they change. All reforms contain this preservation/alteration contradiction. Consequently we have to ask of them whether their primary purpose is one of preserving, and if so, what it is they seek to preserve. For example, comprehensives changed the tripartite system of educational provision but they also sought, according to the relevant D.E.S. Circular (10/65), to preserve all that was valuable in the grammar school. The pressure groups which had campaigned for the comprehensives did not necessarily wish for such a preservation to be part of the new comprehensive approach; it would be incorrect of us, however, to see the state as having somehow highjacked the campaigners' aims after having yielded to them. Such a process may well be present in reformism but the major thrust of much reformism has to be seen as the preservation of, what could be described as the 'baseline', by its being re-presented in a new manner. In the final analysis reform is not the straightforward result of pressure from below, weakened and adapted by the 'powers that be'; rather it has to be seen as part of an on-going process, the aim of which is the reproduction of the capitalist structure with its relations of production, and this reproduction has to be achieved in a manner appropriate to the particular economic, social and political conjuncture. To this we must add the fact that campaigning pressure groups are invariably composed of a whole range of people with differing political views and analyses who have come together on one issue. Political compromises will have been made in order to get their campaign off the ground, further compromises made in order to gain publicity, and even more made to give the campaign a chance of success. Given such a string of likely compromises, if a campaign is successful, then just what will it mean?

Reformism is as much about preserving as it is

about changing. Reforms do not resolve struggles; they move them on. If we appreciate the contradictory nature of reformism then we are able to comprehend the often apparently contradictory ways of pursuing a single particular goal. Again, to give a practical illustration of our point: parents were once kept out of schools so as to allow the professional uninterrupted control; parents are now being encouraged to get involved and come into schools so that they can understand why the professional exercises control in the manner he/she does. The base-line remains intact but its preservation is achieved by methods opposite to those which had been used. In this case, how would we judge parental access to schools - as an uncomplicated reform?

Reforms have their contradictions; though they seek to preserve, they have to do so by making some changes. For those who wish to understand the world as it is, not as it seems, it is essential to have a clear view with regard to reforms, as to what is being changed and what preserved. We have to be sharp-eyed as to the benefits and costs of reforms, and capable of identifying their contradictions so that we are able, if we so wish, to exploit such contradictions. If clarity of vision is absent we will confuse epiphenomenal change with change to the base-line, which such epiphenomenal change actually serves to preserve and protect from change. We can see the consequences of a lack of clarity of vision in the criticism of comprehensives in Britain which argues that these schools are 'failing' their working class students by somehow not functioning properly according to their role. This criticism totally misses the point of the comprehensivisation of schooling in Britain. It was not supposed to change the educational practice of failing working class students; it was to preserve all that was valuable in the grammar school so as to make it available to all regardless of class, gender and race. Working class students would fail within a school attended by all children (except those attending fee-paying private schools) and so would do their failing as individuals. Comprehensives can be seen as mechanisms to draw the sting of socialist radicals who criticised the tripartite system as being blatantly class biased, if not class based. Our comments here are not intended to suggest that comprehensive schools represent no progress at all; rather they are to underline and emphasise just how important it is to

18

begin to examine critically reforms and reformism. As we progress we will see how necessary this advice is with regard to reforms enshrined in legislation and to the various reforms claimed as the property of community education.

The Educational Expert and Rights to Definition

With education being an arena in which classes struggle, what role is played by the educational expert and how did this person come to be an expert with such a role? A part of education's constant effort to negate the cultural existence of the working class has been the denial of validity to the experiential knowledge of the class. The masters of any situation, we are advised, are those with the rights to definition of it, and of course, with the power to ensure their definition prevails over that of others.17 In Hannah Moore's time it was the right of her class, as a whole, to deny the validity of the experiential knowledge of the working class and to label it as antithetical to 'real' knowledge. As such crude ways of describing education and the social world become no longer appropriate, the rights of definition as to real knowledge come to be held in trust, as it were, for her class by the educational expert. The working class, as a class would no longer be deemed ineducable but a large proportion of it would be deemed unsuccessful in the arena of education by those who defined education for and on behalf of the bourgeoisie. The educational expert would come to produce reasons which denied any class bias but which accounted for the educational failure of the working class, or rather, for individuals who happened to be working class. And the reasons for the educational failure of these individuals would reside within them as individuals. If the job of the sociologist is to take individual and personal problems and translate them into social questions, then the job of the educational expert is a mirror reflection of the sociologists. His task is to take social questions and problems and translate them into individual facts, to de-socialise them and psychologize them. Thus the working class does not fail educationally, rather individuals do so. The educational expert, then, seeks to locate the characteristics, the pathologies even, within the individual to account for educational failure.

It is central to our argument that the role of the educational expert is seen in this light and we will later explore the material which will substantiate our assertion on this matter. The expert has to be seen as one whose work consists in an attempt to replace a class explanation with one which deals only in terms of the individual. From the first days of competition for free secondary education to those of community education, the expert has accounted for educational failure within the working class as being the result of a low level of inborn ability, a low intelligence quotient or the result of wrong attitudes towards education and lack of parental know-how: the accounting method is one which refuses to question seriously the arena in which the failing takes place and emphasises only the individuals who fail. The expert is part of a process which wishes to deny class explanations for social phenomena and to insist they are replaced by ones which deal in terms of characteristics within individuals. The expert tells us that education is there, to be enjoyed by all, with access to it equally available to all. Consequently, when some fail to enjoy it or cannot obtain access to it, it is the task of the expert to explain why such people have failed. The expert is to tell us what it is within such people, or about such people that is responsible for them failing to take advantage of what is offered to them. The would be consumers of education's offering pose a problem for the expert; the offering itself does not.

Ideology

By far the major contribution to education's ideological armoury has come from the expert psychologists with their explanations of characteristics, individual abilities and pathologies. With an ideology surrounding education which claims for its subject an independence from class and a concern only with the individual, not surprisingly, comes the particular 'sub-ideology' of equal opportunity. The notion of an equality of opportunity or equal right of access can be seen as valid provided we do not question education on any levels other than the juridical and mechanical. (The Law gives children the right to education and examinations determine the levels of success.) Teachers and educationalists generally do not question this notion, yet despite this lack of questioning they cannot but help see that equality of opportunity cannot be working in practice for those who fail educationally are strongly over- represented by the working class. Unfortunately this does not cause them to examine the concept at any depth. Instead they embark upon a never ending quest for the philosopher's stone which will allow them to make equality of opportunity work in the real world; though the search, not surprisingly, is restricted to the social and cultural world of the working class. By failing to examine the concept at any depth they blindfold themselves before they begin. Thus they look for adjustments to be made which will make the concept a valid description of how provided education works. Their refusal or inability to subject the concept to a rigorous analysis means that they deny the class implications of what is a class concept and the more they search the more they add to this denial. They look for the pedagogic key to enable the working class to succeed, or for that particular something in the working class home which facilitates the occasional working class educational success - the right attitude, parental know-how, early childhood experiences...the list may have no end. Their concern is with the failing of the working class within provided education; they are not concerned to ask how an education is provided which fails the working class.

As we have already stated, we cannot accept any natural correspondence between what people say they are doing and what they really are doing. With our searchers chasing an educational holy grail, they believe they are engaged in assisting the chance to educational success of the working class: in reality they are engaged in adding more rubble to the educational barricade which exists to deny such educational success to the working class. The search for this form of pedagogic key, where only the working class is held to be problematic and not education itself, is a distraction and actually compounds the problem it purportedly addresses. It cannot be compared to a worthwhile search for a new pedagogy such as that discussed by Simon.18

The most important educational ideologies can be grouped around this denial of class and its relevance. Children are judged to fail and it so happens to be the case that the majority are working class. Education has to have an ideology which denies class in any conflictual sense: it can exist as attitudes and know-how, but it cannot be allowed to exist whereby classes oppose each other with real, differing and antagonistic interests.

An Elaborate Facade

As we have stated, the educational struggle of the classes parallels and reflects the economic struggle between the owners and controllers of the means of production and the owners and sellers of the capacity to labour. The overall capitalist ideology denies any real validity to conflict in the economic arena, proclaiming the two interests of the two classes to be compatible. The ideology insists that the lot of the workers can only be improved as a result of increased productivity on their behalf: if they are to have larger slices of cake then they must produce a larger cake. This ideology attempts to refuse any discussion or questioning of how the cake is divided, let alone any debate as to who owns the bakery. In the educational arena, opposing classes are denied and it is held to be the case that the educational improvement of the working class can only come about as long as 'educational standards' are not threatened. Again, what is meant by educational standards, is not open to debate. We are asked to take it for granted that they are independent of class in their construction and do not serve class in their operation. Economic and educational ideologies both make claims to universality for economic and educational systems which serve the interests of the dominant class in capitalist society. Educational ideologies have to be understood within the context of a class structured capitalist society with a class based education system. In their practice these ideologies struggle to legitimate the claims to universality which they make for the belief and value system of the bourgeoisie.

Community Education

The emergence of community education is as important as many of education's changes which we will encounter and discuss, and it is so, because like them, it will be concerned, if not to negate, then at least to diminish radically any class argument concerning education. Psychological theories and notions of Intelligence Quotients attempt to do this by stressing the significance of the individual; community education attempts to arrive at the same place by a rather different and more sophisticated route. It appears to move away from an explanation which deals with individuals and towards one which deals with collectivities. However, this move is more apparent than real for community education does not challenge bourgeois hegemony in education, but as do the psychological theories, explains how it is no such thing. It does this in two ways which can be seen as aspects of its route. First, it puts forward education as the pursuit of value-free knowledge where success need not be class based once the ways of pursuing are appreciated. It seeks to persuade individuals of the working class to adopt and accept views of the world which are antithetical to their own experiential knowledge of it and interest in it. Within community education the working class is not to enter a dialogue but is to be the passive recipient of the educator's monologue. It is concerned with attempting to insist compliance with and acceptance of a bourgeois education system, to the point where the educational failure of the working class will be accepted as valid by it and not seen as a class failure but as one of individual children who, though they might appear to be working class will not have been judged in any manner connected to their class position. In this sense community education does not depart from the tradition of education regarding the individual as the only valid material for educational work.

The second aspect to community educations denial of class and its relevance to education, lies in its attempt to deny class in any conflictual sense. It claims to be concerned with certain problems of capitalistic society but refuses to deal with them as normal aspects of that form of society. It ignores the fact that "poverty, unemployment and inter-racial tensions, for example, almost all have their origins in institutions at the macro-level".19 It fails to address these issues correctly and then compounds this error by offering inappropriate solutions which leave the macro-institutions intact. It works against a class analysis for it posits a community explanation whereby remedies will be found for our ills if people get together and behave as communities. Its message tells us that conflict is pathological and harmony the norm. Thus, when it seeks to involve working class people in schools it does so in order for them to understand and accept as needing no challenge, that which schools say are doing. Similarly, when it chooses to involve itself in a discussion on unemployment, it invariably accepts the TINA (there is no alternative) argument and its practice seeks to educate the unemployed into being unemployed. "The idea of community obscures the most important social and economic relationships."20

Finally we must point out that community education frequently claims to be concerned with changing fundamentally the nature and practice of schools; yet it informs teachers with the same frequency that it does not wish to challenge the professional status of teachers nor their rights to definition concerning educational philosophy and practice. That these two claims of community education are not seen as inherently contradictory by its advocates and practitioners does, at least, tell us something important about community education.

> One must understand the tendencies inherent in present institutions. Criticism is not a matter of arbitrarily condemning an institution or belief, but of understanding it.21

What follows aims to facilitate a better understanding by way of a critical analysis.

REFERENCES

1. Lawrence, D. H., The Rainbow. Penguin 1975, pp. 382-383.
2. For an account of the founding of the first community colleges see Rée, H., Educator Extraordinary: The Life and Achievements of Henry Morris. Longman 1973.
3. Manley, F. J., Reed, B. W., Burns, R. K., The Community School in Action: The Flint Programme. University of Chicago Press 1986.
4. The Plowden Report. Children and Their Primary Schools. HMSO 1967. Paragraph 1152.
5. Ibid. 1157.
6. Burns, T., From the British Journal of Sociology. Quoted in G. Bernbaum, Knowledge and Ideology in The Sociology of Education. Macmillan 1977. p. 28.
7. Gramsci, A., On Education. From Selections From Prison Notebooks. Lawrence and Wishart 1982. p. 35.
8. Marx, K., Grundrisse. Pelican 1973. p. 87.
9. Giddens, A., The Class Structure of Advanced Societies. Hutchinson 1973. p. 35.
10. Thompson, E. P., The Making of The English Working Class. Pelican 1968. p. 939.
11. Lefebvre, H., The Sociology of Marx. Penguin 1969. p. 76.

12. Ibid. p. 76.
13. Dickens, C., Dombey and Son. Oxford University Press 1974. p. 59.
14. Bowles, S., Gintis, H., Schooling in Capitalist America: Educational Reform and the Contradictions of Economic Life. RKP. 1976. p. 116.
15. Vincent, D., Bread, Knowledge and Freedom: A Study of Nineteenth Century Working Class Autobiography. London Europa Publications 1981. p. 36.
16. An Official Report Concerning Wales 1840. Quoted in Evans, D., The Life and Work of William Williams. Llandysul 1940. From Curtis, L., Nothing But The Same Old Story: The Roots of Anti-Irish Racism. Information on Ireland 1984. p. 64.
17. This way of defining the masters of situations is offered by Hamilton, I. and Carmichael, S., in Black Power. Cape 1968. p. 36.
18. See particularly Why No Pedagogy in England and Marx and The Crisis in Education. Two Chapters of Simon, B., Does Education Matter. Lawrence and Wishart 1985.
19. Entwhistle, H., Gramsci, A., Conservative Schooling For Radical Politics. RKP. 1979. p. 45.
20. Jackson, K., Some Fallacies in Community Education and Their Consequences in Working Class Areas. From Fletcher, C. and Thompson, N. (eds) Issues in Community Education. Falmer Press 1980. p. 42.
21. Bernstein, R., Praxis and Action. From Entwhistle op. cit. p. 45.

Chapter Two

SOME FUNDAMENTAL FORCE

"Not because I love sticking out my tongue, but
because I have yet to see a building of your's at
which one could refrain from sticking out one's
tongue." (Dostoyevsky. Notes From Underground)

With community education having the potential to
mean all things to all people there is, naturally,
a difficulty in securing a meaningful understanding
of it. In Britain when we look to community education's literature for identification as to its
origins we find them explained primarily by reference to Henry Morris and the Cambridgeshire Colleges. Harry Rée's biography of Morris and his
short paper on the origins of community education,
though containing interesting material, deal exclusively with Morris, the man, the innovator and
original thinker; Morris, the individual - as the
real 'father' of present day community education.1
Detailed biographical studies of talented individuals can be fascinating but they are of little
help to us as we seek to understand the social
world and account for change within it. Rée tells
us how the 1924 Morris document was delivered to
all members of the education committee and "by
chance, and also because of Morris's political
skill" the document went on to become the bricks
and mortar of the Cambridgeshire Colleges. Interesting, but it tells us little. Rée does not
enquire as to why a man called Morris should have
had the ideas he did have at the time he had them.
Rée's explanation of the origins of community
education is not particularly valuable, even in
terms dealing solely with the community education
of Britain in the 1930's. To accept Rée's explanation as to the aetiology of community education for
Britain in those days is one thing; it is quite
another thing and even less satisfactory to accept
the Morris theory as being significant in accounting for community education's 'take-off' in the
1970's.
    However, this explanation for community educa-

26

tion is the unquestioned, taken-for-granted one to which the vast majority of community educators subscribe. Other factors are added to it by various writers but the base-line of Morris as the father of community education remains in their work. Widlake[2] traces the Morris connection in his offering on the origins of community education by showing how Mason and Western brought community education to Leicestershire; both men having worked with Morris in Cambridgeshire. In dealing with the community education of Britain in the 1970's and early 1980's he adds the contributions of Plowden and Halsey([3] and [4]) but for him it is still Morris who explains the birth of community education. The difficulty with such an analysis, lies in the implicit assumption that community education would not exist had not Morris's parents, as individuals, met, married and produced Henry. Their chance meeting seems to account for community education in Britain. This we regard as totally absurd. Yet we should not be surprised by such a notion put forward in all seriousness for it is very much a part of the bourgeois analysis of the world which wishes constantly to understand it in terms of the sacred individual with his or her individual action for which he or she alone is responsible.

However, within Widlake's account we find a much more worthwhile indication of where to look for the aetiological explanation of community education.

> The flash points in a post industrial society are more usually found in urban areas, especially the inner city; and in the search for fresh approaches education authorities naturally turned to community schools.[5]

Widlake elaborates on none of the issues raised here, though within them we would see some of the keys to an understanding of community education. What are the flash points to which he refers and just what is a post industrial society? Unfortunately he does not tell us. Nor does he explain why it should be education authorities searching for fresh approaches, nor why they should 'naturally' turn to community schools. The questions suggest themselves in Widlake's work but he does not discuss them: it is possible, of course, that he sees them not as questions to be addressed but simply as statements of fact. Widlake, like many community educators, is happy to see community education as part of a tradition of liberal, progressive education: but he, along with many others, is unhappy when it becomes identified with "more radical left-wing beliefs"[6] for such an identification has a negative value for community education. "Community education has tended to be most effective when a bipartisan approach has been adopted."[7]

(Could Widlake here have identified one of the 'chance' reasons for the success of Morris, in that Morris's idea aimed to be non-political to the extent that all parties could feel free to support it?) Again this interesting point raised by Widlake is not discussed by him. Why should the tendency exist and what is a bi-partisan approach?

A bi-partisan approach is very much the norm within education; with the result that any proposed educational change represents a departure from the status quo and so has to justify itself in terms of and to the status quo. This helps to sustain the inherent conservative nature of education. The bi-partisan approach, for its own sake, is one which has to favour the powerful, for as the powerful are the custodians of the status quo then the bi-partisan approach can only be sustained with the permission of the powerful, thereby ensuring any changes remain relatively insignificant if the bi-partisan approach is not to be abandoned. The concept of the bi-partisan approach generally obscures an unequal power relationship for one partner to the approach controls its definition and so permits or refuses elements of change to it. (Later in this chapter this will be made abundantly clear by Midwinter as he asks permission of the powerful for community education to come to the front of the educational stage.)

Widlake's explanation of the origins of community education has its contradictions, and these do indicate a more rewarding form of explanation than his explicit Morris theme. And more rewarding because they place community education in a wider arena than Britain, by way of flash points and bi-partisan approaches; and crucially by suggesting a driving mechanism behind community education in widely different nation states.

> Elsewhere, the drive towards some form of community education is strong and persistent, covering countries with very varied geographical and social conditions, from the U.S.A. to India, from Canada to Australia, from Italy and Germany to Malaysia. The ubiquity of this

phenomena suggests that some fundamental force
in human affairs is being tapped, one with the
potential to provide a counter balance to the
rush to violence which is the norm in human
affairs.[8]

For Widlake community education seems to be a paci-
fist army riding to the rescue of a doomed world,
the expression of a fundamental force in human
affairs mystically rising to the surface when its
hour is at hand. This fundamental force is little
more than Ideology in action. It is to be the
mechanism to counter the rush to violence which,
along with Hobbes, Widlake seems to see as the
natural condition of man regardless of context.
De-coding his language we see this rush to violence
as little more than a radical, unco-ordinated
demand for social justice and the fundamental force
as a way of denying such demand without recourse to
repression.
We can understand Widlake's interpretation of
the world if we accept at face-value the claims
which are made throughout the world for community
education. The similarity of the claims and the
language in which they are made could lead to a
belief that they reflect a process taking place
beyond national boundaries. Indeed this is our
argument. However, we categorically refuse to
accept the claims at face-value, unlike Widlake and
many community educators. Methodologically, we
should be as sceptical of accepting community
education's claims concerning improvements to the
quality of life followed, as we are of accepting
South Africa's claims with regard to democracy and
'The Homelands'.
In 1979 the Minister for Foreign Affairs in
Australia told us:

> Community education is not an end in itself.
> It has the broad objectives of improving the
> quality of social life, providing equal life
> opportunities for all..."[9]

From Japan, a Professor of Education and Communication informed us that:

> The primary aim of community education... is
> to help each individual, man, woman and youth
> make the best of life. By helping
> individuals, community education activities
> thus cover all forms of betterment required by

the community.10

And from U.S.A. Roland Frank informs us that:

> The process of planning for community educa-
> tion centres on the basic belief that commun-
> ity education can and will improve life for
> all in the community.11

The aims and claims here are staggering in their
width and confidence. It is fortunate for educationalists that they are not subject to any Trades
Descriptive Legislation. To embark upon a strategy
of action which aims to improve the life of all in
a community, whatever that may mean, is a significant step, and if that is what is taking place, it
is particularly adventurous given the epiphenomenal
analysis as to the causal factors of the wrongs of
the world, which lies behind the fine rhetoric of
the community education advocates. To criticise
the aims and objectives as put forward by such men
as these, is surely akin to answering the age-old
question 'Have you stopped beating your wife?'
However, this is only so if we are questioning the
integrity of such community education advocates.
This we are not doing. Rather, we are seeking to
begin to explain how such claims come to be made:
what is it which produces them?

The claims from Japan and Australia were made
at the same community education conference as were
those which now follow.

From The Philippines:

> The main concern of non-formal/adult and com-
> munity education in the vital task of up-
> grading the skills of individuals already
> possessing basic training, and of developing
> fundamental skills in the untrained, is to
> ensure the maximum utilisation of available
> manpower in the country by enhancing the em-
> ployability of the participants/trainees with
> respect to efficiency and productivity.... All
> of these programs are intended to improve the
> economic productivity of individuals and com-
> munities through self-reliance, self-discip-
> line and work.12

And from Singapore, a member of the Vocational and
Industrial Training Board, explains with regard to
Singapore's somewhat famous 'national campaigns',

30

which interestingly are seen as part of Singapore's
community education strategy.

> In this way, the community as a whole is drawn
> in to participate in a change, may it be to
> change from a bad habit to a good one, to
> adapt to a new idea or concept or just to
> adopt good working procedures for safety, all
> of which are ultimately aimed to benefit so-
> ciety as a whole.13

These extracts concerning community education in
five very different countries bring two crucial
issues to light. First, community education can
mean very different things to different people in
that all can be claiming to be concerned with
improving the quality of life; what then is meant
by such a claim. We cannot look at these various
claims and allow them to be treated as non-problematic. Secondly, we note that with regard to the
Philippines and Singapore, neither of which is well
known as a paradigm of democracy, their claims deal
very much with the economies of their countries.
Their community education relates primarily to the
drive for increased productivity. As such it appears to have much in common with the claims which
were made for education in Britain and the U.S.A.
in the last century and early in the present one.
It suggests that their community education is very
much a matter of rationalising educational provision so as to enhance its service to industrial
production. In doing so it places against the
community education of the other three countries,
the possibilty that they might have a similar role
to play. Could it be the case that they do, but
that their representation is more sophisticated
than that of Singapore and The Philippines because
those two countries do not believe it yet necessary
to accompany drives for increased productivity and
a better disciplined workforce with progressive
liberal rhetoric?

Midwinter and Community Education

For a considerable time in Britain, Midwinter
was the most important spokesperson for community
education and like his counterparts in other
countries he too was committed to a community
education which would improve the quality of life,
but again, like his counterparts, he would be committed to a particular notion of community educa-

tion and a particular concept of life and its quality. As Midwinter constructs his political and philosophical model of what he holds his world to be, he is both confusing and confused. He attempts, in a way, to define the nature of man in the abstract and to provide a definitive statement interpreting the history of his life thus far on the planet earth. Absurdly ambitious and inevitably doomed to failure! Nevertheless it is an interesting account for it leads to and allows us to make more sense of what he understands by community education. Briefly he argues that it is neither capitalism in the West nor communism in the East which is responsible for the barriers to the improvement of life for all; rather it is the drive for centralisation on behalf of the state which is the inhibiting factor here. If this is the case, of course, it is rather futile for radicals in the West to pursue any strong socialist/communist path towards the re-structuring of their society.

> It is likely that, a thousand years hence, the future historian will see more clearly the similarities of two huge, federalised states, with cash economies and a centrally controlled government, and of a membership and approach differing in degree rather than kind.[14]

In both forms of society Midwinter sees under-achievers, people who, for one reason or another cannot cope; he notes various forms of inequalities and ways which the forms of society have for dealing with such issues. Because he insists upon a basic similarity, however, between the two systems, he does not treat such problems within their contexts; rather he treats the existence of under-achievers as an expression of a universal. "Put another way, there has been so far, no equal society."[15] To us this lack of an equal society would pose a problem and we would wish to know why this was so, what processes and devices had worked against such a society being created. To Midwinter, this does not lead to a questioning; rather it tells him that equal societies cannot be created. They are utopian phantoms, not to be pursued.

Midwinter is firmly opposed to any prescriptive remedy for Western societies which would attempt any radical restructuring and this despite his occasionally acute comments on the present structure of his own society.

By enjoying and sustaining their wealth, by
using it to protect their health, by erecting
legal barriers to preserve their rights, and
by manipulating educational systems, of whatever kind, in favour of their offspring, the
upper classes have run much less risk of suffering social casuality.16

We see here Midwinter recognising, to a degree, the
role of the upper classes vis-à-vis the state; yet
he is also able to fail to retain his own recognition of the same. The state must never be allowed
to become, in his mind, any form of agent acting on
behalf of the capitalist class and for this to be
the case he has to stretch his own logic to its
limits. Thus, with regard to the 'haves' and the
'have-nots' of British society:

By their control, overt and covert, of the
economy, the media, the political machine and
so forth, they command the situation accordingly. It is not necessarily a vicious phenomenon, to be delineated in class war terminology. Much of it happens spontaneously,
automatically, even accidentally.17

Overt and covert control, yet the action can be
described as an accident! It would seem, even from
his own language, that there is little room for
accident. In place of any Marxist nonsense which
talks of class war Midwinter locates disagreements,
often resulting from communication problems and of
course the resolution cannot be a class one which
might threaten the existing order of society.

His community education is part of his overall
notion of community development and it is this
which offers us solutions. He suggests that a form
of community development might act as a checking
mechanism on the drive of the state to further
centralisation, resulting in an improvement in the
quality of life. He believes that a better future
can be secured without any alterations being made
to the relations of production in capitalist
Britain; and he believes this because capitalism
has nothing to do with the problem and the ceding
of such equalities as he requests will help the
state to preserve its fundamental nature and purpose. The problem here, of course, is that the
fundamental nature and purpose of the state is to
guarantee the reproduction of these inequalities as
part of the overall reproduction of class relations

and the relations of production. Midwinter is aware of how the ruling class uses and manipulates, as he sees it, the state apparatus, yet his strategy is to ask this class to dismantle many of those devices which allow it to be the class that it is.

> The question remaining is whether, or to what extent, these groups are worried and saddened by the symptoms of urban decay, violence and collapse. Here the community educator and his thoughts meet those of the demographic specialists, the military experts, the prophets of world wide doom, the conservationists and the broad panoply of urban investigators. Across the West the warnings of urban degeneration are sounded, and the degree to which they are heard by the middle classes may well be the key to the degree of community development in our society.18

Given Midwinter's analysis which operates in terms of nation states with cash economies and drives to centralisation, East and West, we have to ask why this scenario deals only with the West. Why are not all nation states so threatened with violence and decay. Could it not relate to the class relations of capitalist society which he would have as irrelevant to the issue? It would seem to be so. What other reason could there be for the deliberate omission of the Eastern socialist bloc from this sketch. He is not, however, writing about urban degeneration per se; rather the threat which he sees as existing is related only to the capitalist mode of production. Not only does it only threaten the West, according to Midwinter, but it directly results from the inequalities which capitalism must produce and reproduce. As Midwinter pays no particular attention to the characteristics of capitalism he is unable to differentiate between it, society and the nation state. Thus any perceived threat to capitalism is a threat to society where society represents everything between man and anarchy. This thought horrifies Midwinter, and not surprisingly, for his model of man is similar to Widlake's and that bears a close resemblence to the one held by Hobbes. It is enough to send him willingly into the arms of the military experts, and of course, they have their own favourite theories of anarchy, degeneration and disorder and the remedies thereof.

In 1975, when Midwinter was committing his thoughts to paper, he felt that there was, as yet, no real threat to the 'haves' of his society, but he believed that if that society failed to advance on the community front, then such a threat could well become a reality. How then was such a potential situation to be resolved?

For Midwinter a community approach to education would hold the key. This approach would seek to involve the home in the education of the child thereby changing the attitude of the home to education. Midwinter saw that parents already, as parents, must have some form of educational engagement with their child; the inter-action of the child and parent could not help but have an educational dimension to it. The difficulty was that this parent/child educational dimension might be "woefully feeble, even crucially damaging"[19] to the child. Community education would aim to lessen the chance of any educational damage being done to children by their parents. It would intervene in the parent/child relationship so as to ensure that the parent's educating of the child was in line and at four square with that being carried out by the school.

Some parents, for Midwinter, if left alone, are woefully feeble in their educational efforts towards their children. If he were writing of a small, identifiable minority, then it's possible we might agree: this is not the case for he does not identify it in any empirical sense but suggests it to be the working class, generally. Not all working class parents are crucially damaging the education of their children, but all are insufficiently supportive, in an educational sense, of their children. The educational standards and aims of the middle class home are, he notes, likely to be in harmony with those of the school: thus, the middle class home is not at all problematic in the educational sense; there is no need for professional intervention. Not so, with the working class home.

> I am now, sadly forced to confess that on balance, the child in the happy, secure, interested working class home is still at an acute disadvantage, academically speaking, even against the child in the dry, riven, sullen middle class house.[20]

Surely this situation should tell Midwinter some-

thing of the class bias, if not base of education.
Unfortunately it does not. It simply tells him how
much in need is the working class home, of knowledge and know-how as to how schools and the education system operate. The working class parents
need help so that their well-meaning efforts are
not wasted; assistance so that their efforts match
and support those of the school. In talking of the
working and middle class home Midwinter raises the
crucial issue, the dialectic of class and education
but instead of addressing it, he ignores it, or
rather reduces it to a matter of parental know-how.
Like many educators before him, he looks for the
explanatory factor regarding the educational failure of the working class; and like them he refuses
to examine the area in which the working class
actually fails, that is education itself. Rather
it is the failing of the working class which has to
be studied and the reasons for it located within
the class itself. So, in Midwinter's community
education the 'home-school' contact is central.
The professional working in this area, the 'home-
schooler' in Midwinter's language, has to help
parents understand education so that they
are able to help their children in their education. "If informing parents is the main aim, then
the teacher retains professional status."21 However, if a more adventurous community education
path is followed, whereby parents are involved so
that the whole family becomes a target for educational intervention, "then there is a chance that
the teacher status may be heightened".22 How such
a heightening of teacher status interfaces with
Midwinter's desire to de-mythologise the profession
of teaching is most interesting. Is it not likely
that an education which claims relevance and authority and a right to intervene over more areas of
life might well, by adding to the professional
status of the teacher, further increase the gap
between the teacher and the working class client
and thus further mythologise the profession? Midwinter's community education here is no cultural
exchange or dialogue; rather like the missionaries
who went to Africa and other countries, his emis-
saries are to inform people about their subject,
they are to tell them about education and the
people are to accept what they are told. He is
sharply critical of middle class educational intervention of the past for having, what he sees as a
'lady bountiful' image; yet his proposals are not
far removed from such middle class intervention,

though they do have a more sophisticated ideological support and theory than had that of the yesteryear lady bountifuls. His home-schooler is to
persuade more working class parents to know more
about education; to persuade them to bring their
education of their children into line with the
school's education of their children; to persuade
them to make the necessary cultural adjustments to
their homes so as to make them correspond more
closely to the culture of the school.

Midwinter's community education has two major
strands to it. The first is the home-schooler and
the second, though a strand in itself, serves the
home-schooler approach. It is concerned with publicity and advertising. Its aim is to present the
citizenry at large with education's "most fluent
explanation possible".[23] It is in his own terms to
sell education to its consumers.[24]

Man as consumer, is the quintessential image
of man as projected by the ideology of capitalism.
It is one whose power lies in its implicit message
of personal and free choice. Within production,
overall, it is held to be the determining factor:
the wish of the consumer is held to be the deciding
factor in the success or failure of productive
enterprise. Against such an ideology of consumer
power we can posit the consumer, firstly taking
what is available and secondly being 'educated' to
desire those things which he comes to desire. The
image of man as a consumer is a capitalist image
projecting an abstracted concept of man: it is
alienated man boasting of his alienation. To see
people as consumers of education, rather as the
market sees them as consumers of baked beans or
soap powder, is neither progressive nor educational. Salesmen from both reputable companies and
'cowboy' outfits, offer fluent explanations for
their products, and within their explanations the
image of the product is at least as important as
its reality. The second-hand car salesman is,
however, selling only a car: Midwinter's educationalists aim to sell education so that the working
class home will begin to identify with it and so
alter its own culture and ethos so as to closer fit
it to that of the school. To sell education
schools must be presented "in as spanking and as
life-enhancing and as vivacious a mode"[25] as
possible. This advertising must take place in a
whole variety of locations; pubs, clubs, shops,
factories, holiday camps and works canteens. Working class venues are Midwinter's premier sites for

it is to the working class that education has to be sold.

Advertising generally has a tenuous relationship with the product being advertised: it is concerned with the product only from the point of view of its sale. Midwinter's advertising does not depart radically from this relationship: any class education complexity disappears and the sole task becomes one of selling education by presenting it in a radical and innovative manner. If this advertising is successful then the work of the home-schooler will have been made less difficult. The parent will be educated to understand and accept as valid what the education system says about itself. The advertising and selling of education, valuable in itself, will have helped to bring about a situation wherein this parental education can take place. Midwinter's claim that he is not involved in any sort of lady bountiful approach rests upon his overt support for what he sees as the culture of the working class. It is a support which is selective and focuses on non-contentious aspects of that culture; basically, bingo, street parties and music hall. It does not concern him that music hall is a thing of the past nor that street parties are associated historically with nationalist or monarchist fervour. His support for these aspects of working class culture (though whether they can simply be classified as such is another matter) is reminiscent of Wilmott and Young in their dewy-eyed descriptions of the east end of London.26 When Midwinter deals with the culture of the working class it appears he wishes to tie the class to what he regards as its essential culture, and that culture is one with which education can cope, one that has conflict conspicuous by its absence, one in which the working class is either passive (playing bingo) or having a 'knees-up' to celebrate a worthwhile occurrence.

As this advertising becomes more successful, parents will get more involved with education. They will have contact with home-schoolers but they will also have contact with the school itself. They will join parents committees, raise funds and help organise social events. Working class people actually behaving as the lady bountifuls of yesteryear! No, not quite; they will help the school run but will have no real say in how it runs. Community education will provide for parent's rooms in schools for "they bring the parent into intensely direct contact with the teachers, and yet somehow manage to keep the parent out of the teacher's hair".27

The one-sided nature of this new parent-teacher relationship is further illustrated in the context of support for the efforts of the child whilst in school. When dealing with home visiting Midwinter emphasises that not all teachers should do this for a specialised form of approach is needed. He does not explain why this should be so given that home visiting is about two adults discussing the education of a child with which each is involved. Is it because a large number of teachers would find it difficult to relate to working class parents without a degree of cultural arrogance being detected by such parents. This would not surprise us for the purpose of home visits is to insist, albeit by persuasion, the values of the school against those of the home. Thus a message with a distinct element of cultural arrogance to it cannot be delivered by an arrogant messenger.

> It is not only, we should recollect, the lack of re-inforcement in the home for what the school offers; it is the hazard of that offering being contradicted or maimed.28

The home-schooler exists then to state, in an appropriately diplomatic manner, the hard fact that school is right, home is wrong, and home must adjust to fit in with school or be held responsible for educationally maiming the child.

Midwinter's community education will be one where more and more teachers involve themselves in the community to help the community understand the value of education and what the school is trying to achieve.

> Nothing would be more guaranteed to place teachers on a par with lawyers or doctors than this ideal of them supervising the whole educational needs of the community.29

If such parity were to result from the educational efforts of teachers in the community, and of such an outcome we are intensely sceptical, would it be at all possible to see this as contributing to the Midwinter aim of de-mythologising the profession? There is considerable myth attached to the white coat of medicine and the wig and gown of law. The working class does, no doubt, recognise the status accorded to doctors and lawyers; whether it accords them such status is an entirely different matter. Much of the status of the professions in capitalist Britain results from the myths attached to them and those they generate in order to retain such status. It is not possible to de-mythologise the profession of teaching whilst at the same time increasing its status to that of medicine and law. Unless forced by circumstances into contact with doctors and lawyers most members of the working class respect these professions as they do a moving train - they stay out of their way.[30] Midwinter's failure to notice the contradictions within his community education, the result of his own confused analysis, is a serious failing within his work, though it does, on occasions, produce humourous results. Thus, his obsession with the state's drive to centralisation as the key barrier to a more equal society, leads him into suggesting, as part of his community education strategy, that schools may decide to manage without cleaners and cooks so as to use their wages to finance school trips etcetera. Building maintenance staff might similarly be sacrificed; all such work to be undertaken by community volunteers. Large scale redundancy as a strategy to improve the quality of life of the community! Cooks, cleaners and building workers must belong to the non-school community, or maybe they just do not matter. This possibility which Midwinter puts forward in all seriousness is the result of his seeing centralisation as an abstracted process per se, and not as it should be seen, that is, as a mechanism with aims varying according to the specific conjuncture.

> You've been with the professors
> And they've all liked your looks
> With great lawyers
> You have discussed lepers and crooks
> You've been through all
> Of F. Scott Fitzgerald's books
> You're very well read
> It's well known
> But something is happening here
> And you don't know what it is
> Do you Mr Jones.[31]

Within Britain Midwinter has been of major significance with regard to community education. His theories have been taken up by many community education practitioners and a great many of his ideas as to how education can be sold have been acted upon in a practical manner in towns and cities throughout the country. Many who have espoused his notion of community education have done so believing it, like Midwinter himself, to be a radical approach to education. It is, however, no such thing, on any level other than the most superficial. It has to be located as a part of his strategy for improving the position of the have-nots of society; a strategy which is highly suspect for it refuses on principle to consider any class conflict model of societal analysis as it also refuses to consider any necessity for change within the relations of production. It is a community education committed to sustaining capitalism by way of ignoring its existence: as such it is not a community education which offers to its working class consumers the goal of liberation. In the final analysis it translates structural issues into problems of communication and information and in so doing it obscures more than it illuminates.

CEDC and Community Education

Midwinter was, in many ways, the community education figure in Britain during the 1970's. His writings were studied by countless students following courses which would qualify them as teachers; were examined by advisers and policy makers within Local Education Authorities as to courses of action to be pursued; and were frequently followed and translated into action by community education practitioners. Thus Midwinter is a most significant figure, not simply because of the theories which he puts forward but because many of these theories and their recommendations as to practice have, in effect, become educational practice. The ways in which he suggested education go about selling itself have been followed. Many Local Education Authorities have taken school classes out of schools and for publicity purposes located them for a day or two in local shops and teachers throughout Britain have been encouraged to become home-schoolers. In following Midwinter's suggestions to action it has been common practice to accept in a taken-for-granted manner the reasons which justify such action. The reasons are not necessarily examined or questioned, they are simply accepted as 'parts of the package'. His two major strands of community education have become two of the major strands to community education wherever it is practised in Britain. This has happened without any significant analysis having been made of his community education with its identifiable strands.

In the decade of the 1980's the role of Midwinter vis-à-vis community education has been taken, not by an individual, but by an organisation: the Community Education Development Centre (CEDC). The CEDC was established as a result of a great deal of efficient 'hustling' by John Rennie, now its Director. Rennie planned the centre and turned plan into reality by securing funding from the Van Leer Foundation in the Netherlands and the C. S. Mott Foundation in the U.S.A. The centre also 'earns' its living by its publications and its advisory, consultative and evaluative work, most of which is carried out on a contract basis for Local Education Authorities. In 1984, for example, it was very much involved advising a number of cities in Britain who wished 'to go community'. The CEDC acts as a focus for the development of community education in Britain. It publishes booklets on community education as well as a monthly newspaper, Network. It is an important organisation because of the work in which it is engaged, in that its community education is the one model to which many would-be community educators turn: and, of course, it consciously seeks to influence the practice of community education.

CEDC does not have a succinct statement as to its philosophy of community education; this is best gleaned by an examination of its publications. Its philosophy will emerge from its written material on community education. This is a thorny issue in that we will not focus on Network editorials, so will not be analysing the writings only of CEDC staff, but those of Network's contributors as well. Its contributors include Advisers for Community Education, Heads of Community Schools and Community Colleges and others who work as community education practitioners in some capacity or another. Whatever the status of the authors, the factor common to all is their occupation; they are workers in community education. Consequently their articles give us an insight into the philosophy driving community education in Britain in the 1980's. This we have to treat as representing CEDC's philosophy, when placed together with that encapsulated in its editorials, for it is what makes the publications of CEDC what they are. CEDC, for us, is influenced by community education and it in turn influences that community education.

Community Education and Unemployment

In September 1984, six months into the strike by the National Union of Mineworkers, the leading article in Network written by the editor, told us that "full employment for all won't come back in Britain, and the sooner politicians, especially, recognise this the better"[32]. When Network deals with the organisation of production in Britain, specifically in terms of the numbers unemployed it allows us to see most clearly the politics of community education. Network could, no doubt, have chosen not to concern itself with this issue and regarded education in a narrower sense as its only topic for debate. This it did not do. Unemployment is regularly a topic of both editorials and articles. Network is not, of course, in business to compete with overtly political newspapers, but with regard to unemployment, most definitely a political issue, it attempts to avoid taking any political position. It does not appreciate that such an attempt itself is a political position. In Network we do not find any questioning as to the way in which production is organised nor one concerning possible alternatives to mass unemployment. In an educational newspaper a failure or refusal to discuss or even admit the existence of possible alternatives to that belief which one holds, is unacceptable. The unacceptable is the everyday event in Network regarding unemployment. The Chief Education Officer for Oxfordshire in 1982 informed us that "there is quite simply not going to be paid life-time work for everybody in our society".[33] For him, the political question to be addressed is not whether action can be taken to change such a situation but what response can be made to 'live with' such a fact. His response is to offer to young people an education which will enable them to live with this fact of their lives; an education which will prepare them to take their places in a workless world. The disturbing point of this Chief Education Officer's observations is the total unconcern over the subject to which education is to make a response. The inevitability of mass unemployment is accepted with as much ease and as little examination as that of a baby taking a bottle. To this Chief Education Officer there is no alternative; thus his job is to educate people to live without an alternative. His bland acceptance of a politically sensitive idea as an uncomplicated fact is common to community educators the

43

world over. The Director of the Victorian Employment Committee of Australia tells us: "We know that
unemployment is a worldwide problem today." He
might know it but we certainly do not. We have no
evidence to show us that unemployment is a problem
in the Soviet Union or in East Germany or indeed in
many other non-capitalist countries. Where 'educated' people accept 'facts' so readily, we have
need to be suspicious.

The community educator's response to unemployment is generally to attempt to educate an acceptance of unemployment into those who will have to
experience it. The Oxfordshire Chief Education
Officer hopes such a way of educating will lead us
to a society "where there is less violence born of
envy, frustration and intolerance".34

He wishes to achieve this laudable aim, not
necessarily by attempting to remove the factors
responsible for producing such reactions in people:
disparities in wealth, barriers to decent housing,
skills forced to rust - these are not the issues to
be tackled. Instead the concern is to alter the
attitudes of people suffering from inequalities in
his society. For him the problem is not poverty or
unemployment, it is the envy which might be born of
either. Here community education is viewing unemployment out of its political context and com-
pounding its error by then viewing envy, frustration and intolerance as discrete phenomena, again
abstracted out of context. Such abstraction fails
to treat the phenomena as social and instead treats
them as characteristics divorced from the social
milieu in which they occur. Our Chief Education
Officer, like Widlake and Midwinter before him,
views his world, sees violence, decay, envy and
frustration and wishes to play his part in bringing
such things to an end: though without approaching
an understanding as to where they came from. They
are interested in "changing the consciousness of
the oppressed not the situation which oppresses
them".35

Community education, Poster tells us in an
edition of Network, was born in America "as a
response to the social problems of the Depression
in the Thirties"36 and he believes that in the U.K.
community education is only just beginning to
respond to the same problem in the Eighties. It
does not occur to Poster nor to the majority of
community educators to enquire as to why there
should be this educational response to an economic
and political problem. As a consequence, when

44

education does respond, it does so on the terms established by the economic and political concensus of capitalism. These terms allow for no challenge to be made to the organisation of capitalist production.

> The school system is a monument to the capacity of the advanced corporate economy to accommodate and deflect thrusts away from its foundations.[37]

As we are continually informed, by the editor and contributors to Network, of the lack of any alternative to mass unemployment, we see, in this informing, the deflecting away of any potential thrusts against the foundation of Britain's capitalist economy. The editor of Network and its contributors are not, however, conspirators; they are honourable men who believe mass employment to be a fact, who believe there is no alternative to it. The honesty of their belief is not the issue; what such beliefs mean in the real world is at issue. What will such beliefs mean to the education of those already in or about to join the dole queue?

Community educators writing in Network treat unemployment in one of three basic ways. It is either the result of some value-free technological progress which necessitates the use of less labour power; or enquiry is not even made thus far and so it is treated rather like the weather, a phenomenon external to and beyond the control of man; or, finally, it is the result of the inadequacies on various levels of those who are or become unemployed. Community education's response takes two forms. One consists of making educational approaches to the unemployed and is based upon the assumption that there is something within them which results in their being unemployed. These approaches frequently offer help with reading and writing, as if it had been proven that most of the millions out of work were illiterate; offer courses 'linked to the new technology' based on an unquestioning assumption that 'keyboard skills' will enhance employment prospects; or finally offer courses such as one offered to the unemployed of Coventry in 1985 entitled 'Improve Your Interview Skills'. This aimed to show the unemployed "how to find jobs you can apply for, to make a good application and what employers are looking for when they short list and interview."[38] The thinly disguised

45

message of such courses tells the unemployed that
their unemployment is their own fault; that there
are skills and abilities which employers need and
which they, as individuals, do not have. Community
education's second type of response here aims to be
a pastoral and more gentle one. When the rains of
unemployment appear the community college will come
into its own as a provider of shelter. It will
open its doors to these people.

> Thus the wageless and the retired, the often
> forgotten minorities as well as the mainstream
> and perhaps affluent majority would find them-
> selves in a multi-faceted institution where
> each individual would feel themselves signifi-
> cant, both in their own eyes and in the eyes
> of society. At the same time through demo-
> cratic control of the institutions a certain
> social cohesiveness would be attained.39

Apart from the similarity to the inscription on the
Statue of Liberty, this description suggests community colleges almost as sanctuaries from a harsh
world. How will the individuals from the forgotten
minorities, the unemployed and others _feel_ significant in the eyes of society when they are obviously
not significant enough to have their problems addressed directly. It seems to be a matter of
'feelings' not concrete reality. With no examination as to whether mass unemployment is an inevitability, a structural matter which can be addressed,
what would be the likely education offered by such
an institution to capitalism's walking wounded?
Hardly one which encouraged a questioning of the
world. The issue of democratic control is raised,
but in such a way that it offers no cause for
excitement for it is to aim for social cohesiveness
which, naturally, will result in the wageless feeling at one with the affluent. The company director
and the man queueing for work at his gate will feel
part of the same community. Whether such a community college is a possibilty is not the issue here;
rather what is of interest is the posing of such a
community college for this gives us an indication
of the path being taken by community education in
Britain.
      Community education's response to unemploy-
ment, as expressed in _Network,_ is to educate the
unemployed to be unemployed; to teach them that
their lot is inevitable. Then to soften such
teaching with the caring environment of a community

46

college. These responses are part of the overall strategy which seeks to ensure that envy, frustration and potential violence do not become something which could threaten the stability of the capitalist order or society as we know it.

At whichever capitalist country we look, if it has a community education service, we will find unemployment being treated in a very similar manner to that which we have outlined with the help of Network, regarding Britain. Not only is it treated in a similar manner but frequently we can recognise common expressions and phrases which talk of the need for teaching 'life skills' to the young unemployed who are often characterised as having 'unrealistic' job aspirations.40 It is the case, however, that we will also find community educators who strongly challenge community education's passive acceptance of capitalist ideology masquerading as fact; community educators who constantly stress real alternatives to mass unemployment. They are to be found in all capitalist countries but it is undeniably the case that they are a small, if not tiny minority and it is not their voice that can be said to speak for community education.

Home/School and Community Education

Network and other CEDC publications give us no real evidence of any radical break with the home-school approach of community education as enunciated by Midwinter. It is still an approach which has the school as the non-problematic given and the task of the home-school community education worker that of changing the culture and ethos of the home.

> The long term educational goal is that this relationship will mean that parents will be less alienated* from schools, and thus develop a greater understanding of the school's aims, and so become better able to help their children.41

* Alienation for Marx was a way of describing how man's products confront him in such a way that he experiences himself as an object of that which he has produced: his products act upon and coerce him. The term has now been stood on its head and is used to describe men, individually and collectively, who do not identify with and adapt to the products which confront them. Non-alienated man, in the Marxist sense, is alienated man within capitalism and its concept of alienation.

The implicitly present idea in such parent/teacher relationships states that school is doing all it can for children and if they are not to fail educationally parents must support the school in what it does. Again we see how it is parents who pose a problem for schools: parents, who by their understanding or lack of understanding of education, decide, to a large extent, the educational success or failure of their children. The longer we deal with parental attitudes to and understanding of schools as the explanatory factor in educational success and failure the further we remain from any real understanding of the relationship between education and the working class. To explain class and education in terms of parental attitudes obscures more than it illuminates. By totally accepting schools and education as non-problematic such ways of explaining actually constitute a barrier to meaningful explanation and social understanding of the subject.

Community education poses a parent/teacher relationship without dialogue between the supposed partners to the education of children. Parents are not to discourse but are to accept the content of the educator's monologue and the result of their acceptance is to be a lessening of their alienation from schools. "If there is no genuine dialogue... then you can be quite certain cultural arrogance is present."42 The absence of dialogue between teachers and working class parents has been the reality within provided education for over a century. The majority of community educators whose work, in this area, is published by CEDC do not depart from this tradition. Until the 1970's and 1980's this absence was simply due to a failure of the parties to meet; now that they do meet, dialogue is still absent. Parents and teachers meet so that teachers may convince parents that school is a positive place and that negative views of it are ill-founded. Teachers have to "help parents re-assess their attitudes... and promote a better understanding of what education is about".43 If teachers succeed in this new area of their work then the chances for the educational success of working class children will be increased.

This home-school aspect of community education, in effect one of community education's central themes, transforms class into parental attitude and interest in education. A semantic transformation of class into attitude, however, is not a transformation of reality. Parents are being asked

to accept school and education as they are; that is
as class based institutions and systems whose culture is antagonistic to that of the working class
home. Community education is not an education
which talks of the ineducability of the working
class nor of its unsuitability to receive education
but it is one which, in common with the explicit
class approaches of the nineteenth century, locates
the reason for the educational failure of the working class within the class and in so doing it
refuses to believe it necessary to examine in de-
tail just what it is at which the working class
fails. Just as the unemployed become the target
for education's response to unemployment, so too
the working class home becomes the target for education's response to the educational failure of the
working class.
     There is no departure, then, from the home-
school approach of Midwinter. This is not and
should not be surprising. As we stated, much of
Midwinter's philosophy of community education and
ideas as to practice came to be accepted as descriptions of what community education was all
about. The contributors to Network know this is
what community education is about and feel it would
be pointless work to re-invent the wheel. They no
longer write, as did Midwinter, of children being
educationally damaged and maimed by their parents
but they do talk how "teachers often find that they
have to undo what a well meaning parent has tried
to do. How much better then for all concerned, if
teacher and parent get together."44 The language
of educational intervention has changed but the
intervention itself has altered little. Many of
Midwinter's ideas for selling education have also
become the everyday practice of community education
and they have been refined and added to. Community
education in Britain in the 1980's has a number of
strands to it. Home-schooling is most important as
is the making available of school resources to
local communities. Crèches are now often found on
community school sites, and adults participating in
school classes. On first glance schools have
changed radically and community education has been
a causal factor in this change. Whether, on examination such change will remain to be seen as
radical is quite another matter. One crucial question to be asked of community education concerns
whether and how these changes, in effect, additions
to the activities of schools, change in any significant way the educational core of schools: are

they the new decorations of education and schools or do they signify that a meaningful change has taken place.

Rennie and Community Education

The Director of CEDC is, as we mentioned, its founder, John Rennie. Being the individual whose campaigning and fund-raising has resulted in the organisation which has 'taken over' from Midwinter and which is now a major influence and focus for community education in Britain, it is important to understand and place his philosophy of community education. Can it be seen, rather like the work of CEDC, as a continuation of Midwinter's community education approach and if this is not so, then how is it that the Director's philosophy is at odds with that of the organisation he directs. Unlike the editor of **Network** and most of its contributors Rennie does not see Henry Morris as the father of community education in Britain but instead sees him as one of its sons. He sees present day community education having its roots in a series of educational phenomena of the past; from the Mechanics Institutes of the nineteenth century to the night classes held in schools at the opening of the twentieth. He pointed out that, for him, the best example of community education he had ever seen evidence of was located down a slate mine in Blaenau Ffestiniog in Wales, no longer a working mine but an industrial museum. He explained:

> They've got life size models of miners and they're all sitting round the table having their snap and there's about ten of them and there's one guy sitting at the end of the table and he's got a book. And they had a half-hour break out of what was hell and they're sat there in the thick dust and they're using that half-hour to have education - they were educating themselves. And when you see that you think, 'Well, there was real, genuine, grassroots, rock-hard community education'. All the crap that's come since has mainly been led by professionals and there were working people, in the most extreme conditions, saying, 'We need education.'

From him community education's roots are very much located in such self-educating activity of Britain's working class. Most important to him is the notion that one's learning needs change throughout one's life and he sees this present in the Blaenau example as he does in a community education which talks of schools acting as neighbourhood learning centres. "One of the important things that community education believes - that someone who's a pensioner still wants to learn something - as much as a pre-school play kid does." Rather than attempt to give a precise and clear-cut definition as to his philosophy and understanding of community education, Rennie talked to the things he felt to be significant about community education; the things that had to be parts of community education.

Thus community education had to be about the right to learning throughout one's life. It also had to recognise that everybody was not only capable of learning but of teaching also. "In places like Cuba you've got that notion, that the ordinary fellow out there has got something to teach other people. And I think that's a very, very important aspect of community education." He felt that community education should beware of ever writing people off as having no talent for if practiced correctly community education would show that such people did have real talents that were of value. Rennie also stressed that, just as "whatever you do has a political dimension" so too did community education have such a dimension.

> And that's to do with a whole range of things and not the least of which is that it ought to be giving people the confidence and skills and the opportunities to learn about how they change: their life style, their community, the society that they live in.

He explained that he no longer believed, as he had done in the 1960's, that education, of itself, could bring about significant change: that schools were not the vehicle capable of fulfilling such a role. It wasn't possible to educate a generation, confident in the knowledge that it would bring about change as a result of being educated correctly. For, of course, when it left its schools, "much bigger forces in society screw them to the floor". He did believe, however, that education could play a complementary role to other forces in society.

Turning to the place of home-schooling in community education, Rennie felt that for schools

not to have regular contact with parents, was for
them not to be educating properly. He explained
his own background in this area of work. He felt
that there were two elements to it. The first was
concerned with raising standards, with improving
children's education: the second, concerned with
the parents themselves, though this only came to
light as his early work progressed.

> What happened was: as we got more and more
> people involved we found out to our astonish-
> ment that the biggest effect was on the par-
> ents, not on the kids. And they started
> making demands then and saying, 'I want to do
> something - it's interesting. I never had a
> chance to do that.' And realising they'd got
> potential themselves. I remember taking
> Robert Aitken* up to Eburne School, the most
> disadvantaged school in the city - proved
> scientifically - and showing him parents up
> there building Maths games and Reading games
> for teaching their kids, which on the confes-
> sion of the teachers, were infinitely sup-
> erior, not just in the practical way they had
> been made, but conceptually, to the ones the
> teachers themselves had invented. Once you've
> got parents to the stage where they're confi-
> dent enough to do that, they suddenly start
> thinking, 'I've got talents'.

To Rennie, the home-school approach, was as much
about informal adult education as it was about
better school/home relations and improving the
education of children.

Discussing the way in which community education related and responded to unemployment Rennie
did not simply view this matter differently to most
community educators; his view was diametrically
opposed to theirs. There was no acceptance of the
inevitability of mass unemployment, on the contrary
Rennie told us:

> There's no question about it, we could have
> full employment tomorrow in this country. It
> would mean massive re-distribution of income;
> it would mean changes of attitude on a scale
> that isn't conceivable at the moment. But it
> would mean first and foremost political

* Robert Aitken was Coventry's Director of
Education.

change.

Rennie stressed that there was nothing community education could achieve in macro terms regarding unemployment. The most it could hope to do would be to make the lives of the unemployed more interesting whilst they were unemployed and it could be of assistance in advising and helping moves towards worker co-operatives, "getting people involved in saving their own employment possibilities". Rennie was strongly opposed to many of the community education responses which had received publicity in Network. Such responses were part of an overall way of viewing unemployment for which Rennie had little time or sympathy.

> I'm ashamed of how patronising it is. Some of the things they're doing in some unemployment centres are... - well they start off with the assumption that what they need first and foremost is adult literacy. That's not my experience of unemployed people. There's four million unemployed people in this country: there's not four million adult illiterates. It'd be a remarkable coincidence if those two matched....Most of the unemployment centres I see start from the assumption that, I'm afraid it sounds terrible this, but they actually start by blaming the unemployed. They really start by saying - though they don't actually use these words - but what they're really saying to people is: 'Let's look at your shortcomings and see how we can do something about it to stop you being unemployed.' Well that's criminal.

Bringing the discussion of community education back to schools, we asked Rennie about his expectations of it making a difference to what is taught and the way it is taught; a difference, in effect, to the 'real' business of schooling. Rennie felt that the community education practice of encouraging adults to participate in school classes did offer distinct and hopeful possibilities here. He gave us an example of a particular community college.

> When they first started they used to say they liked it because it made the kids behave better. But when we looked at it, it wasn't the kids behaving better, it was the teachers behaving better. Because what they started

doing was preparing their lessons and making
them interesting and not saying, 'Sit down and
read'.

In addition to adults in classes, Rennie believed
it important that schoolchildren learn about their
own communities. If done well this would:

Change the whole nature of what kids perceive
schools to be about. Unfortunately most community educators don't see curriculum as being
anything to do with them. What they think
it's about is night school classes; that's
community education, not what happens to 4J on
Tuesday afternoons. I think that's very important what happens to 4J whether they've got
parents in there or not.

If the slate quarry in Blaenau was Rennie's best
example of rock hard community education from the
past then competing with it on behalf of the
present was the Moss Side Family Centre in Manchester. Its community education has "very little
to do with what we'd regard as traditional education", it revolves in the main around "social action" and is run by local women. To Rennie it is
among the best examples to be found anywhere of
genuine community education.
    The difficulty posed by Rennie's professed
beliefs should be apparent. How can the beliefs of
a Director stand in such clear contradiction to the
practices of the organisation he directs. To
briefly summarise those beliefs:

1. Community education has its roots in processes
   of working class self-education.
2. All people can teach others; therefore working
   class people need not simply be recipients of
   educators' monologues.
3. People have talents and community education's
   job is to bring them out.
4. Community education has a political dimension.
5. Parents are capable of teaching teachers.
6. Mass unemployment is not inevitable and the
   unemployed are not to blame for their unemployment.
7. Pedagogy and curriculum need to be changed by
   community education.
8. Community education can be run by local, non-
   professional people.

Not only do these beliefs of Rennie contradict the practices of CEDC but they are totally at odds with the belief system of that which we have called bourgeois provided education. Instead they seem to fall within the tradition of a working class self-education, an education for liberation not subservience. These two types and ways of approaching education are not ones which simply differ, each from the other: they are ways which oppose and are antagonistic to each other.

Our question about the clarity of the contradiction concerning the beliefs of Rennie, as Director of CEDC, and the practice of his organisation, has its answer in explanations which account for matters social and educational and not in any form of explanation which works in terms of the personal and psychological.

When CEDC was still only an idea in Rennie's mind, then its practice could 'fit' his philosophy: however, as soon as that idea is being translated into a real organisation staffed by real people then the contradiction cannot but be present. Organisations, of whatever variety, do have an existence which is more than the simple sum of their constituent parts. They do have, in some ways, a life of their own. But more important than the life of organisations, is the crucial issue of education itself and organisations which would deal with it. The 'Director belief/Organisation practice' contradiction tells us a great deal: the very fact that we 'see' it as a 'problem' is important. We see it as something which we feel should not be present - the Director is not in total control of his organisation. Throughout our work we will be concerned to stress the control which systems exert upon men and women and the control exerted by education is exceptionally strong and in many ways as substantial as a bag of smoke: all aspects of the educational system constantly and consistently tell us that there is no system; tell us that everything about the edifice works in terms of the individual. Children are assessed as individuals, teachers teach in their individual way, Heads have individual responsibility for their schools etc. Not only is there a systematic agreement about the individual nature of it all (surely a way of asserting that contradicts the assertion), but also there is a systematic concensus as to the language of education. And the language of education is intertwined with its ideologies. Contained within the everyday terminology of education are unwrit-

55

ten, implicit ideologies, the very word 'education' is not a value free, class-interest free noun. It is a value-loaded term and the values which load it, we will see as we progress, are essentially the values of a class with a class interest in the society in which class and education are located.

And the relevance of this to John Rennie? We need a special word here; one that conveys more meaning than 'constraint' for to be constrained suggests we are, or can easily be, conscious of the constraints. We would suggest that education's constraints are subtle enough for us to be unconscious of them most of the time. Most of them we take for granted as facts within the world and pay them scant attention. We have to use educational language to talk to educationalists and that language is filled with educational value-judgements and ideologies carrying class interests disguised as value-free educational truths. And it is all these 'constraints' which are most relevant to Rennie and the CEDC contradiction. In our physical world, the fact that we do not spend most of our waking hours consciously reflecting upon the constraint of gravity does not lessen the power of that constraint. So too, with things educational. Rennie and CEDC have to deal with teachers, Heads, Directors and LEA's. It would be a total impossibility for CEDC to attempt to insist upon an agreement as to the meaning of the words to be used, each time it came to talk to those involved in the practice of education. Even if CEDC thought such a path the correct one to follow, and we have no evidence for this notion, its life would be very short if it tried to follow the path. Professional educators would soon tire of talking about how to talk.

It is education, as it already exists, then, that, to a large extent, sets the terms upon which CEDC can be admitted to the debate. As a body committed to reform, the parameters of reform, are externally decided by the system targeted for reform. CEDC has, in effect, to agree to abide by the rules before being admitted to the game. It also has to show that it is qualified to play and that it agrees that the game is one for professionals only. The self-policing, self-defining nature of education is not the result of some form of conspiracy; it is, as we shall see, the product of history, and a history driven by class struggle. Rennie is as much constrained within CEDC as is a radical community tutor in a community college. We expect him not to be so constrained because we cannot help believing, to some extent, the myths concerning education and the individual. As Rennie is the Director, we expect him to be able to direct as he might wish. We, of course, would never be so naive with regard to the Ford Motor Company, for example. There, we would know and readily admit that a Director could only direct as he/she wished as long as it fitted the Company plan and purpose. CEDC is very different to the Ford Motor Company, but there are common elements. The Rennie/CEDC contradiction, to us, is real evidence that the significance attached to the individual by and within education is so attached, primarily for ideological reasons and purposes.

Rennie, we believe, is no more free to direct as he might wish to direct, than was Ursula Brangwen free to teach as she might wish. To attack either of them as individuals who have freely made an incorrect choice, would be unfair and unrealistic. Fictional Ursula Brangwen's or non-fictional John Rennie's; both are individuals operating within an educational system; both have sharply critical opinions of that system; and both are constrained in that neither can carry out an educational practice that is guided by their own philosophies of education. How could it be otherwise; could we realistically expect individuals acting alone to change significantly the system in which they work? Ursula has to 'put to one side' her beliefs if she is to teach in a way that her colleagues will recognise as teaching and which will allow her to survive as a person. Rennie, we assume, must have to 'put to the back of his mind' many of his beliefs as he operates in an educational arena peopled by many who would disagree fundamentally with him on matters educational.

This should not surprise us. If the education system did not work in this manner, then there would be few problems to be addressed: liberally minded teachers would simply teach in accordance with their beliefs and schools would reflect this. Such a situation would, of course, be a practical demonstration that the social sciences, and particularly sociology were irrelevant for it would show that the individual with his or her beliefs was the key to understanding the world. Institutions would only exist as the sum totals of the individuals within them and analysis of them would have to be by the way of an analysis of the individuals and their beliefs. This would soon be shown to be absurd and in everyday world of men and women, teachers or not, its absurdity is known. We are regularly aware of being constrained in our actions by things beyond our control; by institutional and societal forces and pressures which demand that we behave in a way that varies to some degree or other with our beliefs. These constraints can be such that in order to continue our action in a particular arena we have to come to regard our professed beliefs as separate to the action in which we are engaged. We drive to our place of work despite believing in the sense and sanity of public transport systems.

As we stressed in our first chapter it is crucial to comprehend that 'the educated' are actors in the social world; they are not special people exempt from methods of analysis deemed valid when applied to others. They do not create their worlds as they would wish despite ideologies which might insist the opposite. In their work as educators, they are not independent professionals making up their own minds. They are social actors working in an educational system which is more than their sum total as individuals. The myth of teachers teaching as they wish, the ideology of professional independence has to be exploded: if a few hundred thousand people in a country or a number of millions in certain countries - all working in a similar capacity - insist that, individually, they have the same belief on a particular subject - then we betray everything of value in the social sciences if we do not make such an assertion of common belief problematic.

We have, then, Rennie, as CEDC Director, with his beliefs on community education which are at odds with those of Midwinter, in many areas: and CEDC, itself, which has modified and altered Midwinter's community education, but not radically changed it - individuals and centres for community education. What of the real world of teachers, children, parents and schools? What is a community school and how does it stand in relation to community education thus so far discussed?

REFERENCES

1. Rée, H., _Henry Morris: Educator Extra ordinary._ Longman 1973. And The Origins of Community Education (1) in _Outlines._ CEDC 1981.
2. Widlake, P., The Origins of Community Educa-

tion (2) in <u>Outlines.</u> CEDC 1981.
3. Halsey, A. H., <u>Educational Priority; Vol. 1.</u>
   HMSO 1972.
4. Children and Their Primary Schools: The Plowden Report. HMSO 1967.
5. Widlake. op. cit.
6. Ibid.
7. Ibid.
8. Ibid.
9. A. S. Peacock MP. A Declaration of Interpen-
   dence. <u>1980 Plus Series. Community, Participation and Learning.</u> Book 6. p. 97.
   (The Six Books in this series are based on
   the proceedings of the 3rd International
   Community Education Conference held in Australia in 1979.) (Further references will be
   to '1980 Plus'.) Published by The Australia
   Assoc. for Community Education.
10. Dr Y. Nishimoto, Development of Community
    Education in Japan. From <u>1980 Plus.</u> Book 5.
    p. 70.
11. Frank, R. G., <u>Planning For Community Educa-
    tion: A Lay Citizen's Guide.</u> Pendell Pub-
    lishing Co. 1979. p. 18.
12. Diquiatco, I. S., Non-Formal/Adult and Com-
    munity Education in The Philippines. From
    <u>1980 Plus.</u> Book 5. pp. 46, 47.
13. Chew Keng Sung, Community Education in Singa-
    pore. From <u>1980 Plus.</u> Book 5. p. 66.
14. Midwinter, E., <u>Education and The Community.</u>
    Allen & Unwin 1975. p. 46.
15. Ibid. p. 59.
16. Ibid. p. 27.
17. Ibid. p. 73.
18. Ibid. p. 74.
19. Ibid. p. 86.
20. Midwinter, E., <u>Education For Sale.</u> Allen &
    Unwin 1977. p. 14.
21. Ibid. p. 15.
22. Ibid. p. 15.
23. Ibid. p. 17.
24. In <u>Education For Sale</u> the language of the
    salesman is regularly used by Midwinter.
25. Midwinter, E., <u>Education For Sale</u> 1977. p. 31.
26. Wilmott, P. and Young, M., <u>Family and Kinship
    in East London.</u> Penguin 1962.
27. Midwinter, E., <u>Education For Sale</u> 1977. p. 68.
28. Ibid. p. 87.
29. Ibid. p. 91.
30. The analogy is borrowed from Paul Corrigan, in
    conversation with the Author in 1972.

References

31. Bob Dylan, Ballad of a Thin Man. From High-
    way 61 Re-Visited. CBS. Long Playing Re-
    cord.
32. Rée, H., Network September 1984. CEDC.
33. Brighouse, T., Network April 1982. CEDC.
34. Ibid.
35. Freire, P., quoting Simone de Beauvoir in
    Freire, P., Pedagogy of The Oppressed. Pen-
    guin 1982. p. 47.
36. Poster, C., Network October 1982. CEDC.
37. Bowles, S. and Gintis, H., Schooling in Capi-
    talist America: Educational Reform and
    the Contradictions of Economic Life. RKP.
    1976. p. 5.
38. This Course was offered in Coventry in Septem-
    ber 1985 and was organised by a Community
    College in the City. The hidden curriculum
    may have escaped the notice of the Course
    Organisers: the local unemployed of the City
    were more critical, not one turned up for
    the Course.
39. Rée, H., Network February 1984. CEDC.
40. Kearsey, D., How do you Meet the Educational
    Needs of the Unemployed. From 1980 Plus.
    Book 2. pp. 141, 140.
41. An Article on Walsall (no by-line) Network
    February 1982. CEDC.
42. Pantin, G., Network September 1983. CEDC.
43. Robinson, F., Education Visiting in Outlines.
    CEDC 1981.
44. Ibid.
45. Rennie, J., Home and School: The Essential
    Link. Outlines. CEDC 1981.

Chapter Three

THE COMMUNITY SCHOOL

"Needs-meeting is most likely to re-inforce
prevailing definitions, distributions and
evaluations of knowledge, if the analysis remains
conducted at the level of professional ideology."

Colin Griffin. Curriculum Theory in Adult and
Lifelong Education.

The value of educational research lies in "establishing appropriate questions to be asked"[1] rather
than attempting to provide specific answers to
well-tailored questions. Consequently, though we
were interested in how our community school related
to the homes of its pupils, as well as other
specific concerns, we wished to approach the school
in such a way as to allow unplanned questions and
issues to emerge. Thus we were flexible in our
approach. We wished to discover the issues raised
by community education in the context of one school
as opposed to asking exactly how certain issues had
or had not been raised. We were concerned to
discover questions not test out hypotheses. As a
result we did not adopt a particular and exact
methodological approach; instead ours was a prag-
matic one which combined a questionnaire to all
staff with sessions talking to some members of
staff. We did not 'interview' these members of
staff, asking exactly the same questions in the
same manner; rather we talked with them and tried
to ensure they talked of specific themes within
community education. We wanted to discover and
illuminate important questions within community
education, "not display proofs or technically correct propositions on the basis of simple numbers
made incomprehensible by arithmetically exact
formulae."[2]

In focusing on only one community school we
are open to the charge which states that the sample
is too small or unrepresentative to allow for gen-
eralisation. This charge would be valid if we were
conducting research which aimed to generalise in
such a manner. This is not what our research
attempts to do. As we unveil our community school

with its particular identity and problems we hope that aspects of many community schools will be recognisable within it; that it will show to us some of the difficulties of community education in the community school. It will pose questions of relevance to all community schools; it will not posit answers to questions concerning all community schools.

We assured the staff of our community school that its responses to our questions would remain confidential and to this end we have altered the name of the school, that of the town in which it is located, and those of the staff who gave their time and help. The school was sited in Derbyshire and before we can look at the school itself it is essential to locate it, in an educational and philosophical sense. Briefly, in Derbyshire, what is education trying to achieve and what role is envisaged for community education. We must have an understanding here if we are to be equipped to make sense of our community school when we encounter it.

Derbyshire and Community Education

In November 1982, Derbyshire County Council published the Report of its Working Party on Community Education. This Report gives us a background to the community education service in Derbyshire and so helps us set the scene for our community school.

> Fundamentally we believe that schools should be an integral part of their community and that all schools are community schools. They should be open to all and should help to provide life-long opportunities for education. Parents should be significant partners in schools and be fully involved in the education of their children.[3]

There is some confusion here for the authors believe schools 'should' be a part of their community, thereby implying some are not, yet they assert that all schools are community schools; they then switch back to tell us what community schools 'should' be. If not all schools are integrated into their communities nor are they all open to all, then it is not really helpful to describe all schools as community schools. We are not being unnecessarily pedantic; we are simply illustrating the lack of clarity which can be encountered in the area of community education and stressing how important it is to read carefully community education's literature. The lack of clarity we encounter in community education literature should not surprise us for the absence of such clarity allows a degree of elasticity to community education, as a concept, thereby permitting it to be all things to all people. Consequently, we see here how the authors' own idea of the community school is softened by the description of all schools as community schools. By describing them all as community schools it is suggested that though some may be more successful than others, all schools serve their communities in the way that they 'should'.

Like most Local Education Authorities concerned with community education, Derbyshire wishes to involve parents in the education of their children. However, unlike many LEA's such education is not regarded as static; room is allowed for change.

> We believe that as community education develops there will be a significant change in what is taught and how it is taught, with a marked improvement in young people's attitude to education.4

This most interesting point is repeated in the Report but no explanation is offered as to how such educational change will take place. It is the case, however, that Derbyshire perceives a problem in the attitude of young people towards education and believes community education has a role to play in improving the attitude of young people in this area. We do begin to encounter some difficulties: the Report wishes to see increased parental involvement in education as part of an increased community involvement.

> The community does, of course, include local commerce and industry, and schools should foster their links as fully as possible.5

Parents will be involved in schools as individuals, as parents of particular children: industry will be involved in a more organised manner for managing directors and personnel officers will not speak and act as individuals, but as representatives of companies with policies. It seems to us that such representatives will be listened to more carefully than will individual parents for they will be able

to claim to be speaking for someone other than
themselves. Will local companies come to have much
more influence on schools and education than will
parents? Within the Report this becomes a likely
possibility.

> It is vital that each individual's gifts
> should be developed to prepare him/her for
> life in a society that increasingly demands
> adaptability and resourcefulness.6

For us, society demanding more adaptability, is the
result of the way in which industry and commerce
are organised and to us the Working Party's formu-
lation of this question is evidence already of the
existing influence of industry on education. Adaptability is not an abstract concept; it relates to
demands made of labour power by capital. To seek
to involve industry directly in education by relating community schools to local firms carries the
possibility that industry's influence will become
powerful in determining educational practice and
educational change. As most schoolteachers are
genuinely concerned with the future of their pupils
in a world of few employment opportunities, this
seems a likely result of such involvement. We
would not simply advocate schools severing links
with local industry or behaving as if it did not
exist; rather we are drawing attention to the influence which can all too easily accompany such
links as suggested by the Working Party. The theoretical questions concerning the relationship between capitalist production and education are not
only relevant to academics in universities; they
must be seen as important in the day to day inter-
face of industry and school, which the Working
Party sees as part of community education. Especially so when the local firms may well be owned
and controlled by parent companies located anywhere
in the capitalist world; possibly with subsidiaries
in The Philippines also having links with local
schools. Seeing local industry as part of the
local community, then, is not without problems.
There is an ideological aspect to this; one that
has been present since provided education's earliest days; and it suggests the essential harmony
and community of interest between capital and
labour power - bosses and workers part of the same
community.
    Though the Report envisages the school curri-
culum changing as a result of community education,

this change seems somewhat remote, and for two reasons: first, the Report does not discuss how such change might take place nor what kind of change it might be and so suggests implicitly that change will happen automatically - this is hardly likely. Second, the Report concerns itself with community education in a very 'day to day' manner: primarily it is about the use of school facilities and this suggests that such usage will be a large part of community education. How curriculum change will result from such usage is not explained and we can see no logical connection between these things. The Report contains some fine rhetoric for innovative community education but, more importantly, it contains a good indication of what will be the practical reality.

> The main constraint that we face in developing community education is that there have in the past been few resources allocated specifically to this aspect of the service.7

In its context, this suggests a view of community education concerned with resources, be it cleaning or caretaking or the extra wear and tear of plant in general. Important though these matters are they relate only to community use of facilities, not to what is taught nor how it is taught.

The need for parental involvement in education, a crucial aspect of community education, and the whole issue of curriculum change are given little serious attention in the Report. The authors wish to involve parents, do believe community education has implications for curriculum and pedagogic method, but seem to regard these issues as ones which will somehow be taken care of once the more mainstream, mechanical aspects of community education are put into motion. The authors believe there to be a causal relationship between open school facilities and educational content and method of delivery. Whether such a relationship does exist is not the question here: that it should be implicitly suggested in such a taken-for-granted manner is cause for concern. Schools as educational institutions, have over a hundred years of history to them: is it likely that significant change will come about in such a casual manner? This off-hand, unthoughtout way of regarding educational change is regularly encountered within community education as is the unclear way in which educational philosophy is treated. If change

65

to significant, aspects within education is treated as something which happens almost 'naturally', then, from the point of view of the teacher, what reason is there for a commitment to community education as a process of education. Will it not simply become part of education regardless of teacher reaction to it.

> We are anxious to state long term aims, certainly, but we also wish to ensure that our objectives are achievable and will represent real progress when we have reached them.8

When we decide objectives and state that they must be identifiable to the point where we can say we have concretely reached them, then we may be limiting our objectives and so restricting the nature and scope of our work. For example, a community education objective could be a particular number of evening classes in a school: once this objective has been stated there are a limited number of ways appropriate to its pursuit. Will these 'fit' the long term aims of community education or will they come to replace them. Many community educators are aware how easily a community education philosophy can degenerate into a 'numbers game'. Community education can lose its overall purpose and come to consist of sets of achievable and identifiable aims. It can abandon any philosophy which would seek to guide it as a process and can embrace pragmatism so that community education can be measured in numbers according to timetables and days of the week.

In this Report community education is identified, primarily, with those activities which are able to be easily identified and which revolve around the use of the plant: that is evening classes and community use of facilities, youth clubs and play schemes. It discusses in depth issues such as letting arrangements for schools and the acceleration in the capital depreciation of plant which comes with community use: it pays little attention to parental involvement and curriculum change. It does contain, however, two interesting points as part of its approach to community education. First, corporal punishment will not be permitted for it is "not acceptable in the context of the personal relationships which make up any community".9 Secondly, a move is made towards opening up the closed system that is education, by allowing parental access to pupils' records. "We regard confidential records as inconsistent with our view of school as a caring community."[10]

In November 1984, Derbyshire was beginning to discuss ways of discovering community need and strategies for meeting it, and community education was being discussed in the light of it being driven by client need, and buildings were being talked of as hoped-for community buildings.

> For the more a building reflects in its activities, displays, exhibitions, etcetera, the interests and concerns of local people, the more it becomes theirs rather than ours.[11]

The relationship between professionals and community was being examined in a radical manner.

> If a community's wishes are dominant the professionals have failed to enter into an iteractive partnership and undersell their skills; if the professionals are dominant then community participation or even representation becomes meaningless, doing no more than give a spurious acceptability to inflexible professional decisions; if politicians dominate, again there is partiality. Genuine participation and decision making calls for new structures.[12]

The aim put forward here is exceedingly difficult to make real in the social world, and presents even more problems in the educational world with its tautological methods of allowing rights to definition. Midwinter's community education where professionals tell people about how they, as professionals, make their decisions would be under attack from the new kinds of structures outlined here. In our next chapter we will be concerned with education's historic refusal to allow miners and mechanics to contribute to education's debate; with regard to community education in one school in Derbyshire we will now be concerned with the extent to which community education allows such contribution. Within education does community education help achieve a genuine participation, a true balance between professional and community?

Huntingdon Community School

I have learned, over the years, to realise

that the learning process is complex and that
it can be considerably reinforced when
conflicting attitudes are avoided. These
conflicts can arise between school and home
particularly when parent and teacher fall into
recognisable groups. There are, for instance,
those teachers or parents who think that
school is the teacher's business and that it
has nothing to do with the home. Yet so many
children during adolescence pass through a
phase of being difficult. How much better it
is for the teacher, therefore, to have the
support and help of parents during these
troubles.13 (Our emphasis).

Though the Headteacher of Huntingdon School, Mr
Rollings is writing about conflicts between school
and home, it is to the home he looks for support
for the school and the schoolteacher. We would not
expect him to do otherwise for the home, as a
supporter of school, has been a taken-for-granted
educational aim since the earliest days of provided
education. In the words of the Headteacher we see
the continued presence of an area of educational
struggle; specifically the home/school relationship
and the claim that it is for the home to be supportive of the school. Also present here, the
individual/class dialectic.

All children are, of course, different. They
have different talents and skills, different
likes and dislikes, different ideas and interests....Some will achieve great success; some
will realise modest aims and some will bring
disappointing results, but each one will
have had exactly the same chance.14 (Our
emphasis)

It is not the job of the Head to locate and critically question the individual/class dialectic. However, the fact that he might not feel able to
publicly recognise its existence does not negate it
nor lessen its meaning educationally for the working class pupil. As we will later see in our
discussion there is a particular assertion being
made here, which has been a constant in education's
ideological armoury, from the 1924 Committee on
Psychological Testing For Educable Capacity to the
Report of Spens in 1938 to the community education
of the 1980's: this constant states that the thing
in which an individual fails is non-problematic.

The failure is on his or her head. Children are seen as different, are given the same chance, some fail and some succeed. Huntingdon School can be seen as part of a tradition, within education, which offers individual explanation for phenomena which are class based. The personality and beliefs of Mr Rollings are not being attacked; rather we are showing how the role of Headteacher has to be seen as contributing to the continuation and reproduction of an ideological explanation for the way in which education functions. The aetilogical base for this form of explanation will be discussed in our next chapter but it is important for us to note that simplistic analyses and accounts such as this one dealing with reasons for educational failure, should be treated sceptically and should be suspected of being more ideological than they are explanatory. Though it is Mr Rollings who puts forward the assertion that Huntingdon School gives all of its pupils the same chance, we must not assume that Mr Rollings has blandly accepted a true equality of opportunity as being an accurate description of reality. Rather his assertion is of the type which all Headteachers must feel under pressure to put forward. The very word, 'school' carries an implicit message that all children in such places will be treated equally. Although the actual words are frequently written by individual Heads of schools, we are not able to explain the reproduction of educational myths and ideologies purely by reference to their words alone. We must consistently stress that we are dealing with an educational system within which the freedom for individuals to operate is limited: and that includes Headteachers. The Headteacher, then places the responsibility for failure with the individual who fails.

There is no radical departure here from traditional educational explanation. There also appears to be little chance of radical curriculum change.

In order to allay anxiety about adversely affecting the future prospects of all children, changes in the curriculum must be open to parental and community review.[15]

Here we see the Head re-assuring his readers that any changes to the curriculum will not adversely affect the future prospects of the child. To us, this suggests change will not be allowed to affect

69

the consensual base-line of the curriculum. The comprehensive school was to retain all that was excellent in the grammar school: it seems the community school will retain a curriculum necessary to the future prospects of children. How curriculum relates to prospects is not a clear issue: whilst it would be unfair to the children of one school to so alter their curriculum as to destroy their chances of success, we are concerned with the way in which this problem is posed. It seems that the debate is narrowed before it begins, by the suggestion as to how parents should approach it. They are being invited to monitor the curriculum to see that it does not change too much. We are not criticising the Head here for we understand the problems and pressures of curriculum reform. We feel he is conscious of the fact that there are groups of individuals who are greatly concerned to protect education against any slide which would seek to take it further away from the apparently sacred '3R's'. Let us not forget that we have had teachers, in effect tried, judged and convicted by the mass media for pursuing curricular reform.

More critically, from our position, for the working class child the curriculum has not been the arena for success: though we understand why the Head feels he has to defend it from all but the most gentle reform, we see the defence of it as not particularly relevant for the class which fails educationally. This class can be said to have no vested interest in the retention of the curriculum as it is at present constituted.

Huntingdon School and The Questionnaire

Huntingdon School is situated in Rochester, North Derbyshire. It is a split-site school and has approximately 40 teaching staff and 600 pupils. The organisation of education within the town is somewhat unusual; there are six Junior High Schools and two Senior High Schools, the latter being single sex schools. The Junior High's take children from the ages of 11 to 16 and the Senior High's, children from 13 to 18. At the end of their second year at Huntingdon approximately 50% of pupils transfer to one of the Senior High's. As a consequence of this system neither Huntingdon nor any of the other Junior High's has a Sixth Form, and, we were assured, they lose the vast majority of their academically able pupils at the age of thirteen. This way of organising a town's

education system deserves a chapter in itself to do
justice to the issues raised. Though unable to do
this, we will discuss, later in this chapter, the
effect this form of organisation has on one
specific area of community education.
Our questionnaire was designed to discover
ways in which school teaching staff viewed community education. We were concerned with the potential for change which was or was not offered by
community education. When we drew up the questionnaire of particular interest were community education's two major claims: that parents would be
involved increasingly in the education of their
children, and that standards would rise. When
completed the questionnaire demanded of us that we
pursue different questions in our follow-up interview for the responses here did not indicate a
great deal would be gained by further pursuing
these questions. The responses did, however, offer
to us areas to pursue which suggested interesting
views of teachers on community education more generally. With regard to the two specific community
education claims the responses were as in Tables
3.1 and 3.2.

Table 3.1. Teacher Contact With Parents.

Teachers Having Contact With Parents   21
Teachers Having No Extra Contact
    since Community Designation of School   20

Table 3.2. Community Education: Affect on Academic
            Standards

Teachers believing standards will rise   5
Teachers believing standards will not rise   6
Teachers unsure about this matter   11

Table 3.1 shows us community education has not
increased teacher contact with parents. One member
of staff did have more contact with parents, but as
this was the Head, it is fair to say that community
education had not increased contact between teachers and parents. Though community education has
not increased contact between teachers and parents
at Huntingdon, we were informed that considerable
contact existed prior to the school receiving its
community designation. With an already high level
of parent/teacher contact, it is hardly surprising
that the level did not rise further with the community designation. In Huntingdon then, community

education retains a parental contact system; it does not initiate it.

Of our respondents only the Head had had any experience of working in a community school and of all the staff, only he had received any in-service training for community education. Given this lack of experience in and contact with community education, on behalf of the staff, it is helpful to explore whether many of the staff are 'touched' by community education. Eight of the staff, approximately 32% of our respondents, either taught evening classes at the school or worked in the school's youth club; four worked in both areas. Only two members of staff had any experience of adults participating as students in their classes and this occurred with Computer Science and Pottery. In answering our questions concerning adult students, the pottery teacher wrote:

> This is an area where great care has to be exercised as it is a vexed question whether it is right or wrong. I tend to take each case on its merits.

It would seem, from this comment, that the acceptance of adults into school classes is very much a matter to be decided by the individual teacher. The positive aspect to leaving such 'policy-type' decisions to the teacher is that teachers unsympathetic to the practice will not have to participate and so will not teach adults, resenting their presence as they teach them: the negative aspect is that teachers are allowed to make community education policy and so deny adults the right to participate in school classes, which can mean that teachers unsympathetic to this practice will continue to have negative feelings with little hope of such feelings undergoing change.

Of the six teachers who had adult voluntary help in their classes, the help fell into three types. First, a local clergyman gave assistance with particular aspects of the humanities courses; second, assistance was given in child development courses and third, parents helped out when classes went out of school on educational visits. We did encounter one particularly interesting example of assistance and will describe it when we come to deal with our interviews.

Table 3.3 Departmental Staff Meetings

    Regular Departmental Staff Meetings   18
    Occasional Departmental Staff Meetings   1
    No Departmental Staff Meetings   2

Table 3.4 Agendas of Departmental Staff Meetings

    Community education always on the agenda   0
    Community education sometimes on the agenda 5
    Community education rarely on the agenda   12
    Community education never on the agenda   3

With none of the teaching staff having any community school experience or any in-service training, Tables 3.3 and 3.4 show how few of them seem to be in a position where they can develop their knowledge and understanding of community education through discussion with colleagues. Apart from the Head no member of staff believed the department in which they worked had a community education policy. Community education does not appear to touch a great many staff in the school. Though this is probably the case, twenty of the twenty-three teachers who completed our questionnaire did believe community education to be a sound educational idea, or at least to be one with some educational value; yet, at the same time, twenty-one of the twenty-three felt community education made little or no difference to the way they taught. We have to ask, how can community education be a worthwhile educational idea if it makes little or no difference to the way teachers teach? This question is not only being posed with regard to one community school in Derbyshire: it is asked of all community schools and of all staff in them. Rennie, we will remember, pointed out that 'most community educators' saw the curriculum as being nothing to do with them and indeed community education's literature makes this clear. Thus, we could argue that teachers who see community education making no difference to the way they teach, are reacting to it as community education would have them react. If this is so, then just what is community education. That it can still be a worthwhile educational idea, to us, is indicative of the ideological strength of all things pre-fixed with 'community'. Community education is ill-thought out to the point where it can be all things to all people and when one attempts to discover just what it is one is left with only a vague notion that it is a good thing. Apart from youth clubs on site and night classes by a new name, it is very difficult to grasp community education.

The questionnaires showed community education to have made little or no difference to any say teachers might have in the management of the school. Indeed only one teacher felt she/he had more say in school management and this was, in effect, cancelled out by another who felt their say in school management to be less since community designation.

The attitudes of staff towards a community say in teacher appointments was what we had expected. Educationalists seek to ensure that only 'the educated' are allowed any rights to definition or dialogue concerning education; the professional teacher has been trained to believe education to be the business of professional educators, and the ethos of school daily reinforces this belief. At Huntingdon fifteen of our teachers were opposed to any community say in teacher appointments, five were unsure and three were in favour. One teacher wrote:

> The Community are not the best people to have a say in this. This is an area I feel strongly about. I feel education is far too political already and would become increasingly more so were any inroads made in this direction. Such inroads of the community tend to be the thin end of the wedge and teachers might be hired and fired for entirely wrong reasons... whichever way I look at this; as a teacher, parent, governor or union person, I see no merit in it as an idea.

And another:

> All schools have governing bodies - these people are part of the community, therefore the community has always had a say. I don't think any more powers should be given to people who do not fully understand educational philosophies, etc.

Though the staff generally feel community education to be a good educational idea, it is difficult to understand how they can feel so. Most staff are in departments without any community education policy and where there is little discussion of community education; community education does not affect the

way they teach; the majority does not believe, or
is unsure, that community education will raise
standards; community education has not brought
staff into increased contact with parents; and,
finally, most staff are opposed to any community
say in appointments. The world, however, is far
from being a simple place; thus Huntingdon's
teachers are also able to hold the following
beliefs.

Table 3.5 Community Education's Effects

Improving Children's experience of School

Yes	17
No	2
Unsure	4

Table 3.6 Community Education's Effects

Improving the life of the Community

Yes	19
No	0
Unsure	4

The completed questionnaires suggested that
staff experienced community education in a very
indirect way; experienced it as something 'out
there', something external to themselves. Most
staff were in favour of community education in a
general sense but did not see it as something
particularly relevant to themselves as teachers.
They appeared to believe community education was
something which now happened at Huntingdon because
Huntingdon was a community school. If community
education has a distinct lack of impact on a school
teaching staff, then it is difficult to actually
say what community education is, in such a situation. Is it much more than the sign on the board
at the gate. In Chapter Two we consistently stressed the way in which community education attempts
to secure support for the school without changing
the school and its educational practice in any
significant manner. Huntingdon's questionnaires
support our argument here for the staff believe
community education should both improve children's
experience of school and the general life of the
community without changing greatly the way in which
the school operates and seeks to educate its
pupils; and, crucially, without teachers making any
real changes to the way in which they do their job.
If schools carry on their educational business as

usual, then just what is community education.

Talking To The Teachers

In talking to the staff we were keen to explore some of the issues raised in the question- naires. We will deal with the comments of the Community Tutor last for they offer important con- trasts to those of the mainstream teaching staff. These contrasts will indicate some of the diffi- culties community education has, even on its own terms. The views and beliefs of the community tutor allow us to see some of the important contra- dictions of community education in practice, and will be shown to be particularly significant when we come to deal with our Sheffield projects, in Chapter Six, where we will see how certain strat- egies contain the possibilty whereby these contra- dictions can be exploited to the benefit of the working class. In reporting our talks with staff we do so according to the themes we explored with them. In our conversations we expressed few opin- ions and spoke as little as possible, though enough to allow our conversations to be recognisable as forms of social intercourse. We do not believe we influenced any of the teachers in their comments, which were freely offered.

Parents in School

Mr Steel was in favour of having adults join- ing school classes as students, believing it would "help maintain discipline which is good and it would give the kids a much better working environ- ment". He believed an adult presence in the class- room would be a demonstration, to the benefit of the children, of how education was valued. It would also help him for it would offer "another pair of eyes. Anything that helps maintain discip- line is a good thing."

Mr Wall is assisted by parents in organising and running school educational visits. "They help out wherever they can; generally just keeping an eye on the kids." This 'teacher assistant' role of parents is also mentioned by Mr Kennnedy who told us that the humanities library could not function without parental help. "The amount of help given is fairly considerable." He also raised the subject of school visits and pointed out how important it was to have some-one at the back of the 'crocodile' as well as at its front. Though parents assist him in such ventures he did not expect any to join his classes as students for he regarded the curriculum as being geared to people of school age and so unsuitable for adults.

The interesting point mentioned on page 73 concerning parental assistance in school visits, relates to a child whose parents make their living by farming. Mrs Rich asked the boy's parents to come into school and take a session with pupils on issues related to farming. The father did not feel confident enough to 'teach' in the school but the mother did and so took the class. Teacher/parent contact increased in this case.

> They were so interested in it and had enjoyed it so much that - we were running a trip to Iona and they said they'd always wanted to go there and so I said, 'Well why don't you join us on the trip?' So they joined us - it made a nice relationship.

This example of what Mr Rollings would probably call 'organic community education' is worthy of attention for the social and educational become blurred here. It does, however, appear to be far from Huntingdon's norm. Few adults participate as students, even less take an occasional role as teacher, and go on from this to join students and staff on an educational holiday. Most adults/parents who are in Huntingdon School are there as voluntary workers. "I have parents that do voluntary work in the library", Mrs Rich tells us and then outlines the hours of assistance given by these helpers. From her comments it appears that the school receives from parents the services at least equivalent to those which would be provided by a full-time paid librarian. She was not unaware of this, nor of its problems.

> There's really a need for paid people to be doing those jobs: so I'm in conflict with myself because I can't run that library without them because we never, ever, have bottomed the work. We've always got a pile of work. Now I think that's not on: politicians should pay. Alright, let's supplement it a bit, but not to the extent of all those man and women hours.

Mrs Rich is sceptical concerning the unpaid labour aspect of community education. She sees jobs, essential to the running of the school, only being carried out because of the goodwill of parents. If community education in this area is about saving money, in Mrs Rich's view the same can be said in relation to adult students in school classes. She spoke of the differences in salary between the schoolteacher and the college lecturer and to her, teaching adults in schools instead of colleges, was "education on the cheap". Since Huntingdon received its community designation the number of adult helpers has not really changed nor have those individual adults who do the helping. Mrs Rich told us that the helpers were generally middle class mothers; though she had had one working class mother who assisted her. "I thought how refreshing it was to have her; and we lost her because, I think, she was aware of the differences." These differences, to Mrs Rich, were very much class differences. A working class mother was trying to operate in a middle class environment, and she knew it.

The Way Staff Teach (Including What is Taught)

Only one member of staff felt that community education should really involve a change here, though Mr Steel did tell us how he would like community education to make a difference to the way he teaches, but for him "community education has not encroached on my area at all". Again this should not surprise us, nor should we feel inclined to criticise Mr Steel for community education has, since Midwinter, attempted to 'sell' itself to teachers as a 'good thing', which would not challenge their professionalism. As we have seen in our discussion of Midwinter, his community education is, to a great extent, a method of advertising education as it is: it is not a strategy for changing it.

As we have said, the staff tend to perceive community education as separate to themselves and Mr Steel shows this. He sees community education as a thing which is capable of encroaching upon his area. He does not fear it; rather he would welcome it, but nevertheless it is a thing which may or may not affect him. It is not a philosophy of education which he feels, as a teacher, able to embrace. Thus he would like it to affect the way he teaches: he does not believe he could alter the way he teaches in the light of the philosophy of community education. Mrs Collett, who had experience of

teaching two adult students in her school computer
class, felt community education had not made and
would not make any difference to the way in which
she taught computer science.
Staff talked about teaching method being part
of one's personality and about the unsuitability of
many school courses for adult students. As we
talked with the staff it became clear how, in most
cases, they equated community education with two
phenomena: first, adults joining school classes as
students and second, increased use of school
facilities by members of the local community. The
one member of staff of the firm opinion that
community education should involve a change in the
way teachers teach was Mrs Wood: though she was
unsure what such a change might mean.

> I think the curriculum needs changing here and
> I think if they thought about involving the
> community more then the curriculum could be
> altered in a way which would, sort of enhance
> the community somehow. I see a much greater
> involvement as possible. Maybe it's idealis-
> tic, but I mean, ideally I see the community
> could have more say in the running of the
> school.

If staff equate community education with
adults in classes and increased use of school facilities, then it is difficult to see how they could
believe community education might be about changing
the curriculum and the way it is taught, especially
when the majority of staff have no experience of
adult students joining their classes, which could
possibly offer them the 'spark' they might need to
cause them to question the curriculum.

The Experience of School

For Mr Steel community education was very much
about adults joining classes and he expected such a
presence to "change the ethos and atmosphere of the
school". A scepticism towards such possible change
was evidenced by Mrs Rich who believed any adults
who came into school as students would tend to be
middle class and so would accept the ethos and
smoothly fit into it. She spoke of a miner who was
an expert at creating all manner of traps and
snares, tools of the trade for a part-time poacher,
a man with extensive skills and knowledge of the
countryside. Because schools do not generally

involve working class people she believed "people
are doing these things and we miss out on all that
richness". She was unconvinced community education
would significantly increase working class
involvement in education. Mrs Rich was the only
member of staff who talked explicitly of class. It
seemed she saw community education as a way of
attempting to involve the working class more in
schooling but she did not expect such an attempt to
succeed. For Mrs Rich, one problem here was the
inability or unwillingness of education to
recognise the skills and abilities of working class
people as valuable. For example, the snare making
skills of the miner would not be recognised as
being artistic, as would those of, say, the potter
or painter.

Mrs Wood believed community education,
particularly adult use of day-time school, would
change the school atmosphere for the better.

> I think school can be a very isolating insti-
> tution for kids ... little relevance for the
> kids to the outside world. I think a commun-
> ity school should lessen that isolating in-
> fluence ... There's the awful case when some-
> one says, 'OK - well you've got to be on your
> best behaviour today, kids, because there
> are visitors in the school'. It shouldn't be
> like that. There's no reason why it should be
> like that. Surely if the place is open to
> everybody then there's no need for anything
> like that. (Her emphasis)

She stressed how the presence of ordinary people in
school should not be the cause of extraordinary
behaviour. For her, a constant adult use of school
would be of benefit to all.

> I just think it's good to see, I love it. In
> fact, if I feel happier about seeing mums
> walking in and out past my classroom - just
> ordinary people - if I feel better about it,
> then the kids are going to feel better about
> it; my pupils are going to feel better about
> it because I am happier because I can see
> ordinary people about, so I don't feel iso-
> lated either.

Mr Rollings hoped community education would help in
a move away from a "layering of society" and looked
forward to:

> Seeing a whole range of age groups from the
> mothers and toddlers, through the youth
> clubs, through the adult classes, through the self-
> programming groups, through the senior
> citizens - all enjoying working together in
> the right kind of atmosphere without there
> being any apparent generation gap.

As we have said staff at Huntingdon do identify
community education with adults in school classes
and it is this, which for some staff, offers hope
with regard to changing the ethos of school and
increasing the motivation of the school's pupils.
Mr Steel is representative of the staff when he
tells us that "having people who want to learn in a
room" will increase the desire of others to learn.
Not only does this relate to Derbyshire's desire
for an improvement in young people's attitudes to
education (see page 63) but it is central to
community education in general. There is an element to it which reminds us of Midwinter's methods
for selling education in that the adult students
are to advertise the real value of education to
those who have a statutory duty to be its consumers. However, with regard to Huntingdon School
this advertising/community education practice is
threatened very much by the way in which the education of Rochester is organised. Mr Kennedy began
to explain.

> I think for a community school to be success-
> ful it needs to raise its academic standards
> before it starts; it needs to be respected by
> the community. The people who know the Ro-
> chester set-up, regardless of the abilities of
> their children, if they have an ambition for
> their children, send them to the Grammars. As
> a result you get a massive outflow of ability.

For Mr Kennedy this means community education cannot raise standards at Huntingdon for the vast
majority of academically able children transfer at
the end of their second year. For him this means
few adults will wish to become students at Huntingdon for there is no Sixth Form, nor for that
matter, suitable courses for adults provided as
part of the Fifth Form curriculum. There are two
crucial points here. First, Huntingdon staff perceive community education to be about adults in
classes and if it is likely that there will be very
few such adults in classes, then this has implica-

tions for community education at the school. The
teachers will not experience adults in classes and
so will not alter their way of teaching nor what
they teach. Consequently Derbyshire's aim for
community education to change these things might
well be an unrealistic one. Secondly, if Mr
Kennedy is correct, in a general sense, then the
already successful schools should be the ones which
come to be designated as community schools for it
is they which will attract adults as students.
This, of course, stands in total contradiction to
the practice of and rationale for community education: in that community education was to be a way
of working educationally on and with the working
class. Mr Kennedy's comments would seem to suggest
community education as a strategy for engaging even
more in an educational relationship with the middle
class and those aspiring to middle class status.
Fortunately, however, for community education, few
cities or towns in Britain organise their education
as does Rochester. Thus community education does
not face a situation where schools can be clearly
identified as being, in effect, for the less academically able or academically competent and so a
situation does not come about where adults only
join classes in particular schools. However, Mr
Kennedy's point does force us to ask, for example,
of the inner city community school - what proportion of its adult students in school classes reside
in the immediate inner city area. Are they locals,
or are they middle class people who have commuted
to benefit educationally from a community school?

So, even on community education's own terms
just who is it that is actually served in the real
world by community schools? Returning to Huntingdon, with few adults in classes what will community
education be? It will probably come to constitute
evening classes, play schemes, voluntary parental
labour, youth clubs and youth activities. Though
we do not have the empirical data to sustain the
following; we suspect that underneath the sophisticated explanations of community education in many
of the older and better established community
schools and colleges, the actual practice of community education is broadly similar to that practiced at Huntingdon. Again, let us remember
Rennie's point: if most community educators don't
believe community education to be about curriculum,
then what can it be about? What can community
education's practice be concerned with - other than
the activities we find at Huntingdon? This is of

course how community education is perceived by many; a series of extra activities grafted onto a school but not of it, not something which changes the school itself in any appreciable manner.

A Community Say in Teacher Appointments

It was not possible for us to talk to all teachers who were willing to discuss community education with us, but we were able to talk to eight of this group. We selected, in so far as we ensured we were able to talk to, those teachers who had expressed an opinion favouring a community say in teacher appointments. We did this because we saw the issue as important in itself, but primarily we saw it as a barometer which would allow for a broader reading on attitudes towards community education. The opinions of the staff on this subject show us again how the educational world has its own contradictions. Mrs Rich, the teacher most keen in many ways to see an increased working class involvement in education and an educational recognition of working class skills and knowledge, was strongly opposed to any community say in teacher appointments. Nor was Mr Steel in favour of any community say:

> The number of adults in the community that I am being specifically appointed to deal with is small; so, therefore, I find it rather bizarre that that group of people that I deal with, in fact will have, seemingly a disproportionate say in my appointment.

Mrs Collett argued:

> I don't have any say in how anybody else gets their job so I don't really see why anybody out in the community should have anything to do with my appointment.... I don't think the community as a whole has, perhaps, the knowledge to choose the teaching staff.

Mr Wall's view on this matter lay at the other end of the spectrum to that of Mrs Collett.

> We're providing a service for people in this area and, therefore, surely they should have a say in the way things are done and who is appointed to do the jobs.

As community education does not really touch the majority of Huntingdon's staff it is not surprising that little reason is seen for the community having a say in teacher appointments.

This issue allowed us to gauge staff attitudes to broader and more contentious areas of community education, those which have the potential to challenge the professionalism of teaching, and staff attitudes present a particular problem. If community education in Derbyshire is to talk seriously about participation then it has to begin to consider operating with a model of education as a service, as described by Mr Wall. Indeed his comments fit well into the idea of participation and decision making as outlined in Derbyshire's Community Education Document of November 1984 (ref.12. page 67). The problem, of course, is concerned with translating the ideas of a document into teacher belief and if no real attempt is made to do this then we have to ask whether the stated aim is a real one or whether it is primarily rhetorical in purpose. All the teachers working throughout Britain have been trained to do a particular job, and, in the main, that training has not had to take into account notions of participation nor theories of community education. It would seem, to us, that even within education as it is, some attempt at training is necessary. To expect teachers who have been trained not to consider participation, to suddenly embrace it, seems unduly naive and optimistic. If we see L.E.A.'s espousing notions of participation and pursuing the practice of community education, then we would expect them, if they are serious in their espousal and pursuit, to be engaged in providing systematic in-service training. In effect this training would be a re-training: teachers who had been trained to believe and operate a practice of professional autonomy, would need to become operators of a de-professionalised, co-operative approach.

Mr Kennedy was also in favour of some form of community say, preferably by way of "some extension of the governing body", to allow for the representation of community groups. The thinking behind his contribution relates specifically to Huntingdon School but it is relevant to most schools where Headteachers have considerable power.

The present Head's policy has been very much, 'I shall decide who I get', and there has been some disquiet in fact with his interviewing

techniques and there has been a feeling, in
fact, that there is a certain amount of nepotism. It's who you know if you want a job at
Huntingdon not what you are. I feel strongly
that Governors should be involved; they are
the representatives, and important representatives, of the community. The question that
begs is who else could be considered a representative?

For Mr Kennedy a community say would act as a
balance to a charge of nepotism resulting from the
Head appointing alone. For Mrs Rich, however, the
Head appointing alone would be satisfactory for it
would retain professional control over
appointments.

> Even with Governing Bodies there are very
> often people on governing bodies who, in my
> opinion, have no right to be there. They
> don't understand education itself; they are
> not particularly interested in the education,
> just interested in being on a body... but I
> think it's a professional thing. I also think
> politicians have too much to say.

Mrs Wood could see no reason for the community not
to have a say in this area. Rhetorically she asked
herself, 'Why shouldn't they'? and answered:

> Would people say that they shouldn't because
> they don't know anything about it? It would
> depend on what you were expecting of that
> teacher. If you were going to say that all
> teachers in a community school – its like
> saying, 'Right, from September 3rd 1986 all
> teachers employed here are going to be commit-
> ted to community education and who are going
> to have, not only to teach first year maths,
> but also be involved much more fundamentally
> with other community groups'. Then that would
> be OK, wouldn't it? That would be fine. You
> could then have a representative (on the in-
> terviewing panel) I think that would be good.
> But while you're in a state where the school
> has simply been designated a community school,
> and there are lots of teachers who don't agree
> with community education, it's difficult then.
> Perhaps you could say, 'From now on the only
> teachers we are going to appoint are the ones
> with community bias'.

The Community School

On this issue, as with many other community education issues, we do not simply have a group of staff
in favour and another opposed; rather we have staff
taking different positions for different reasons
and with different motives. If community education
is to have a chance of succeeding, even on its own
terms, then ways have to be found towards making
the teachers in schools such as Huntingdon, parts
of a whole which has a coherent philosophy and
staff policy towards what it means by community
education. We believe this critical comment could
well be applied to any community school or college
and this is primarily due to two factors. First,
the schools and colleges themselves often do not
attempt to create a coherent philosophy and staff
policy: secondly, and more important, community
education, as it exists, is not constituted as a
coherent whole. On its own terms, community
education must become considerably sharper in
definition if belief in it is to be something more
than an act of faith and declaration of intent.

Community Education

Only three of the twenty-three teachers who
completed our questionnaire believed in some community say in teacher appointments. If we treat
this as an indication, but not <u>the</u> indication, of a
strongly positive attitude towards community education, then we can appreciate some of community
education's problems at Huntingdon. However, there
is a difficulty here. It is possible that well
established community schools and colleges would
produce high numbers of teachers supporting a community say in teacher appointments. We are tempted
to speculate that such hypothetically high numbers
would be obtained as a result of teachers telling
interviewers what they wanted to hear. We believe
that at Huntingdon, teachers told us what they
really believed and felt about community education.
Teachers in a school recently designated a community school have not had the time to become fluent
in their answers. We are not able to address this
issue here but we must raise the possibility that
changes in teacher attitudes claimed for community
education might be more about increased fluency of
explanation than real change of attitude.
To those who completed our questionnaire we
must add the seventeen questionnaires which were
not returned. We cannot theorise much about these
but it is probable that some were not returned

owing to lack of interest in community education. Mrs Wood told us that there were 'lots' of teachers who didn't agree with community education, yet our responses had twenty of the twenty-three agreeing that community education was of value. If Mrs Wood knows her colleagues' opinions then many of those with negative feelings towards community education failed to complete our questionnaire. A low level of support for community education was also mentioned by Mr Kennedy as he outlined the beginnings of community education at Huntingdon.

> There's no secret about it; that it's been the Head's pet and it was something that he, in a sense, has pushed. He didn't get a lot of support from many staff because of the sorts of things he was saying when he was trying to push it - like 'it will mean flexi-time' and this and that. It put off a lot of staff and made them feel threatened. Although there was discussion it was very much a one-man show. He didn't even have the full support, I don't think, of his deputies. Though they liked the idea, they haven't actually backed him up in a way that he would have liked if he'd been able to appoint his own community deputies...I think there's a gradual softening of attitude toward community education.... I don't think the in-service training was in any way adequate.

Thus far we have suggested how community education is seen by Huntingdon staff, primarily in the light of use of facilities and adults in classes. These two aspects of community education are among the least contentious; yet, if Mrs Wood and Mr Kennedy are correct in their assessment of their colleagues and their attitudes, even these aspects cause problems for some staff. Not all the antagonism towards community education will be found with those teachers who did not complete our questionnaire: contradictions can exist within individual teachers so that they are able to believe community education to be a sound educational idea yet fail to support it, and in their everyday teaching work, be antagonistic to it. Mrs Rich, we remember, was critical of schools for their failure to involve working class people, yet was firmly opposed to involving them in any governing capacity.

For Mr Steel community education was "making people within the community, part of school,

whether it be in passing in break-time, using the
same buildings at the same time, or hopefully,
being involved in the lessons themselves". This
idea of community education is a 'one-way' notion
where the community comes to and uses the school;
the school does not go out into its community. In
this model community education is not concerned
with any change to educational provision; rather it
seeks simply to allow increased access to that
provision. Like Mr Steel, Mr Wall believes "we
ought to be looking for more and more ways of
introducing the local community into school". But
he goes on to suggest that school should also be
"taking as many opportunities as we can to use the
local community". By this he meant, seeing the
local community as a resource, something of value
in terms of the school curriculum. He drew attention to what he perceived as a problem in community
education: his problem, to us, was an indication of
a beginning of a questioning as to the purpose or
function of community education. He talked of how
schools were once much smaller and how teachers
lived in the locality of their schools.

> I think in a way we're actually going back in
> time. I get the impression that we went
> through a stage of excluding the local commun-
> ity from school; possibly because teachers
> themselves were not involved in the local
> community, whereas in the past, teachers used
> to live more in the communities they served
> and I think in that way the community was more
> involved in the schooling. Communities are
> different now to what they were then.

It is not important here to discover whether communities existed in which teachers and taught were
very much constituent parts; what is important is
Mr Wall's idea of community education as almost an
attempt to turn the clock back to such a time. The
passage of time does pose a problem for him because
he believes it probably necessary for teachers to
be a part of the community if community education
is 'to work'; yet he recognises that most teachers
live some distance from their work. He was aware
that this situation could not be changed by Local
Educational Authority directive. Even if such an
option were available and practical it could not
ensure that teachers became parts of their communities. Mr Wall told us of teachers who did live in
the immediate locality yet were not really part of

it. "I can think of examples of people that do live in the catchment area of the school who have very little to do with the local community." Indeed this was echoed by Mrs Collett who does live on the same estate as many of the school pupils and their parents. "I don't have a great deal of social contact with them."

We see Mr Wall as moving towards a recognition of the contradiction between the rhetoric of community and its reality, or rather its lack of reality. He was one of the few members of staff who had begun to think about community education in any sense theoretically. He was examining the problem of how schools should and do relate to their 'communities'. Mrs Collett, a teacher who had had two adult students in one of her classes, seemed untouched by community education. For her it was, "the community coming into school and being around the school, not just in the classroom, and using the school's facilities". She described her experience of community education thus far:

> You see the old age pensioners coming in one afternoon a week; you see them walking past your window; you see, possibly the mother and toddler group - but really, once you're inside your classroom it has no effect on you whatsoever.

Mr Kennedy's ideas on community education have much in common with those to be found in CEDC's Network:

> At its most basic level, which is not what community education is about - on the use of facilities, it obviously makes good sense that they should be made more widely available, the doors shouldn't be locked when the P.E. staff go home. I think it is good in the more broad sense. I feel that to have people from the community becoming involved in the pupils' education leads to a greater understanding of what a school is trying to do for the 11 to 16 age group. It is important that, if you have the facilities as a community school, or any school, that are being used at night, the people, the children in particular, will see education as less than a thing that stops... but as a lifelong process.

Community education should be about giving people "the right sort of approach to education. One of

89

the most important things that I see the community
school actually doing is to change people's attitudes."

Mrs Collett and Mr Kennedy are fairly untouched by community education; insofar as they
might see it as altering the attitude of people
towards education but not necessarily altering
education itself in any way. People come into
schools and as a result better understand what goes
on in them. Community education does not 'touch'
them for they know what education is about and the
job of community education is to educate the uneducated into an understanding of what education is
about. This is not a harsh judgement; either of
Mrs Collett and Mr Kennedy or of community education. Midwinter's work and a great deal of material printed by CEDC informs us that the task for
community education is the bringing about of maxi-
mum parental support of schools. Community education aims to ensure more people understand why
education is as it is. As professional teachers
already 'understand' this, it is to be expected
that they will not feel particularly 'touched' by
it.

In Chapter Two we drew attention to the public
relations/advertising nature of Midwinter's community education and criticised the way in which the
culture of the working class was treated. The
views of Mrs Rich pose similar problems here. She
is concerned at the lack of working class involvement in schools:

> If they're coming in for sport, then yes, you
> will get all kinds of different people, but if
> they're coming in for education, they're
> generally people who could, perhaps, learn by
> themselves anyway. They're generally the
> middle class.

Her strategy for working class involvement is, in
many ways, strikingly similar to Midwinter's.

> I honestly think that you should put on your
> bingo and darts matches if that's the way to
> get them in, and then graduate from there. We
> don't seem to do that, do we? Get them in
> with the things they like, not that we think
> they ought to have...Do you ever see beer and
> darts at school?

Mrs Rich, like many educationalists, honestly believes the only way working class people can be gotten into educational institutions is by way of beer and bingo. Chapter Six will show this not to be the case. She, again like many community educators as well as mainstream educationalists, aims to use a method to 'get them in' on their own terms in order to involve them in education on the school's terms, not their own. This is an example of a very common phenomenon within education: that is the working class is seen as insufficiently intelligent to allow for an honest and open educational approach and instead is approached by devious paths and with some stealth in order to capture it in the educational sense. Or it is possible that educators implicitly recognise that the education on offer is antithetical to the interest of the working class and so seek to offer it in a devious manner?

For Mrs Wood a community involvement in school is seen in a more radical manner. She does not treat the school as a non-problematic given to be supported by the community.

> I think I see it as the school being a focus for the community and the community being involved in the running, in every level, in the running of the school.

The Headteacher

With community education being a series of discrete good things it is hardly surprising that the staff of Huntingdon does not have a coherent view of community education; rather individual staff members hold different and often contradicting views and attitudes towards the subject. Different teachers think community education means different things and they have different perceptions as to what is going on at Huntingdon. It is important, then to see how the Head of the school views community education, how he perceives its problems vis-à-vis Huntingdon and how he proposes to deal with them.

> The thing that has, I think, perturbed me a little has been the reserve of the teaching staff in building their obvious skill level and taking advantage of the professional situation that has been presented to them. If I can enlarge upon this without being critical of my colleagues, because I've got the great-

est admiration for my colleagues, but the
history of the school is this.

We began five years ago as a school
threatened with closure. I came to the school
at that point with some clear community education experience; made it quite clear to all
the staff that while falling rolls and the
threat of closure could be staved off by
adopting a community education stance, I was
not going to introduce community education as
a philosophy simply to avert closure and
simply as an antidote to falling rolls; that I
happened to believe in the philosophy of community education; explained what it was, built
a consensus, and then, as a school staff we
did for two years work on an outreach programme which convinced people that we were
capable of becoming a community school. And
the fascinating thing was, that while it was
voluntary and because it was a 'backs to the
wall' situation, there was an enormous amount
of dynamism, imagination and effort that produced a quite outstanding situation - so much
so that the school was designated a community
school, the community tutor was appointed, and
those self-same staff who had shown their
ability and willingness suddenly felt that
they could no longer give the same amount of
commitment. Hard to analyse whether this
coincided with the national disenchantment
...I'm never sure...But I'm disappointed at
how, having been designated as a community
school, and having worked for that position,
some staff then, only then, began to query
whether we wanted to become a community
school. They started asking the question far
too late.

To us, it seems the staff, when working for the
community designation, understood community education as a thing which could be 'achieved'. The
Head was seeing it as an educational method while
the staff was seeing it as an educational end.
Consequently, when the school received its
community designation the staff believed community
education had 'arrived'.

The problem with perceptions within the school
becomes apparent. Mr Kennedy, we remember, believed the Head received little support from the
start but that staff attitudes towards community
education had since softened: the Head believes he

received support from the start but that attitudes
have since hardened. Thus we have, within the
school, different perceptions of community education and different perceptions as to how community
education is perceived.

> I'm not aware of many of my staff taking an
> active interest in the Community Education
> Association. I think they feel it's tinged
> politically. And the reserve that has come
> into the school I think is surprising, partic-
> ularly when one sees that the Authority is
> going to appoint Headteachers - only those
> with community education experience and we
> have the opportunity to train ourselves... But
> I can't believe that community schools are so
> different that there is some magic training
> available somewhere that is in fact going to
> produce or change the outlook of the teacher.
> We've got to get away from the idea of teach-
> ing and into the business of learning. We've
> got to re-inforce the idea that learning takes
> place in the most unexpected places, the most
> unexpected times, both day or night or stages
> in your life.

If there is no magic training method, then how is
the Head to educate his staff into a philosophy of
community education? For himself, he is beginning
to see education as not so much teaching but more
the facilitation of learning; how is he to take his
staff with him down this road? Mr Rollings is no
radical Headteacher but he is beginning to recognise as valid much of the learning which occurs
outside educational institutions and he is asking
how we can move from seeing teachers as simply
those who teach to seeing them as those who help
others to learn. Though Mr Rollings does not form-
ulate the issue as we do, it seems to be one we can
summarise thus: the staff's community education
asks for support from the community; the Head's
community education asks for the same support but
recognises the need for educational change in order
to ask for this support. His willingness to accept
the need and possibility of change is made clear.

> The organic community school, from my point of
> view, is a school which is responding to the
> needs of the community and it has to be in the
> context of the day to day situation. Schools
> change when there's a mining strike, schools

change when there's a schools dispute on,
schools change when there's rate-capping. So
what kind of school we shall eventually be, I
don't know. So we're organic, we're growing
like anyone else. But what we're doing is
working on the idea of partnership, networking
and using our facilities because school facilities should be open all year round...I don't
regard school as being <u>the</u> centre of the community. I would like to see Huntingdon as a
centre of the community and part of a network.
I am not a de-schooler; I happen to believe
that there is such a thing as a good school
and that if we get the relationship right
between the staff, the students and the wider
users, then, in fact, I see schools very much
as centres of learning where we're maximising
the use of the facility. (His emphasis)

The questionnaires, the interviews and the comments
of the Head lead to the major problem facing community education at Huntingdon and it is concerned
with the attitude of staff to community education.
This is not a criticism of the staff for like
teachers in any school the members of staff were
trained to do a particular job in a particular way:
to criticise teachers for failing to welcome community involvement in education would be to miss
the point, for when teachers are trained they are
not trained to make such involvement welcome. And
within the writing on community education itself we
have seen how little departure there is from the
model which refuses meaningful involvement to non-
professionals. Nevertheless for the Head to develop community education at the school it is necessary that the staff be won over to a philosophy of
community education at least in sympathy with that
held by the Head. Mr Rollings does not believe in
a magic wand of training but tends to believe in a
training by doing: however, this presents him with
difficulties given the reserve he sees among his
staff and the fall-off in commitment. If not many
are doing, not many are being trained. The crucial
issue concerning community education as expressed
by the community school emerges. For community
education to begin even to do that which it believes is its task it is necessary that it convince
teaching staff of its value to the point where they
become its supporters and advocates. How is this
to be done?

94

The Community Tutor

In our conversation with Helen Gould, the community tutor, a number of ideas emerged as she explained her strategy aimed at winning over the school's teaching staff. We explained to her how many of the school staff equated community education with adults in classes and community use of plant, and asked her how she saw community education.

I see it as a strategy for changing communities, changing for the betterment of society in general. I see it as political. I think it's empowering people to do something about their world; it's people having a say about what happens to them in their learning centre... What I'm saying is that I'm prepared to go along with people who have fears about working alongside people who are so-called non-professional, and wouldn't want to confront anybody like that with too much of a change. I don't see any point in doing that. I think if I can help them come to terms with, and eventually experience the fact that non-professional people can actually educate, not by telling them that they can do it but by showing them; that there are benefits from working alongside those people, doing it in a fairly subversive way I suppose, because I don't think you get anywhere by saying, "Now look here you must, you've got to, it's reactionary of you to think that a mum of an eleven year old hasn't got something to say about the education of her child or about the community or life of the community". There'd be no point in me telling a teacher that, however I might think that they were being reactionary. There'd be no point in me doing it. What I would prefer to do is to gently show them that, actually it's quite possible and it isn't threatening and that the people have got ideas to contribute.

Helen explained how she saw the need for educational change and how she felt this had to be attempted by changing the attitude of teachers by way of practice not debate. With regard to how the staff saw community education, she told us:

Obviously there's a hell of a lot more to it

95

> than that and I'm surprised, given the number
> of times I've ferried information out to the
> staff about the sort of thing I'm doing, I'm
> surprised that they still see it as that.
> Maybe they see it in their terms, what it
> means to them: the other developmental things
> are perhaps what they think it means to me -
> for the moment they don't particularly want to
> be involved in that.

In the context of her 'persuasion by practice'
approach to staff education regarding community
education she began to explain her work.

> Dual use is the very first primary stage that
> you would be going for and even if you're
> going for dual use, you're not going for it
> just for the sake of using plant; because,
> although that's important - it is important
> that resources shouldn't be wasted - it is
> only a very small part of the story. If that
> is the beginning then the end point is that
> the school or college, or call it what you
> will, should have a curriculum which reflects
> the idea that learning is for life, that you
> do continue to learn throughout the whole of
> your life; so that the curriculum for the
> young people and the older people should re-
> flect that.

Community education has to be seen as essentially
ideological, as a mechanism which attempts to involve the working class in education without making
any fundamental change to that education. There
are, of course, contradictions within community
education, both its philosophy and its practice.
Helen Gould's concern is not simply to explain the
curriculum to parents; she is interested in changing it and in the role parents can play in this
changing.

> Once people do start to learn and start to
> come together, and particularly when adults
> start to come together, then obviously their
> confidence is built, their awareness of their
> world is sharpened and they become more aware
> of the things they want to change.

Helen's comments here echo those made by John
Rennie in our last chapter. She is locating
aspects of the continuous thread of working class

96

self-education; a coming together for a collective
identity, an increased confidence born from the
collectivity, a sharpened awareness and, crucially,
a desire to change the world. The process she
describes is, however, far from straightforward and
it is one which schools historically exist to pre-
vent: thus it is a process in which schools are
ill-fitted to assist, for the school's educational
model is far removed from this self-education process and is, in fact, antithetical to it. Schools
deal with individuals and are concerned not with
changing the world but with adapting to it and they
provide education and do not facilitate self-education and learning.

Where John Rennie talked of Eburne School and
the lessons learned there (see page 52), Helen
Gould talks of work on play schemes. In 1985 a
group of local women came together in order to set
up and run a scheme for 4 to 7 year olds. It
would run parallel to a similar school organised
scheme for children aged 8 and over.

> And for some of them it will be the first time
> that they've been involved in anything; act-
> ually planning for, executing something which
> is normally done by professionals. Running a
> playscheme is really quite a technical job and
> in lots of areas it's provided for by, say the
> Local Council who employ play leaders; but
> here we are doing it using voluntary help,
> which I know has got all kinds of question
> marks over it, but it does mean that the
> people themselves gain confidence through
> doing it and, as I say, meet together. And
> then all the other issues start to come out as
> well. Women's issues are beginning to come
> out of that group; plus the fact that we've
> got a mother and toddler group and a playgroup
> and the women tend to meet one another.

This form of learning by doing is interesting: we
must point out, however, that the learning which
takes place cannot fail to be influenced by its
location and professional input.

> Then we've got the outreach work team and
> their job is specifically to make those sort
> of contacts within the community, to find out
> what's going on, to find out what people are
> talking about, what issues they're mobilising
> around and to actually work alongside them.

The way in which the members of this outreach team
work alongside people from the community and the
issues in which they choose to involve themselves,
are critical aspects of educational intervention.
The problem here does not concern the individuals
who make up the team, though that can be important,
rather it concerns a school actually working in
this area. An ever present ideology within education is the denial of class in any conflictual
sense, and the insistence of consensual harmony.
This ideology is part of the drive of the bourgeoisie in capitalist society for hegemonic control.
This 'theoretical' point is relevant in the day to
day practice of education in schools. (Indeed we
have already encountered the Head stressing the
need to avoid conflict. Ref. 13, page 68.) With
an outreach team being school based it is almost
inevitable that the team will come to be more
concerned with explaining education than changing
it. Such a team will have to be politically sensitive as to which areas it gives its attention, to
the point of possibly avoiding altogether those
areas which could be most important to the working
class members of the community. Such a team will
not be able to work alongside local people should
those people be attacking, or be perceived to be
attacking, the school to which the team belongs.
These points are important, but the most important
critical comment concerns the notion that an outreach team can be established, sent out into the
community, finds out what is going on, joins in
with the people, and works alongside them. If it
simply worked alongside, then it is doubtful
whether it would be putting any of its expertise to
the useful benefit of the community and we would
have to ask what it was doing there. In fact such
an educational outreach team will not be able to
avoid making contributions: the question is, what
kind will it make and how well qualified will it be
to make it. A community education which attempts
to bring people together so as to 'have a nice
time' is of little use to the working class. "The
only knowledge which is of service to the working
people is that which makes them more dissatisfied,
and makes them worse slaves."16 Such a team needs
to be able to help people educate themselves; to
help them as they seek an understanding of their
world. This aspect of community education; the
notion that teams of professionals can assist in
the process of working class self-education is
incredibly complex, littered with theoretical and

methodological mantraps. Yet we frequently find it
included in the community education approach of the
community school and it has often been placed there
in the most cavalier fashion with little thought
given to the complexity of the issue. It is often
there simply because someone thinks it is a good
idea. To us basing such teams in community schools
seems most inappropriate. The community school is
first and foremost a school and as such can have no
real interest in a self-educated group of working
class parents. Consequently we have to question
the function of these teams.

Helen Gould continues with her community
education strategy.

> People who have become confident through
> making alterations in their lives - I think
> will then want to have some sort of say with
> what happens with the children of secondary
> school age, what happens to the actual curric-
> ulum in the school, both for those children
> and the adults within it. And I suppose, the
> point beyond what I said was the original
> final point, is where you get a community and
> parental participation in what their learning
> centre is providing.

In working as a community tutor Helen Gould is
attempting to pursue a strategy which we regard as
the most likely to offer the possibility of educational change to the benefit of the working class:
that is, one which talks of a working class say in
the educational content and delivery method of
educational institutions. However, we do not believe such a strategy pursued only by community
tutors in community schools has any real chance of
success. How such a strategy might have some solid
chance of success will be suggested in Chapters Six
and Seven.

Concluding Comments

Many points concerning community education
have emerged from our investigation of Huntingdon
School. We will not re-cap them; though we must
comment on the most crucial issue raised. This is
the critical contradiction which community education brings to the front of the educational stage
and it concerns the question of a working class say
in educational provision. Midwinter, CEDC and
community education, in general, regard the notion

of parental involvement in education and schools as central to the philosophy and practice of community education. It is community education's way of working educationally on the working class. Whilst Huntingdon School has a high level of contact between parents and teachers it does not appear to have a great deal of parental involvement in school: few adults attend classes and the structure of education in the town does not suggest that attendance will come with the passing of time. But we are given evidence of a type of involvement being sought which departs from the normal restricted model of community education. It shows how a community tutor is striving to involve parents in such a way that they can contribute to both education and educational change. It shows us a community tutor who believes working class parents have a right and an ability to contribute to the debate concerning education. However, we note that the community tutor is subject to the same kind of constraints as those we outlined with reference to John Rennie at CEDC. In her efforts to change the perceptions of the teaching staff, the method she adopts is, to an extent, determined by those very perceptions she wishes to change. She has to start 'where the staff are' and this means that she has to operate as if she shared their perceptions. Thus, as she tells us, she has to work slowly; she has to demonstrate to her colleagues the validity of her beliefs in a concrete way and it has to be demonstrated according to the firmly fixed views and perceptions of the staff. She has to do it according to their rules. It is compromised before it begins. Huntingdon School brings to the fore the central contradiction of education and community education; that of control. There can be little room for optimism here for it is unlikely that parents will be able to become involved to the point of helping alter the curriculum etc., purely as a result of coming together in play groups or evening classes. To bring about change in as closed a system as is education is no easy task. Highly motivated and organised sections of the British working class made regular attempts in nineteenth century Britain without any major success; and this when politics was still very much manifestly present in education and educational debate. There are few chances of any real successes being secured by groups of parents at the present time for it is the case that for a considerable period the political dimension to education has largely been denied. The Labour Party, as the party claiming to represent the working class, has disengaged itself from any political analysis of education and has embraced a consensual model which exists to serve those with an interest in the preservation and reproduction of the status quo. As the community tutor had to approach colleagues on their own terms, what chance for groups of mums? Would they not have to show how 'educated' they were, according to the teachers' definition of education, in order to be able to enter into a dialogue on education?

It is unreasonable to believe mums groups and community groups, assisted by outreach teams from schools, will achieve in this area more than did the organised sections of the working class which operated with a model of education and class that was a great deal more sophisticated than the model offered to mums groups by community education. The potential for change as is offered by the community tutor's scenario is little for it relies upon community tutors as highly motivated individuals. Whatever their motivation and skill, they are only individual human beings, and ones who have to work in a manner and at a pace that is, to an extent, determined by those whom they aim to change.

If, however, the contradictions concerning control, opened up as they are by community education, are to be better exploited, then it is possible the potential for change will enter a new stage offering greater promise of such change being to the educational benefit of the working class. Such a situation would see the power of the individual community tutor welded to the collective power of organised groups of working class people, self-educated away from the influence of the community school, who would be capable of entering into dialogues with teachers about education, without the entrance being on terms established by teachers alone.

REFERENCES

1.   Nisbet, J., Educational Research and Educational   Practice. From B. Simon and W. Taylor (eds) <u>Education in the 80's.</u> Batsford 1981. p. <u>167.</u>

2.   Finn, D., Leaving School and Growing Up: Work Experience in the Juvenile Labour Market. From I. Bates, J. Clarke, P. Cohen, D. Finn,

References

R. Moore and P. Willis. Schooling for the Dole: The New Vocationalism. Macmillan 1984. p. 20.

3. Report of the Working Party on Community Education, November 1982. Derbyshire County Council. para. 6.
4. Ibid. para. 6.
5. Ibid. para. 7.
6. Ibid. para. 9.
7. Ibid. para. 11.
8. Ibid. para. 5.
9. Ibid. para. 20d.
10. Ibid. para. 20d.
11. Community Education in Derbyshire, November 1984. Derbyshire County Council. p. 2.
12. Ibid. p. 3.
13. A Parent's Guide to Huntingdon School. p. 1.
14. Ibid. p. 3.
15. Rollings, J., What Might Happen to the Curriculum of a School That Goes Community. p. 1.
16. O'Brien, B., Destructive 7/6/1834. From p. 7 Hollis (ed.) Class and Conflict in Nineteenth Century England 1815-1850. RKP. 1973.

Chapter Four

NEITHER MINERS NOR MECHANICS

"We make revolution if we realistically win the battle for education." Fidel Castro.

We have argued that community education is no radical educational innovation and have suggested it to be located very much within the tradition of bourgeois provided education, where it can be seen to be playing a part in the overall bourgeois attempt to negate culturally the working class. Time then to locate it thus.

We will do this by taking a number of definite moments in history, specific conjunctures, where we can see the coming together of the important problematics of education where the contradictions can best be illuminated. We will identify unbroken threads which run from education's early days to the present, and so comprehend how things may change yet remain basically the same. We will examine the education/state/ideology relationship and in so doing construct a model of education and educational change. "We must know how we arrived here so we may discover how we may move on."[1] We are concerned then with why provided education came about and how its coming about was explained, and how changes occurred within it once it had been provided. In this chapter we are only concerned with the education of those classes unable to avail themselves of the education already offered by well established institutions; only concerned, then, with the education of the lower orders.

We will not re-tread the steps taken by Simon[2] in this historical enquiry; rather we will offer an account for what is taking place within the history of education which Simon has documented so well.

Education and the Lower Orders in Late Eighteenth and Early Nineteenth Century Britain

The conditions of the labouring poor during

103

this period are well recorded and their repetition is unnecessary. Until recently, however, the labouring poor were treated only as those who were done unto and who did little themselves; they were treated as people without consciousness, people without ideas, and this resulted in a very one-sided history where the opinions and ideas of a whole set of actors were ignored. Fortunately this is no longer the case and we are now able to understand how many of them defined their own situation for we can read and study the pamphlets, books and articles which were read, and occasionally written, by the literate among them. Many of them were engaged in an educational struggle for ideas with their masters; this was not, however, a struggle in the abstract for it was related to ideas of increasing radicalism in the economic and political arena as to the way in which the world was and should be. The educational debate and struggle took place very much within this economic and political context.

During this period many secret societies were formed by members of the lower orders and oaths of allegiance were seriously sworn; negotiation by riot was almost becoming a traditional and normal way of conducting business with the landowner.[3] Suggestions for an educational provision for the lower orders were treated as dangerous: it was argued that if more of them were able to read then even more of them would be discontented with their station.

> This mass of people was liable to be infected with Jacobin doctrines, and if the State was to be made safe from revolutionary agitation, it was essential that the proletariat should be excluded from all opportunity of dis-cussion, association, education and remon-strance.[4]

The fear of literacy among the lower orders had a certain validity, for the desire for literacy was related to political discontent. "Nothing can be accomplished but by Union... Men must meet each other, unite their knowledge and their powers."[5] During this period rapid industrialisation was resulting in a dramatic restructuring of society, century old ways of living were being forced to change; this, tied to the fear of Jacobin doctrines, is crucial with regard to education, helping to explain how the notion of mass education comes to be an important topic for debate and how it is debated as it is.

Only after the French Revolution did education have to be discussed significantly in the context of the political protection of property. Education as an antidote to crime was to remain, of course, a central feature of nineteenth century educational discussion.[6]

The challenges being made to the authority of the higher orders came from articulate spokespersons of the lower orders; as a consequence, the education which such spokespersons had, was seen as inherently dangerous. Such education aided the rush to violence; were not France in 1789 and Ireland in 1798 warning enough! To educate the lower orders:

Would teach them to despise their lot in life, instead of making them good servants ...instead of teaching them subordination, it would render them factious and refractory ...it would enable them to read seditious pamphlets, vicious books, and publications against Christianity; it would render them insolent to their superiors.[7]

The speaker here, Whitbread, puts his metaphorical finger on what soon became the button of the educational debate. He notes, though without realising it, how subordination has to be taught: it is not something which is simply there, a happy occupation of one's place in society is not automatic - the incumbent has to be educated for it. His opposition to educational provision is not surprising for he was faced with many thousands of the lower orders already reading literature of exactly the type he mentions and abhors.

Whitbread and many of his class saw education for the lower orders as a handmaiden to revolution. Others of his class, such as Hannah Moore, saw it as a bulwark against such revolution and acted accordingly by providing sections of the lower orders with education.

My plan of instruction is extremely simple and limited... they learn, on weekdays, such coarse works as may fit them for servants. I allow of no writing for the poor. My object is not to make them fanatics, but to train up

the lower classes in habits of industry and
piety.8

Central to Hannah Moore's education was religion.
"The political value of religion can never be too
firmly believed, or too carefully kept in view."9
Whitbread, and those of his class with a similar analysis, viewed the activities of the lower
orders who had some form of education, and in
horror determined not to provide any education so
as to limit the numbers engaged in such activities.
Hannah Moore, and others like her, viewed the same
phenomenon as Whitbread and determined to provide
such an education for the lower orders as to ensure
they would not behave in such a way. We have,
then, two distinct and opposing ways of trying to
guarantee the same outcome to a situation, a conservative or a progressive method. These opposing
ways of attempting to work towards one goal are
most important within education and need to be kept
to hand. We must also note the correspondence
between the statements of the Whitbread's and the
Moore's and what they did in their world. As
education comes to be provided by the State and
changes occur within that provision, such a clear
correspondence will no longer be present. The
words of the educationalist will come to describe
what is provided in a very different manner than
did Hannah Moore, but what is being described may
not be that different to that which she described.
Comprehending the educational debate of this period
is relatively simple because of the correspondence
factor; a similar comprehension today is not so
easy for we have to hack our way through the jungle
of ideological presentation before we can get at
our subject. Not so in education's early days.
There we have a dispute between sections of the
higher orders as to an educational response to the
possible threat of revolution from the lower
orders; a dispute which was eventually won by the
Hannah Moore progressive approach: and a struggle
for ideas, not least one of which concerned the
question as to what was meant by education, between
the higher orders and the labouring classes.
This struggle for ideas, for education, concerned the role education would play in society.
Would it be its custodian or undertaker?
This would depend, naturally, on the class position
of the questioner. That this question was posed at
all was primarily due to the industrialisation
process which was rapidly bringing about a drastic

restructuring of society. It was this restructuring which was so significant to the importance of the education question. From the being-formed working class it brought questions as to the origins and causes of what it was experiencing in this industrialisation, and to its future within it: from the being-formed bourgeoisie it brought questions as to how this new structure of society could be conserved so that it did not go the way of that which it was replacing. Education, for both interested parties, was held to be crucial here: it would help to liberate the class or domesticate it.

This period which leads to the first State provided education in Britain is terribly important; and it is so because it does exactly that - it leads to provided education - and in so doing it establishes a basic definition of what is meant by education with regard to the working class of the country.

The Report by The Society for Bettering the Conditions of the Poor, of 1809, began to construct the footings on which a definition of education for the lower orders would be built.

> But in political commotions, the uneducated pauper has neither principle nor motive to induce him to respect or defend that state of society, the benefits whereof he has not been taught to appreciate.10

This Report argued strongly against the negative influence of the home environment of the children from the poorer classes and its author wished for an education to counter the influence of such an environment on the children so that the children, once educated, would bring their educated influence to bear on the home environment and thus change it. Sir Thomas Bernard, the author of the Report, simply saw the negative influences to which children were subject and in his own philanthropic way wished to make them positive. However, these negative influences were those of parents, friends, relatives and neighbours; in sum, they represented the life style and culture of the class to which the children belonged. Consequently, Bernard's concern was likely to be experienced as an attack upon the culture of the home and the class; and indeed this is what it was regardless of the sincerity of Bernard's concern, for this concern was, after all, with changing utterly, and to the interest of his class, the culture of the working class, which, constituted as it was, posed a threat to him and his class. The explicit aim was to teach the uneducated pauper how he had a real interest in the society in which he was a pauper.

The finding of the working class home environment problematic, and the purpose of education being to change it, is the major theme of this Report; and it is one which remains significant in education from that time to this. Indeed, education appears on the agenda as a method for undertaking this task; it is first and foremost introduced into the political debate concerning the protection of the being-formed industrial society, as a possible mechanism whereby the influence of the working class home will be beneficial to those whom the society serves; and they are not the working classes.

For Bernard, children should not be removed from their environment, to do so "would unfit them for a cottage life and cottage fare. It disqualifies them for hard labour. It raises their views above their conditions wherein they were born."[11] Not only should the children not be removed from their environment, but the environment itself was not to be confronted; instead the children were to be educated in such a way that they themselves would cease to reflect such an environment, and hopefully would influence it as it existed, and in time, actually bring it to an end as they as adults no longer reproduced it.

This 1809 Report, in many ways, is Newsom, Plowden and Midwinter all rolled into one. It clearly states in crude class language that which has since become educational orthodoxy - the need to change the environment of the working class home. This aim has been central to education since it was first provided for the working class; though the language in which the aim is articulated is very different to that which Bernard used in 1809. What the aim might mean in the real world, especially when linked to Hannah Moore's point concerning the value of religion, becomes clear in a document written by J. A. James in 1822.

A cheerful resignation to the irremediable ills of their situation, a frame of mind that looks as if they were so grateful for the blessings of grace, as to be almost insensible to the privations of poverty, is one of the many ways in which poor Christians may signally glorify God.[12]

The clearly argued class preservation tactics of
Bernard later became the taken for granted notions
as to the nature and purpose of education vis-à-vis
the working class.
Over a period of time the bourgeoisie ceased
to regard education for the lower orders as a
threat to society and began to see it as a remedy
for the evils in society. And most of the evils
could be attributed to the home environment and
culture of the working class. Part of this culture
was the process of working class self-education and
it was against this that provided education was to
struggle.

The Struggle for Educational Definition

Working class self-education consisted of a
number of strands: the home and the immediate
cultural environment were important, for this was
where children began their journey to adulthood
acquiring values as they went; also important were
the working class schools. These were often no
more than the front rooms of working class homes
where a few children would be taught by a working
man, incapacitated by an accident in factory or
pit. How efficient he was in his teaching of
reading and writing is not important here: what was
important was the fact that in his teaching he
passed on the values of the culture from which he
came and in the case of workers injured in
capitalism's drive for profit, it was unlikely that
those values would be in accord with those who knew
what 'real education' should be. The most significant strands were those which reflected the more
organised aspects of self-education for these were
grouped around an education for liberation, and as
such were identified with the publication of the
seditious pamphlets much loathed by Whitbread.
The Female Union of Blackburn, a self-
educating body akin to a trade union branch in its
activities, had as one of its declared aims, "to
instil into the minds of our children a deep and
rooted hatred of our corrupt and tyrannical
rulers".13
Provided education had to seek to destroy
organisations which could have such aims.
Expressions of discontentment with the established
order are treated by provided education advocates,
not as expressions of discontent, but as requests
to be better informed about the established order
so as to no longer be discontented with it. A

provided education would aim to resemble Hannah Moore's:

> Merely a sufficient portion to give their minds a right bias, a strong sense of religion and moral honesty; a horror of vice, and a love of virtue, sobriety and industry; a disposition to be satisfied with their lot; and a proper sense of loyalty and subordination.14

The struggle of the bourgeoisie towards a provided education was indeed a struggle, and it was fought on more than one front. The Corresponding Societies were revolutionary in their activity, and their growth was rapid; they were, however, hamstrung by the legislation of 1799. From their ashes, though there is evidence that some did continue as underground organisations, rose the Hampden Clubs. These were not banned as such but with the passing of the infamous Six Acts of 1819 their existence was made problematic. Two agencies of working class self-education were thus attacked with the instruments of law. The Mechanics Institutes, however, were de-radicalised in a different manner. In their days they were, to a large extent, centres of critical political education for the working class. Thus, Hodgskin lectured at one Institute in Yorkshire on 'Labour Defended Against the Claims of Capital', and this in 1825. A process was underway which would reduce the number of lectures of this type until ending them altogether, for local philanthropic businessmen began to be able to force upon the Institutes their definitions as to what they should be and how they should conduct themselves. They saw the Institutes as potential centres for technological innovation and scientific discovery. With their help they felt the Institutes could produce many more Watt's and Stevenson's from the ranks of the working class. As their power over the Institutes increased the reputation of the Institutes as forums for radical discussion decreased and by the late 1830's the Institutes were all but totally incorporated into the capitalist process, in its broadest sense, and men like Hodgskin denied access.15 An organisation with a strong potential to offer a liberating education to the working class came to offer little more than a chance to individual members of the class, to escape from it, as a reward for being of service to their capitalist masters.

As the bourgeoisie attacked the self-education of the working class, fully frontal by the use of law and stealthily by the exercise of influence, it was not, in its own eyes, attacking education: rather, it was attacking sedition, blasphemy, lawlessness and totally unscientific notions as to the operation of society. To the bourgeoisie real education stood antithetically to that which could countenance many of the beliefs of the supposedly educated working class. Only something masquerading as education could produce a belief such as this one:

> The capitalists of all kinds will be our foes as long as they exist and carry on against us a war to the very knife. Therefore, they must BE PUT DOWN. Therefore, we MUST have class against class - that is, all the oppressed on one side, and all the oppressors on the other. <u>An amalgamation of classes is impossible where an amalgamation of interests is impossible also.</u>16 (Author's emphasis)

Thus working class self-education is attacked for its political beliefs for they stand opposed to the political beliefs implicitly present in real education. Real education would show that there was no war to the very knife; that, not only was a class amalgamation possible but that there was no conflict of interest between master and man anyway. Real education knew that there was no conflict of interest; instead there was only a community of interest which simply was not understood by the working man, and real education would help to remedy this misunderstanding.

Prior to State provided education, against the working class organisations of self-education, stood the organisations of bourgeois provided education. These included the schools of Hannah Moore, The Society for the Diffusion of Useful Knowledge (frequently caricatured by its working class enemies as the Society for Useless Knowledge17), the Ragged Schools and those of the two societies (The National Society, which was Church of England and the British and Foreign Schools Society, which was Non-Conformist). There is no need to locate each of these in its exact period: all were similar in that they were concerned to imbue the lower orders with a deep and lasting respect for law and order, respect for their superiors as superiors deserving of respect, and a mor-

ality in line with their superiors' definition of
Christianity. Their common educational concern was
a reflection of the bourgeois drive to guarantee
the stability of the developing capitalist economy.
The validity of our analysis does not depend alone
on the theoretical concepts within it, but is supported by the very material of historical enquiry,
which itself informs our theory. Thus, at the end
of the nineteenth century, looking back on the role
of the Ragged Schools teachers, Lord Shaftesbury
tells them in his address:

> They followed the neglected children to their
> homes, got them into the ragged schools, in-
> culcated the first principles of morality and
> religion, imparting such an education and such
> habits and diligence and order as to put them
> in the way of getting an honest and decent
> living and so become useful and loyal members
> of the Nation... All this time these people
> were working from pure love to the perishing
> ... (to the teachers) You are making it pos-
> sible to keep the vast population of the lar-
> gest city on earth in order with the fewest
> police and the smallest armed force to be
> found in any other large community in the
> world.18

In 1833 the first Central Government grants for the
education of the lower orders were made. The date
is significant for it is only one year after the
passing of the Reform Act, which symbolised the
victory of the industrial and entrepreneurial bourgeoisie over the landed aristocracy. The recipients of these grants were the two major providers
of education; the Church of England and the Non-
Conformist churches. From 1833 the grants grew as
the education provided 'touched' an increasing
number of working class children. The bourgeoisie,
by this time, was in support of provided education
and the debate within it was no longer concerned
with the correctness of such provision; it began to
concern itself with how the provision was made. A
voluntary system, varying in its impact on the
working class, area to area, began to be seen by
fractions of the bourgeoisie as insufficient and
voices began to be raised in support of a State
provided system, uniform throughout the country by
being compulsory. Though France of 1789 was becoming a memory for the bourgeoisie of Britain, it was
a fresh one and very much revived by the activities

of the Chartists. Radical ideas abroad among sections of the labouring classes had to be combated.
The Times commented:

> Cheap publications containing the wildest and
> most anarchical doctrines are scattered broad-
> cast over the land, in which religion and
> morality are perverted and scoffed at, and
> every rule of conduct which experience has
> sanctioned, and on which the very existence of
> society depends, openly assailed, while in
> their place are sought to be established doc-
> trines as outrageous as the maddest ravings of
> furious insanity - as wicked as the most
> devilish spirit could possibly have devised...
> Let a prudent spirit of conciliation enable
> the wise and the good to offer to the people a
> beneficial education in place of this abomin-
> able teaching.[19]

When the bourgeoisie focused its attention on the
class that worked in its factories and produced its
wealth it saw furious insanity, blasphemy and dis-
respect for property and the order of society.
These things did exist, of that there can be no
doubt; what is interesting, however, is that these
things were seen as phenomena, regardless of their
context. The bourgeoisie did not ask why such
ideas were abroad, nor why they should be attractive to sections of the working class, often the
most educated sections; instead, the bourgeoisie
could only look for an effective way of countering
such ideas. Briefly, we can say that the ideas of
the radicals among the working class reflected
their experience which told them an oppressing
class of capitalists stood against them. So too,
with the class of capitalists who saw standing
against them a class of wage labourers with a real
interest in bringing to an end the system which
produced the situation in which they found themselves. Real interests made the two classes opposing ones and this state of affairs was reflected in
the struggle for ideas of the classes. It was not
a struggle for ideas in the abstract. Education
has been seen, then, in the light of this class
struggle. A working class anxious to improve its
knowledge so as to improve its existence; a bourgeois class anxious to educate its workers so as to
ensure they continue to exist in their present
manner. The material conditions in which the working class existed were not of particular interest

to those who would educate them; the cultural conditions were of interest, however, for they had to
be at fault if they could allow the working class
to accept anarchical doctrines and blasphemous
beliefs. Thus the culture of the working class had
to be the target for educational intervention, no
longer area by area or city by city, but nation-
ally. All aspects of the working class environment, which were conducive to an acceptance of such
doctrines, had to be challenged and altered. Education would play a part in the struggle of the
bourgeoisie to regulate, destroy or replace the
means of cultural reproduction of the working
class.20

> We cannot let farmers or labourers, miners or
> mechanics be judges of our educational work.
> It is part of that work to educate them all
> into a sense of what true education is... We
> are not trying to make solely chiefly skilful
> mechanics or intelligent miners, - no, nor
> faithful servants; but, God helping us, to
> train up Christian men and women to fill their
> appointed place in life, as those who have a
> higher aim than that of self-interest, and a
> nobler motive than that of prudence. It is
> then a struggle; are we carrying it on to the
> best advantage?21

Education and 1870

Prior to 1870 we have essentially two forms of
education, each standing antithetically to the
other: a working class self-education and a bourgeois provided one. Eventually, in an organised
sense, only one would stand where there were two,
but it would stand in an altered form, for the
contradictions which existed between the two forms
would continue to exist, albeit in a changed state,
within the one which remained. The working class
desire for a liberating education would not disappear with the compulsory schooling brought about
by the 1870 Act; it would remain and so remain
problematic for the providers of education. Thus,
as providers, their struggle is an on-going one.
We are not offering a conspiracy theory of
history as we, to an extent, contextualise the
legislation of 1870. An extra dimension was added
to the educational debate in the period immediately
leading up to the extension of the franchise in
1867. Opposed to the proposed franchise extension,

Robert Lowe (later to become Viscount Sherbrooke) wrote:

> Once give men the votes, and the machinery is ready to launch those votes in one compact mass upon the institutions and property of this country.[22]

His opposition achieved little and the legislation of 1867 was enacted: his attention now turned to ensuring that the votes were not launched in one compact mass; that the franchise benefited little those to whom it had been extended.

> We cannot suffer any large number of our citizens, now that they have obtained the right of influencing the destinies of this country, to remain uneducated... it is a question of self-preservation.[23]

The key to ensuring this preservation was education as Lowe wished it to be understood. Here he advocated weighting knowledge in order to ensure that the education received by the working class was of less value than that received by its masters.

Lowe's contribution here allows us to see the ideological/educational dialectic of the period and so we quote at length.

> I have said I am most anxious to educate the lower classes of this country, in order to qualify them for the power that has passed, and perhaps will pass in a still greater degree, into their hands. I am also anxious to educate in a manner very different from the present, the higher classes of this country, and also for a political reason...Power has passed out of their hands, and what they do must be done by the influence of superior education and superior cultivation; by the influence of mind over mind - 'the sign and signet of the Almighty to command', which never fails being recognised wherever it is truly tested. Well, then; gentlemen, how is this likely to be done... Is it by confirming the attention of the sons of the wealthier classes of the country to the history of these old languages and those Pagan republics, of which working men have never heard... Is it not better that gentlemen should know, only know them infinitely better in their

115

their principles and in their details, so that
they may be able, in their intercourse and
their commerce with them, to assert the su-
periority over them which greater intelligence
and leisure is sure to give, and to conquer
back by means of a wider and more enlightened
cultivation some of the influence which they
have lost by political change?
      The lower classes ought to be educated to
discharge the duties cast upon them. They
should also be educated that they may appreciate and defer to a higher cultivation when
they meet it; and the higher classes ought to
be educated in a very different manner, in
order that they may exhibit to the lower
classes that higher education to which, if it
were shown to them, they would bow down and
defer.24

What a beautifully clear statement of education
operating to support and reproduce class society; a
society in which education will almost serve as a
badge of class to be acknowledged by all. Lowe
writes of how all knowledge can be weighed and of a
science of ponderation which will allow for all
human knowledge to be weighed according to its
relative importance: this critical importance will
be decided according to class criteria. The knowledge which the working class is to have will weigh
considerably less than the knowledge which is to be
the property of its masters. Not only would the
working class be given lighter knowledge but it
would recognise the inferiority of its knowledge
when confronted by the knowledge of its masters.
Lowe's education would help to give the working
class an image of itself which was deprecatory and
an image of the upper classes which was apprecia-
tory.
      With the educational struggle leading up to
1870 and the setting provided by Lowe, the Education Act of that year no longer can be seen as a
straightforward example of progressive legislation.
In many ways it symbolises the victory of the
bourgeoisie over the working class in the arena of
education. This victory relates, however, to a
battle in the war, not the war itself: though
further battles, from this time will have to be
fought on the home territory of the State. Much of
the substance for the further battles actually is
present within the Act itself. The Act basically
provides for a State organised elementary education

system to be established where it is deemed
necessary to fill the gaps in the voluntary sector
provision. It is the notion of 'elementary
education' which will provide the arena for further
educational struggle and the issues which are
involved here will have ramifications for
educational development from 1870 to the present
day. The two crucial clauses stated:

> Requiring the parents of children of such age,
> not less than five years not more than thir-
> teen years, as may be fixed by the by-laws, to
> cause such children (unless there is some
> reasonable excuse) to attend school.25

> The term 'elementary school' means a school or
> a department of a school at which elementary
> education is the principle part of education,
> there given, and does not include any school
> or department of a school at which the ordin-
> ary payments in respect of the instruction,
> from each scholar, exceed ninepence a week.26

Elementary education is defined as instruction
which must cease when a child is thirteen and which
must not cost more than ninepence a week. The cash
nexus definition "the Government hoped... would
exclude all who were not of the lower classes".27
     The Act, in striving to serve capitalism, was
not without its contradictions: thus it allowed for
children to leave school at the age of ten provided
one of Her Majesty's Inspectors was satisfied with
the level of educational attainment reached by such
children. Consequently, industry was not to be
starved of its diligent 10-13 year old workforce
nor of the surplus value it produced. The Act also
established for these elementary schools to be
administered by School Boards, to be elected by all
ratepayers. Some of these Boards became radical
bodies yet were charged with administering an
education which was far from radical. Bodies which
had, as their task, the tightening of the chains
which bound the class were often committed to
loosing them and they tried to loose them by
exploiting the contradictions within education.
They hoped to use an education which aimed at
social control, for purposes of liberation; for the
members of such radical School Boards still kept
faith with the liberating potential of knowledge.
Such School Boards began to allow substantial
numbers of working class children to remain stu-

117

dents at school past the age of thirteen and they
re-organised the schools to cope with the age
change of their pupils. They created 'de facto'
Higher Grade Schools.

These 'de facto' Higher Grade Schools, in
effect, challenged the right to definition regarding elementary education for they were seen to be
educating children in a manner and to an age not
allowed for by the 1870 Act. Though the Act of
1870 was a victory for the bourgeoisie, the growing
number of School Boards, growing in their radicalism, show how the bourgeoisie's struggle for hegemonic control is never simply won; it is on-going
and it shifts ground according to the conjuncture.
Faced with these School Boards, the bourgeoisie had
to find a way to deal with the situation: miners
and mechanics were beginning to define education.

The Cross Commission which had as its brief,
this thorny issue of defining elementary and secondary education, reported in 1888. Unable to agree,
it presented Majority and Minority Reports. The
Majority Report stressed elementary education as
that suited to the working class and secondary as
that suited to the middle class. It suggested
'Higher Grade Schools' be classed as elementary and
their curriculum restricted accordingly. The Minority Report advocated official recognition for the
'Higher Grade Schools' and support for them as
parts of the State's educational provision. The
Majority Report was keen to impose the elementary
definition on 'Higher Grade Schools' regardless of
what they had been teaching and the attainment
levels reached by their pupils. For the Majority
there was a curriculum which should not be accessible to working class pupils; this would signify
real secondary education. The Minority was more
progressive; though, like the Majority it would be
keen not to threaten the class nature of society
and education. Thus it would recognise 'Higher
Grade Schools' and see them as valuable educational
institutions for the 'artisan classes'. "Higher
Elementary Schools would satisfy the wants of an
entirely different class from those who really
desire secondary education."28

The signatories to both Reports were, without
question, committed to the continuation of a class
structured education system, an expression of their
commitment to a continued class structured society.
They differed over the method appropriate to
guaranteeing a successful outcome in line with
their commitment.

The Church threw in its lot with the Majority Report as it saw its recommendations offering the best way to deal with the blasphemous radicalism masquerading as education as organised by the School Boards. Also to support the Majority were all the Secondary Teaching Associations who "were agreed that the Higher Grade School should be confined exclusively to higher primary work, and that their aims should be 'of a definitely practical character, as intended for handworkers rather than headworkers'".29 Further debate, the Bryce Report and a national election occurred before the not unexpected fate of the School Boards came about with the Education Act of 1902.

Education and 1902

The Act of 1902 abolished School Boards and transferred the control which had been theirs to the local County Councils and County Borough Councils who would now be allowed to aid the supply, or themselves supply "education other than elementary".30 Thus the Act dealt with the contradiction whereby radical School Boards had direct control over the provision of education. The Act did not deny an element of democratic control, but it did remove it a stage back, as it were. No longer could a working man stand in an election to his local School Board. The Act, in abolishing the School Board, gave added importance to the elementary/secondary distinction: as School Boards and direct democratic control were removed from the educational debate by the Act, it emphasised how important was this elementary/secondary distinction, which some of the School Boards had so successfully blurred. This would be a new arena for educational struggle.

The Act did not define what constituted secondary education nor state that it should be provided; rather it allowed for an education other than elementary to be provided. What this would mean in the real world was made clear by Gorst.

While primary instruction should be provided for, and even enforced upon all, advanced instruction is for the few. It is in the interest of the Commonwealth at large that every boy and girl showing capacities above the average, should be caught and given the best opportunities for developing those capa-

119

cities. It is not in its interests to scatter
broadcast a huge system of higher education
for anyone who chooses to take advantage of
it, however unfit to receive it.31

Gorst here is talking about the working class when
he points out that advanced instruction is not for
all; this advanced instruction was that form of
instruction which was deemed suitable for all, if
relating to the middle class. It was, after all
that form of instruction which had to cost more
than ninepence a week. Education here is still a
class phenomenon but it is here where it begins to
receive its ideological clothes. We are not told
how the Commonwealth shall benefit from the provision of advanced instruction nor why it shall be
provided only for the few; nor are we told what are
above average capacities nor how they shall be
recognised. This, naturally, is a crucial issue in
education. How shall it be decided who is to be
allowed access to a position wherein they can benefit from advanced instruction? Why was it that
Gorst was unable to recommend a broadcast scatter-
ing whereby those fit to receive advanced instruction would be those who benefited from it? Why did
the fitness question have to be dealt with before
the instruction began? Surely there can be only
one answer to these questions: as advanced instruction for the above average members of the working
class was similar to that instruction provided for
all members of the middle and, to a degree, members
of the upper classes, then the issue was one of
social mobility. The catching of above average
working class boys and girls is a process which
will put their talents to the use of the class
which opposes the one from which they come. Jef-
ferson, in the United States of America, described
this as "raking a few geniuses from the rubbish".32
      For Gorst the secondary nature of the educa-
tion received by the middle classes was non-problematic, as was the primary nature of that received
by the working classes. The concept of an above
average capacity among working class children could
not be based on anything other than class criteria,
for the middle classes in receipt of secondary
education had to be defined, as a class, as super-
ior to the working class where only a minority of
children were suited to such an education.
      The 1902 Act was a way of dealing with the
contradictions posed by the School Boards over
rights to definition. An education system had been

constructed to educate capitalism's workforce and it was seen as essential to the reproduction of the relations of capitalist production. The way in which it came to be managed was then seen as at odds with its purpose and this raised the question of a social control education being used for purposes of liberation. How could the tools of literacy and numeracy be provided with an assurance that they would be used only to assist in the reproduction of subservience? How could a class education be delivered without having such contradictions within it as to pose a threat to it?

The Act of 1902 was an attempt to deal with these questions. However, they are ones which cannot be answered; ones which the bourgeoisie is constantly struggling to answer. This struggle of the bourgeoisie to answer these questions, to resolve these contradictions, is the motor which drives the engine of educational change; it is the key to the analysis of provided education, whether the provider be Hannah Moore or the State; the struggle to deliver a contradiction free education. For the working class the whole issue is inverted and its question concerns how to exploit these contradictions within a bourgeois, social control type of education, to the benefit, not the detriment, of the class itself.

What of the geniuses being raked from the rubbish? Not only must some working class children have above average capacities if they are to be given the chance to receive advanced instruction, but the State must also have an interest in their receiving such instruction "so that it will get out of it, by the improvement of the child's faculties, a return for the money expended".[33] We must stress that during this period Secondary Schools were constituted on class criteria; thus the moving of the promising working class boy or girl from Elementary to Secondary School was as much a class move as it was an educational one. Working class children had to be fit to receive advanced instruction and the State had to have an interest in their receiving such instruction. If we were dealing with an educational matter totally divorced from class then fitness might be a valuable concept; however, where we are dealing with a secondary education clearly constructed on class lines such a concept is of little value in the educational sense. It is of even less value when linked to the interest of the State. As the move from elementary to secondary represented a class move we have to suspect the criteria of fitness and State interest of being class biased if not class based for we are talking about the potential of certain working class children for social mobility. The criteria to be used for this creaming off process are crucial for they will come to constitute educational standards which will influence education from 1902 onwards. these educational standards have to be seen in the light of their origination in class standards.

After 1902

In 1906 the Report of the Consultative Committee on Higher Elementary Schools was published. When it began its work the Committee had asked for submissions from teachers and educationalists, and from "employers of labour with a view to determining what, in the employers' opinion, is the kind of product most to be desired".34 Interesting to note that the employers of miners and mechanics, with no educational expertise, were deemed capable of advising the Committee; or was it possibly the case that the Committee was there to do what it was told by such captains of industry? And they told the Committee that the kind of product they wished to see coming off education's production line would be disciplined, obedient children ready for work; higher elementary education should "make them efficient members of the class to which they belong".35

We draw attention to the 1906 Report for it is the last report to use such crude class language consistently and the reasons for this to be found in the real world outside the Committee Rooms of the Palace of Westminster.

The pre-war years were characterised, to an extent, by an intensified capital/labour struggle, reflecting, among other factors, the growing Trades Union movement. Larkin and Connolly in Ireland, Mann and Tillett in London, McClean and McShane in Glasgow - these were the militant leaders of the time and the demands which they articulated on behalf of their members, had revolutionary implications. Faced with such increasing radical activity, the language of class arrogance was hardly appropriate. It was becoming no longer possible to dismiss the vast majority of working class children as being unfit to receive a secondary education because of their class alone; an ideological explanation for such a dismissal had to be found. The need for such an explanation was made more urgent by the ending of the First World War. Before the war industrial unrest and class conflict: by the end of it, the Tsarist regime, to the delight of sections of the British working class, had been overthrown, and closer to home, for a time, Dublin had resembled St. Petersburg with Connolly, Plunkett and the Citizen's Army confronting the Army of Britain - for the bourgeoisie, worrying times. When the men who had fought in the fields of Flanders returned to Britain, amid considerable talk of them as heroes, it could not make sense to dismiss the education of their children or explain their educational failure in the crude class language prevalent before the War.

The ideology of educational explanation which came to be provided had two elements to it which were crucial. First, this ideology was provided by the educational expert, in this case the educational psychologist, and so moved educational explanation further from the challenge of the educational layman: second, it offered explanations for phenomena, not in class terms, but in terms of the individual child with his or her individual capacities, and in this area it further developed and advanced the process outlined by Gorst - it began to refine the criteria to be used to allow for some social mobility. This new ideology makes claim to explanation unconnected to class and goes on to allow for differences in educational provision to be explained with reference to 'scientifically' determined criteria which are valid for all and by which all are judged. Thus, instead of a class education system with its inbuilt injustice, there would be an individual system which would be fair and be seen to be so. The service done for an educational ideology supportive of the class structured capitalist society of Britain, can, in many ways, not be over-stated, with reference to the Report to which we turn our attention.

The Report Concerning Psychological Tests of Educable Capacity, 1924.

The radicalism of the working class before the war had, in the main, restricted itself to economics and politics; with regard to education, the demands, somewhat radical in their own context, were for an equality of opportunity. The 1924 Report shows why such demands were as hopeless at the time as time has shown them to be. The psychological theories which underpin and inform

123

the Report are those which look for an individual explanation for a social phenomenon, thus reducing social phenomena to explanatory factors of individual psychology. By such a reduction, the theories effectively justify the phenomena as the products of the behaviour and psychology of the individual: this reinforces the social forces which produce the phenomenon. The theories offer explanations of failing which take no cognisance of that which is failed: they suggest an individual's failing is independent of the thing in which he fails. Consequently the failing is on his own head for the thing in which he fails is non-problematic, it is given and is not subject to analysis or debate.

The critical relevance of this Report to State education and the development thereof lies in its introduction of this new ideology to education. It has been adjusted and modified since the time of the Report, but it has remained within education since its initial introduction. It is an ideology which offers an individual causal explanation for social phenomena. Within the Report itself this individual explanation operates in terms of psychology and educable capacity.

The members of the Committee accepted the concept of an "inborn intelligence" and a given "educable capacity" and we are told that psychologists are aware of certain tests, Binet-Simon, for example.

> When properly prepared, applied and marked, the tests neutralise to a very considerable extent the effects of bad teaching and un-favourable surroundings...In other words the tests, unlike examinations, not merely assess the degree of intelligence, but when applied at an early age detect with a fair measure of accuracy the degree of educable capacity and hence the extent of probable attainment.[36]

The tests, we are informed, are sufficiently developed and accurate to allow for their use in schools, yet it is "hardly possible to explain simply and precisely what is measured by them".[37] Strange! We have tests which measure to a fair level of accuracy yet are unable to specify to the same level of accuracy just what it is they measure. Instead we are offered a general description of what is being measured - "certain mental factors that remain more or less constant during the life time of individual human beings".[38] Would any other 'science' dare to offer such vague generalisations as data? Tests which measure fairly accurately, cannot tell us accurately what they measure other than factors which can be described more or less. It is the case, of course, that the 'scientific' claims of these tests have by now largely been discredited, and specifically with regards to Cyril Burt, chief advocate for such tests for half a century, his data has been exposed as having been faked.[39] That Burt's data was 'fiddled' is not that important: the crucial issue here is, why was his data so readily accepted by educationalists? The answer is simply that it told them what they wanted to know. Thus there is no need to question rigorously the accuracy of the tests nor what it is they measure, it is their usefulness which is important.

> By far the most important public examination is the examination for free places in secondary education.[40]

This examination is most important because secondary education is not provided for all. Hitherto, the reason for the lack of a universal provision of secondary education was given in terms which talked of the unsuitability of the working class to receive it. (It had, of course, been available to all who could pay for it.) This public examination, then, was no longer held to be as efficient as it should. The trouble with the examination was that children could study for it and this led to many passing who should not have passed: in the language of Gorst, children passed who may have been fit to receive advanced instruction but the State had no interest in their receiving such instruction. This is a thorny problem but our explanation approximates to accuracy for just as the capitalist is interested in the 'capacity' to labour, the State education system is interested in the 'capacity' for education: does the child have the capacity to be educated as the State wishes to educate him?

The tests existed to reinforce the class nature of educational provision, whilst at the same time obscuring it by psychological reductionism: crudely, they were ways of 'rigging the rules' even more efficiently. This is supported by the fact that the tests did not have right or wrong answers; they had responses which needed interpretation and

125

this could only be undertaken by educational experts. It was claimed, not unexpectedly, that the tests did not fail children; rather they assessed the educable capacity of the children and so helped them towards that in which they were most suited to succeed. The reality of this helping would mean the majority becoming miners and labourers, the minority becoming engineers and book-keepers.

With Henderson[41] we see the practical use of these concepts of educable capacity and inborn intelligence, as a way of controlling social mobility so that those acceptable to the middle classes would be allowed to become mobile. How else are we to make sense of these tests, useful as they are "for discouraging children from entering occupations for which they are unsuited".[42] They produced a situation in which educational decisions were made 'in camera' and education, as a system, became a closed one. Children could not study for the tests; there were no right or wrong answers only responses to be interpretated: how was it possible to challenge them? With regard to occupation, there were no tests of woodworking skills nor questions about digging coal, so how were the latent carpenters and miners identified? It was all a mystery which demanded that the non-professional take the word of the professional for granted. And it was a mystery associated with 'science'.

> Methods of examination have been discovered by which these factors (innate intelligence and educable capacity) in any individual can to a great extent be ascertained and differentiated from the results of training and education.[43]

The methods have not been constructed by men in the real world; they have been 'discovered'. This discovering is part of the scientific gloss, present throughout the Report.

It was a scientific gloss to cover the fact that the tests would be concerned with a social and occupational mobility, would be concerned with fitting working class children to jobs. They would allow a social mobility to the few, while confirming the many in their status as members of the labouring classes. Most interesting is the concept of an educable capacity divorced from the world in which it occurs. The Committee members and the psychologists who gave them their material believed they were measuring a metaphysical 'something' that was 'there'. They claimed to ignore, as a matter

126

of scientific principle, the educational history of the child, thereby ignoring language itself, without which thought and reasoning are scarcely possible: they seriously believed they were dealing with something which was not the result of an inter-active process between the individual child and his or her environment. In the Report we are witnessing how:

> Intelligence comes to be treated as a quality within an individual rather as a pattern of behaviour... carried out in relation to others, and meeting a specific response from others.44

Intelligent behaviour is a much more useful concept than inborn intelligence, or intelligence of any variety, for the latter is an abstraction and can only explain itself by further abstraction. However, within this abstracted concept is the key to the explanation of it, not as an abstract concept but as something made in the real world. In order to be able to measure the educable capacity of the child it is essential to have a model of educable capacity against which the child can be measured. Such a model, an ideal-type, has to be constructed in the real world for, of course, there is no abstract world. Thus it has to be made by people acting in the social world. Given, then, that you can only measure the child's intelligence against a model of intelligence; that is, before you measure the child, you have to define what it is you are seeking to measure, then the question which has to be asked concerns the production of the model, the very creation of the construct of intelligence. This concept was not the product of value-free inquiry, but of an inquiry which was class deter-mined and class based. The psychologists did not discover concepts and tests, they made them. And they did not make them as men divorced from the world, but as men very much parts of the world and informed by it. A raison d'être for the tests was the simple fact that secondary education was not to be provided for all working class children; one which was deemed suitable for all middle class children. It was the non-problematic notion of an intelligence as exhibited by the middle class that had to become the notion of intelligence, in a universal sense, against which working class child-ren would be measured for secondary education was to give, to some working class children, the chance

127

to become middle class. If we join clubs we do so on the conditions laid down by the management of the club. An intelligence, acceptable to the middle class as an intelligence, was that which these tests sought to identify.

The class nature of the tests and the concept of intelligence as a class concept was illustrated in 1983 in Solihull, England. The Local Education Authority was considering the re-introduction of selective secondary schooling and its feasibility study stated, "there are not enough high I.Q. pupils in the North of the Borough to warrant the establishment of a selective school there".45 Not surprisingly, the North of the Borough of Solihull is where the highest concentration of working class residents can be found.

Post 1924

Psychology, as an academic subject, grew rapidly in this century and there were two strands to its growth: first, it grew with its own internal dynamic as universities expanded and new ones were created and, secondly, as education needed a new ideology in order to continue its class practice, it turned to psychology as the provider of individual explanation for class phenomena. This education/psychology relationship became a symbiotic one making education and educational explanation an even more closed system, even less accessible and open to challenge from the lay person. Psychological testing grew in its practice as did the sophistication of its theories. The Spens Report of 1938 subscribed whole-heartedly to the notion of an inborn intelligence and the tests which claimed to ascertain its level, and of course, refined versions of the tests came to be known as the 'Eleven Plus', an examination system, like those before it, to decide the social mobility question with regard to working class children.

In Britain in the 1980's, as in many other advanced capitalist countries, these tests are no longer used and 'the notion of an inborn intelligence is no longer the bedrock of educational belief. However, the beliefs upon which the tests were based have not disappeared. Intelligence is still viewed by educationalists very much as a thing which resides in individuals as opposed to being a way of describing how individuals behave in the world in which they live. And most importantly, it has become taken for granted that it is with

the individual that education deals, and it is to
the individual education looks when seeking an
explanation for educational failure. Not only is
this incorrect on its own terms, for that which is
failed is at least as important as the person who
does the failing; but the very model of the individual with which education operates was constructed in a class fashion for it was modelled on
the individual member of the middle class. Unless
educational inquiry and explanation attempts to
break out of this individual way of viewing its
subject, it will in actuality remain imprisoned in
a class explanation, provided for it by the bourgeoisie of the last seven or eight decades. Their
explanations and accounts took the individual
member of the bourgeoisie and made him the universal individual against whom all would be
measured.

Education and the Inner City

Education and its attendant ideologies have to
be seen for the parts they play in preserving and
reproducing capitalist society with its class
structure. The education which was first provided
for the working classes was provided so that they
would continue to be working classes and, hopefully, contented as such. This purpose of 'provided
education' has remained very much a part of it, but
it has been obscured by changes within the organisation of the education provided, and by the
growth of sophisticated educational ideologies, one
of the most important of which has revolved around
the individual form of explanation. The world is
not a static place where struggles are won and
problems finally resolved; struggles are on-going
and the resolution of a problem gives birth to
another, as was evidenced by the Education Act of
1870 and the School Boards which it created. Where
then does this place community education?
There are two points to be made to this
placing. First, the appearance of community
education has to be seen as a 'normal' change
within education as the bourgeois struggle continues to attempt to deal with education's contradictions. Our next chapter will deal with community education's aetiology as normal, not unexpected
educational change. Secondly, there is a more
specific placing which locates community education
and places it in a political and economic context.
This placing was, of course, hinted at by Mid-

winter, Widlake and others with regard to the possible rushes ,to violence which they saw on the
horizon. It is made more explicit in a short paper
by Sharpe.46

Sharpe illustrates how, by a displacement
mechanism, economic problems look to education for
solution, thereby re-defining themselves: this
relates to education and the inner city.

From the end of the Second World War the
process of internationalisation of capital had
increased in pace, affecting areas of countries and
countries themselves. Also since the war, and
until the mid 1960's, the economies of the capitalist West enjoyed a relatively uninterrupted boom,
due among other factors to the war itself and the
reconstruction necessary once it had ended. The
capitalist ideology which seeks to link the well-
being of labour with that of capital, was considerably strengthened by the material benefits brought
to the working class by this boom. Experientially,
the lot of the working class improved; consumer
durables, once only affordable by the middle
classes and above, were now within purchase range
of the workers. Sociological myths stating the
death of class abounded and politicians told the
British working men how they had never had it so
good. By the late 1960's, however, the economic
boom was slowing considerably and with it, the
notion of joint well-being was experiencing cracks.
It became visible how not all had shared in the
growth, and this non-sharing could be located in
particular geographical areas of Britain and among
these areas the inner cities were over-represented.
The mobility of capital and its need to constantly
re-structure itself had had a very significant
effect on the inner city. Industries which had
been located at the heart of the Victorian town and
which had stimulated the town's growth to city,
were run down and closed. The means of producing X
were modified or scrapped altogether and the owners
of these means of production located Q their production elsewhere and now produced Y.

> From the point of view of capital, its
> mobility requires the mobility of labour. It
> therefore also requires the continual
> fracturing of the local and more fixed pat-
> terns of reproduction; it specifically re-
> quires the destruction of locality as a major
> form through which working people experience
> their social life.47

Labour cannot be as mobile as capital for labour is labour power and this only resides in people: the mobility of capital is about moving machines and building factories, the mobility of labour is about creating a class of 'industrial gypsies'.[48] The early days of capitalism destroyed locality and fractured village and rural life as it created its cities as centres for manufacturing: hardly surprising that a similar destroying and fracturing should take place as capital re-located away from these city centres. Sharpe argues that this re-structuring of capital and its effects on the inner city give rise to a theory of 'urban crisis', for, of course, large numbers of wage labourers are unwilling to become industrial gypsies and so remain resident in the inner city, but without work. The 'urban crisis' theory does not see the direct effects of capital's re-structuring as direct, but sees them as almost unfortunate side-effects and so it does not challenge these effects by challenging that which produces them. In the inner city, industries close, unemployment rises, skilled workers leave, social security claimants increase in number, house conditions deteriorate and house prices, if they do not fall, fail to rise. The 'urban crisis' seeks to address these direct effects of capital's behaviour by educational and community means.

Community approaches are brought to bear on the inner city, among them, community education. These approaches, to Sharpe, represent:

> The outcome of a new social democratic settlement fashioned out of the political and social struggles which characterised the ending of the Long Boom. What had been brought about was a hegemony of reformist discourse.[49]

But the discourse would be a limited one for it would fail to address the issue of capital's behaviour and this would result only in an attempt at "management, containment and control".[50] The educational/community response came to have two aspects to it, and they were both inevitable given the failure to challenge the behaviour of capital: first, the lack of employment, inadequate housing, general dereliction, etc., came to be held to be responsible for the educational failure of the children of these areas. And second, the educational failure of the area generally, the lack of education among the adults, came to be held as

131

having caused their problems. They were unemployed and badly housed because they did not have the skills and intelligence which could be used to remedy the situation in which they were placed. Once an educational approach has been decided to be the one followed to deal with such problems as unemployment, urban decay, etc., it is entirely logical to arrive at a position where those problems are viewed as the results of a lacking of education among the people having such problems. These two aspects of the education/community approach did not govern the approach at different times; one did not lead into the other: rather both were present in the notion of education as a way of dealing with the re-structuring of capital.

The community education approach to these problems sought to enable the people of the inner cities to improve their own decaying areas, not necessarily in any physical sense, but in a 'community' sense, whereby they would feel pride in their area and a sense of community with their neighbours. Part of the rationale for the community education response lay in the down-town areas of cities in America. The riots which had taken place there were seen as a future possibility for Britain unless action was taken. This is most interesting, for it gives a political and economic context to Midwinter et al. and shows the economic and political factors which might cause a rush to violence, which community education will exist to negate. It places community education as the 'flak catcher' for capitalism. The parallel between this would-be radical change within education, that is community education, and the reasons for the initial provision of education for the lower orders, cannot fail to be noticed. As capitalism grew in the nineteenth century and village communities were broken apart so that manufacturing cities could be born, education was held to be a possible bulwark against radicalism and violence, both the riot as negotiation variety and the Paris 1789 type. As workers assembled in the cities in their tens of thousands, education would help to discipline them. Over a hundred years later, with the workers still assembled but no longer working, education will again seek to stop them misbehaving.

Community education arises as a natural part of educational change and as a specific part at a specific time, targeted, initially on specific geographical/class areas. It treats the effects of capitalism and capitalism itself as non-problematic; rather the people experiencing these effects as problems are treated as the problem. The notion of the urban crisis, and the notion of community education can be seen as essentially ideological for they insist upon treating the effects of capital's behaviour as independent variables, as abstracted phenomena, out of context and divorced from their causes. They both serve the ideological construct of the inner city as a thing in itself, as an entity unconnected to the rest of the world, and they do this by dealing with it on those terms.

Education has served capitalism well: is there any reason to believe it has ceased to do so? Can community education be seen to be playing a part in ending education's servicing role to capitalism, or does it help the reproduction of this role by giving it a more up to date image, a more plausible and fluent explanation as it tries to offer education for sale?

REFERENCES

1. Bowles, S. and Gintis, H.,Schooling in Capitalist America: Educational Reform and The Contradictions of Economic Life. RKP. 1976. p. 152.
2. For an excellent account of the history of provided education in Britain, see B. Simon's, Studies in the History of Education 1780-1870. Lawrence and Wishart 1960 and Education and the Labour Movement 1870-1920. Lawrence and Wishart 1974.
3. For a discussion of the phenomenon of negotiation by riot, see E. J. Hobsbawm and G. Rude Captain Swing. Penguin 1969.
4. J. L. and B. Hammond, The Town Labourer 1760-1832. Quoted in Simon 1960. p. 134.
5. Black Dwarf 21/4/1819. From Simon 1960.
6. Silver, H.,The Concept of Popular Education. MacGibbon and Kee 1965. p. 27.
7. Hansard Vol.9, Col. 798. July 13th 1807. From Simon 1960. p. 132.
8. R. Brimley Johnson, The Letters of Hannah Moore. From Simon 1960. p. 133.
9. Cadell and Davies, Collected Works of Hannah Moore. From Simon 1960. p. 133.
10. Sir T. Bernard, Of the Education of the Poor. The Society for Bettering the Conditions of the Poor. 1809. p. 47.
11. Bernard op. cit. p. 15.
12. J. J. James The Poor Church Members Guide.

References

From P. Hollis (ed.) Class and Conflict in Nineteenth Century England 1815-1850. RKP. 1973. p. 344.

13. Manchester Observer 26/6/1819. From Simon 1960. p. 191.

14. P. Colquhoun, Treatise on Indigence. From Hollis. op. cit. pp. 332-333.

15. For a detailed study of the Mechanics Institutes see M. Tylecote, The Mechanics Institutes of Lancashire and Yorkshire 1851. Manchester University Press 1957.

16. E. Jones, Notes to the People. From Hollis op. cit. pp. 82-83.

17. For a discussion of the caricaturing of such organisations, see R. Johnson, Really Useful Knowledge: Radical Education and Working Class Culture 1790-1848. From J. Clarke, C. Critcher and R. Johnson (eds) Working Class Culture: Studies in History and Theory. Hutchinson 1979.

18. Lord Shaftesbury's Speech at the Guildhall in London on his 80th birthday. From C. J. Montague, Sixty Years in Waifdom or the Ragged School Movement in English History. Woburn 1969. pp. 31-33.

19. The Times 2/9/1851. From Simon 1960.

20. R. Johnson, Notes on the Schooling of the English Working Class 1780-1850. From R. Dale, G. Esland and M. Macdonald, Schooling and Capitalism. RKP. 1976.

21. Minutes of Committee of Council of Education 1857-1858. p. 478.

22. Life and Letters of R. Lowe. From Simon 1960 p. 354.

23. R. Lowe. Primary and Classical Education. From D. A. Reeder. Educating our Masters. Leicester University Press 1980. p. 108.

24. Ibid.

25. The Education Act of 1870.

26. Ibid.

27. Rich, E., The Education Act of 1870. Longman 1970. p. 89.

28. The Cross Commission of 1888: Minority Report.

29. Banks, O., Parity and Prestige in English Secondary Education. RKP. 1967. p. 16. (This incorporates a quotation from The Incorporated Headmaster's Association Report of 1870).

30. The Education Act of 1902.

31. Gorst. From Banks op. cit. p. 51.

32. Tyack, Turning Points in American Educational

History. From <u>Bowles and Gintis</u> op. cit. p. 29.
33. Hansard. Vol. 107, Col. 673. Gorst Speaking.
34. The Report of the Consultative Committee on Higher Elementary Schools 1906.
35. Ibid.
36. The Report Concerning Psychological Testing of Educable Capacity 1924, p. 65.
37. Ibid. p. 137.
38. Ibid. p. 137.
39. For a discussion of Burt and his faked data see B. Simon, The I.Q. Controversy: The Case of Cyril Burt. Chap. 5. of <u>Does Education Matter.</u> Lawrence and Wishart 1985.
40. The Report Concerning Psychological Testing of Educable Capacity. 1924. pp. 111-112.
41. For a discussion of intelligence versus intelligent behaviour see P. Henderson, Class Structure and the Concept of Intelligence, from R. Dale, G. Esland and M. Macdonald, <u>Schooling and Capitalism.</u> RKP. 1976.
42. The Report Concerning Psychological Testing of Educable Capacity. 1924. p. 143.
43. Ibid. p. 137.
44. P. Henderson op. cit. p. 142.
45. <u>The Guardian</u> 16/9/1983.
46. See R. Sharpe, Urban Education and the Current Crisis. From G. Grace (ed.) <u>Education and the City.</u> RKP. 1984.
47. J. Clarke, Capital and Culture: The Post-War Working Class Revisited. In J. Clarke, C. Critcher and R. Johnson (eds) <u>Working Class Culture: Studies in History and Theory.</u> Hutchinson 1979. p. 239.
48. This sharply descriptive phrase is one of Mick McGahey's, National Union of Mineworkers.
49. Sharpe. op. cit. p. 66.
50. Ibid. p. 67.

Chapter Five

TRADITIONAL METHODS OF INDOCTRINATION

"The main purpose of American foreign aid is not to
help other nations but to help ourselves." (Richard
M. Nixon during the 1968 Ohio campaign)

As a natural change within the organisation of
provided education, how did community education
come about and how did this educational change come
to be given the descriptive term 'community'?
Within sociology, community, as a concept, has
been used generally with regard to groups of people
seen as living in close-knit geographically defin-
able areas, often organised around a single industry: for example, a Welsh mining village or a
Scottish fishing village. In such communities
there is held to be a shared experience of the
world, a common condition of existence, and over
significant issues, a harmony of interest. With
such mining and fishing villages there is, to a
great extent, a community of interest, for the
people of these villages are in a similar social
and economic positions, often all working for the
same employer. They can be seen as communities of
the working class: though not without their contradictions and divisions between drinker and tee-
totaller, chapelgoer and churchman, respectable and
rough, they can be seen and treated as relatively
homogenous. It is the case, however, that few
people in Britain live in such communities. The
essential point about them is their harmony of
interest and it is this which is crucial in explaining why community comes to be the term used in
an educational change aimed at being a reformist
method of dealing with capitalism's effects. The
harmony of interest experienced in the 'real' community of, say a pit village, is abstracted from
its setting and used as a way of defining community
in the abstract. Real economic interests which
might be regarded as community interest in a specific and real context, are neglected and the focus
is given only to the notion of a community interest

136

regardless of context. Community ceases to be a term used to describe a real world and becomes an ideal-type construct to measure the world. The abstracted community where harmony should be the norm, comes to be used, not as an abstract concept, but as a description of the world. As such it is a descriptive term which is invariably at odds with what it describes. This does not worry its users for accuracy of description is not its purpose; ideological presentation is. Thus non-communities are so regularly described as communities that it is they which come to be deemed at fault, and not the descriptive term applied to them. Reality has to adjust not rhetoric. All geographical areas then become to be defined as communities and the term becomes interchangable with 'society'. The enthusiastic use of the term, not unexpectedly, must lead to its unmasking as an ideological device for if all areas of society, and society itself, are communities, then there is nothing which is not community, and so, as a descriptive term and a concept, it becomes valueless. This should lead us to ask why it is used? How has it happened that so many services, most of which are supplied by the State, Central and Local, are now prefixed with the term 'community'? In Britain we now have community transport, community health, community housing, community police, community architecture, community relations, community service and community education, etc. Prefixing societal processes and institutions in this manner can be understood as an ideological attempt to secure an identification, on behalf of all, especially the working class, with such processes and institutions. 'Community', then, can be one of the most "potent legitimation symbols of our time".1

Though 'community' becomes a paint spray of legitimation, it does not mean that it works, that it is accepted as accurate or meaningful by members of the supposed communities, or indeed by many professionals. "How can you make a community in school when there's no community out there?", asks a teacher in Salford.2

This is a pertinent question when the term is frequently being used to describe a school's catchment area. Some catchment areas can include poor quality council housing along with private housing in the £100,000 plus range. Community education, in such catchment areas, has the task of bringing together the people of the area so that they might realise the benefits to be had from understanding what they have in common as members of the same community. Community, then, is a term which does not simply work, it is one which struggles to work: it strives to be accepted as a valid description of that which it describes.

With regard to education we have discussed its beginnings in terms of the inner city and the restructuring of capitalism: time, then to turn our attention to community education's birth as a normal educational change. There may be some dispute about its parents but we are sure of their identity: the Reports of Newsom and Plowden, published in Britain in the 1960's.3

Newsom and Plowden

Newsom deals with education of pupils aged 13 to 16 of average and less than average ability, whilst Plowden deals with all aspects of primary education and the transition to secondary education. Though focusing on two different areas of education the Reports have much in common for they are confronted by the classic problems which face provided education and these become themes which are found in both Reports. Thus, throughout the Reports we find an ideological way of viewing the world as a whole, and the world of educational provision. The relationship between schooling and employment is explored in such a way as to try to ensure that education truly serves the capitalist organisation of production. The culture of the working class, problematic since the first provision of education for it, confronts the authors of both Reports and their response is the traditional educational response; that is, such culture is deprecated and attacked and its replacement is sought. The role of parents with regard to the educational process is explored and their support for it becomes an aim common to both Reports. Plowden gives some attention to the organisation of religion and religious instruction in schools and strongly advocates a form of instruction which will aim to inculcate a Christian belief in children and a sense of duty to God. Both Reports deal with the traditional problems of provided education and they do so in a traditional manner. Two themes of the Reports are of particular interest to us: the way in which intelligence is treated and the model of man such treatment suggests, and the moves which are advocated towards some form of community education. There is a relationship between these two themes in that community education can be seen as a strategy aimed at guaranteeing that a particular model of man and intelligence be the one with which education operates.

Intelligence and Newsom

In Newsom the rigid affirmation of an innate intelligence, such as that we encountered in the 1924 Committee which then found such favour with Spens in 1938, has disappeared. No inborn intelligence and given educable capacity here: "Intellectual talent is not a fixed quantity with which we have to work but a variable that can be modified by social policy and educational approaches".[4] It is not, of course, as we would have it; that is, a type of behaviour in a type of situation and it would be incorrect to expect it to be so treated within the tradition of provided education. However, in Newsom, it has at least become something that is amenable to change. Newsom is concerned to find ways of assisting change for the better and wonders whether, with the right educational help, even more people might not achieve even more. He is optimistic here for he informs us that standards have risen and that which was once regarded as average would now be seen as below average. There is an obvious and significant problem here, though one which is not discussed by Newsom. If standards rise in the absolute sense then more people achieve more; but if these standards are then adjusted to take the absolute rise into consideration, then the same proportion of people succeeding and failing can be obtained. If this is done, then, in the overall sense, why do rising standards matter? Five 'O' Levels are needed to train as a teacher; more people pass five 'O' Levels: five 'O' Levels and two 'A' Levels are now needed to train as a teacher. Related to the world of employment and recognised qualifications the notion of rising standards can serve as a carrot, forever dangled in front of a not-very-convinced donkey. This point is, of course, crucial with regards to community education and its drive to involve parents so as to improve the chance of educational success for their children. If community education's strategy were to work on a mass level, then at whose expense would the children succeed? Or would the notion of success and failure be adjusted to take in the new figures without altering the percentages succeeding and failing? But if community education in this area is only aimed at increasing the chance of educational success for individual children, then the issue of standards and percentages of successes and failures does not need to be examined or challenged. And, not surprisingly, it is with the individual that Newsom is concerned. Thus it is most important to have a model for individual intelligence, for community education will actually be a way of working with individuals without troubling to question the standards by which these individuals will be judged.

For Newsom the aim of raising standards is related to the need of industry for an ever increasingly educated workforce. But to this we must add the cultural aspect of education; the sense in which education is about the struggle of the bourgeoisie to have its definition of the world accepted as the valid one. In this sense, raised standards are not so much the result of a deliberate educational aim, pursued for its own sake, but are more the by-product of the bourgeois struggle for hegemony in the cultural arena.

Focusing on the notion of an intelligence and the tests used to assess this so as to determine to which school the child shall be sent, we are told:

> The kind of intelligence which is measured by the tests so far applied is largely an acquired characteristic. This is not to deny a basic genetic endowment; but whereas that endowment, so far, has proved impossible to isolate, other factors can be identified. Particularly significant among them are the influences of social and physical environment; and since these are susceptible to modification they may well prove educationally more important.[5]

Intelligence is still a thing, a variable, but now it can be modified. What it is, is held to be basically the same as it was in 1924; what has changed has been the way in which it is held to come about. Explanations in terms of a fixed inborn intelligence are no longer adequate and can no longer be sustained; the vast majority of the working class can no longer be so cursorily dismissed as uneducated and uneducable. But Newsom, like any shrewd card player, has pocketed, at least in his own eyes, an ace: that is, he has retained the concept of genetic endowment which science at some later date might be able to isolate as a causal factor of intelligence. There is no need for us to deny the possibility of some form of genetic endowment but the wish to discover and identify it is driven less by disinterested science and more by partisan politics and ideology for such a notion could well be used to remove all debates concerning education from the political and socio-logical arena: DNA codes would be deemed material inappropriate to political action.

Intelligence as a thing is most interesting: in Newsom it is an acquired characteristic which can be influenced, but as an acquired characteristic it has to be so acquired in the real world. The real world, of course, is a social one, yet Newsom's acquired intelligence is treated very much as an individual one, divorced somehow from the world in which it is acquired.

> In relation to those pupils whose potential ability may be masked by environmental, and, particularly linguistic handicaps, here is a largely unexplored territory: the evolution of practical teaching techniques will demand the highest professional skills, and might contribute to a major break-through in learning. It is work which can only be done empirically in the classroom, and which, we hope, may qualify for support by research grants.6

For Newsom the environment of some children has reacted in such a way as to block their true potential and he writes of the need for a study of the "pedagogic problems presented by our pupils".7 The role of the environment is, in many ways a minor one, for the difficulty is posed, not in terms of the environment, but in terms of the problem the child poses for education. The problem, for Newsom, resides within the child, not the environment or society and the task for education is to discover the pedagogic key which will unlock and solve the problem. Intelligence exists as a thing, as does pedagogy, independent variables, and as such they can be investigated. Newsom manages to incorporate an environmental explanation into the thing called intelligence, whilst at the same time he seeks to ensure that it remains a thing, and a thing that is taken for granted. Thus any investigation will not be of the thing itself but will be of the individual in whom it resides.

The fact that education, however, has treated intelligence as inborn and not amenable to change,

141

produces some disquiet in Newsom and he writes of
how education must have failed a number of young
people because of seeing intelligence in such a
way. In Newsom's disquiet there is almost an expression of liberal guilt which is the result,
primarily, of a complete lack of comprehension as
to just what an education system in capitalist
society has as its role. We find a similar guilt/
apology in Britain in the 1980's with regard to
education's recently past practice. Some teachers
feel they may have 'failed' their pupils by incul-
cating a work ethic, given the unemployment being
faced by their pupils, and that instead of educating for work they should have educated 'for life'.
Their very expression of liberal concern indicates
changes within the ideology of education which
reflect how education still strives to serve its
capitalist masters even without realising it.8

Newsom serves this master by the assistance he
gives to a new ideological explanation of education, success and failure; for it helps to dangle,
yet again, ever ahead of the class that is failed,
a hope of a new educational Jerusalem for all once
the educationalists have, on behalf of the working
class, discovered the pedagogical key as to how it
can benefit from education. If the concept of
intelligence, whether it be innate or acquired, is
taken for granted and not subjected to any analysis; if it is regarded as a thing residing in
individuals, then how seriously can the search for
a pedagogic key be taken and how much can it be
held to matter?

Intelligence and Plowden

The notion of an intelligence which can be
modified is taken further in Plowden and so we find
intelligence being dealt with alongside the notion
of child development. In the same way as the 1924
Committee had a model of intelligence against which
children were to be measured, Plowden has a model
of child development with which real children can
be compared. Like the 1924 intelligence model,
Plowden's child development model is confusing and
confused. Implicit in Plowden's talk of child
development is a model of man. Thus, of children
and their development she writes: how it can be
understood as "the complex and continuous inter-
action between the developing organism and its
environment".9 The term 'organism' is most inappropriate: children are conscious of themselves

142

as they interact with their environment, changing both it and themselves as they do so. If we cannot characterise man in any other way, we can characterise him as a social and conscious being. Organisms are not conscious of being. In talking of organisms, and using it as a starting point, Plowden establishes, for herself, a one-dimensional view of the world where man, at times, becomes almost unrecognisable. For example, dealing with growth and development of children, information is given on bone and muscle development and we are told with regard to considerations on such matters "it is highly probable that they also apply to emotional and intellectual development".10 To suggest that emotions and intellect, constructed as they are in a real, social and material world, are subject to developmental laws as in a similar manner to muscles and bones is absurd. Even if such a bizarre idea were possible to sustain it would have to take into account the social and economic factors involved in the development of the purely physical characteristics of height, weight, strength and overall health. Bone development, etc., are not unconnected to economic and social class. But most importantly, "minds are conscious: children are aware of themselves and others".11 Bones and muscles categorically are not.

These rather strange notions of Plowden are not isolated examples, out of context and tune with the rest of the Report; they are parts of what will become her model of child development; a model which is a mixture of crude biological determinism and confused notions of socialisation by way of an interaction with the world. An imperative as to what human beings should be is located in her belief in a developmental/chronological age construct. "By developmental age we simply mean the degree to which a child has advanced along the road from birth to full maturity."12 Such a notion is by no means simple, if it involves more than just a physical maturity, as it does within Plowden. Plowden talks of people "attaining their adult ability".13 This is a strange notion: by suggesting such a thing as adult ability which is somehow attained, it posits a halt in development on the part of the individual. Time does not stop when people become adult; they continue to live and for as long as they do, they have a capacity for change. We don't attain an adult ability; as we live, we are forever attaining it.

143

> Biologists are now much clearer than they were
> thirty years ago about the manner in which
> hereditary and environmental factors interact
> to produce a characteristic, be that charac-
> teristic stature or the score in an intelli-
> gence test.14

Like an advertisement for toothpaste, the claim to
legitimacy for what is asserted rests with an association to scientific rigour by telling us that
'biologists are now', rather like 'dentists tell
us'. Naturally, Plowden does not tell us which
biologists are so much clearer about such matters.
She takes their word for it and we are supposed to
take her word for what it is they say. Certain
characteristics are, without doubt, biologically
given; hair colour and height, for example. These
factors do change with the ageing process but they
are given to us; there is nothing we can do to
change them, though we can, of course, use hair
dyes and high shoes to change their appearance.
Are we really to see intelligence in a similar
light? Hereditary factors and the environment
interact to produce a characteristic. There seems
little room here for beings that are conscious of
their being. Plowden's ideas here compromise the
importance of her comments regarding the environment, for the environment is only important insofar
as it interacts with what is given. The ace pocketed by Newsom is still with us. Intelligent behaviour is neglected for intelligence as a thing,
the product of an interaction between environment
and that which is hereditarily given. The one-
dimensional view of man produces strange assertions:

> A particular environment, in other words, may
> be highly unsuitable for a child with certain
> genes, but highly suitable for a child with
> others.15

Thus the suitability of certain environments is
carried along with hair colour and height in the
DNA coding. The consequence of such a belief can
mean that groups of children may be removed from
certain environments for they are held to be con-
stitutionally at odds with the environment: the
environment, of course, does not need to be changed
for it is the genes of the children which make it
unsuitable, not the environment itself. The thinking behind these notions of Plowden has a liberal

144

concern to it which wishes education to provide the right environment for the individual child. However, the individual child has to compare favourably with the constructed model of the individual child.

> The Plowden strategy is to base educational practice upon a certain theoretical view of children and their 'nature', namely, that children's education is the product of their maturation and of their learning, both of which are determined by certain 'general principles' of developmental need which are discovered by experts and which must be applied to particular cases by the teachers of the children concerned.16

It is Plowden's espousal of certain theories which causes problems. She seems to believe that if a reality does not correspond to a theory then it is the reality which is at fault. In Plowden theoretical models of child development and intelligence are put forward, not as theories in the true sense of the term, but more as moral prescriptions for the behaviour of the real world. In Plowden the knowledge of the expert cannot be challenged by the phenomena of the real world. The expert, in Plowden, is the educational psychologist with his or her tests. She informs us that according to a World Survey on Education in 1962, Britain has the best methods of testing for scholastic aptitude and ability: despite being the best, these methods, nevertheless have a margin of error between 10% and 20%. Not only is there such a wide margin of error but there is also a degree of self-fulfilling prophecy to the tests in that they may create the future they predict. It is hardly surprising then that Plowden welcomes the ending of 11 plus examination which based itself upon the use of these tests. Are the experts not discredited along with their inaccurate self-fulfilling tests? Not at all!

> We hope that attention can now be diverted from the design of tests for the purpose of selection to the development of tests suited to the changing primary curriculum, and, helpful to the teachers who need to diagnose children's difficulties in learning. Teachers themselves might devise tests, of an objective type, based on the concepts which they wish

their pupils to form in such subjects as
mathematics. Tests which would help teachers
to recognise inventiveness and originality
would also be valuable.17

Is it not strange that Plowden should be suggesting
testing in new areas and to new purposes; is it not
possible that there will still be errors of 10% to
20% and self-fulfillment to the tests? If it is,
it does not worry Plowden for it is outweighed by
the fact that tests deal with children as individuals with their own individual level of intelligence, and tests make claims to objectivity. They
claim to treat all children in an equal manner and
so aim to be resistant to any attack arguing class
bias. To make a commonsense criticism: is Plowden
really telling us that teachers need tests in order
to recognise originality and inventiveness? Don't
we know it when we see it? But again, this is not
surprising for Plowden's ideology is one which sees
such things as characteristics that can in some way
be isolated from the rest of the person in whom
they are found. To treat originality and inventiveness as discrete phenomena is ludicrous. James
Joyce was noted for his originality in the use of
language, not his theoretical physics: Einstein was
not renowned for his inventiveness with regard to
the form of the novel. Neither man had a characteristic called originality which somehow manifested itself in a certain way; their originality was
recognised in its manifest form and it was impossible to divide it away from the way in which it
became manifest. Plowden is interested in trying
to discover originality as a characteristic in its
latent form. Why should this be? There are two
aspects towards an answer to this question. First,
the more facets of intelligence that can be subjected to so called objective tests, the less objections can be made to the outcome of such tests
for the tests claim objectivity and freedom from
class and cultural bias. Secondly, this notion of
characteristics is crucial to her model of man and
concept of intelligence. To her the world is composed of individuals who happen to have characteristics in common, as opposed to classes that might
have economic interests in common. The notion of
latent characteristics which can be discovered by
tests adds to the argument against class for the
way these latent characteristics are discovered is
above class. As Plowden's model of the world works
in terms of the individual and not in terms of

classes, as it is one which refuses to take the
social seriously, then all her explanations need to
be in terms of the individual with his or her
characteristics; there can be no exceptions. Thus
the ludicrous position where tests are advocated to
discover originality.

Plowden in many ways is a diatribe against any
analysis of the world which talks of class and it
is a hymn of praise for the individual: but the
individual in the world and in education has very
much to be able to measure up to a particular model
of what an individual should be.   Educational
experts are the natural arbiters here.

> He can also give parents and teachers a fuller
> understanding of the needs of children and an
> appreciation of the range of behaviour that
> may be <u>properly regarded as normal,</u> so that
> they can distinguish between minor difficul-
> ties which are incidental to growth and those
> for which outside help may be needed.18 (Our
> emphasis)

Though both the Reports of Newsom and Plowden are
concerned with education in Britain, they do,
nevertheless, have relevance to education in any
capitalist society for they represent a strong
articulation of and argument for education being
seen as solely concerned with the individual.   And
they begin to identify the strategy of community
education as the mechanism to insist the validity
of this identification.   They posit a community
education as a way of insisting that the individual
be seen as the only legitimate target for educational efforts and educational inquiry.   And they
do this without inquiring as to why and how they
have come to be doing it: they do not seek to ask
how an education system which talked of the ineducability of classes has become one which is concerned only with individuals regardless of class
and so they fail to comprehend that this individual
approach might well be serving similar aims and
purposes to the erstwhile class approach.   They
fail to see that the individual with whom they are
concerned is one who has to measure up to and be
judged by the ideal-type individual, a construct
very much based on the individual member of the
bourgeoisie, living in a real class structured
capitalist world where the interests of classes
oppose each other.

Traditional Methods of Indoctrination

Newsom and Community Education

Newsom, in keeping with education's tradition, finds the working class cultural environment problematic and identifies it as being, in the main, responsible for the educational failure of the class. Homes and schools are frequently at cross purposes; children need the civilising influences which schools can provide; the social behaviour of children has to be altered, as do their speech, dress and deportment. The working class home is the source of the majority of education's problems, as well as being the author of the child's.

> Many boys and girls may well appear to be more stupid than they need be simply because of the inarticulate homes from which they come.19

This way of viewing the working class home and the total environment of the working class has been an ever present aspect to the education of the class: so too has been the concern with the ending or total changing of the class' cultural environment, the existence of which is held to be testimony to the need for educational intervention. What is new here is that this intervention should no longer be restricted to working on the schoolchild in the hope that he or she, being influenced by education, will, in turn, influence the home environment. The ideas put forward by Bernard in 1809 are taken further by Newsom. The working on the schoolchild which occurred only during school hours will continue but will be added to by working on the home environment directly, both inside and outside school hours. Community education's home-schooler makes an entrance here; what will be his or her role?

The education provided for the working class has always had to face a particular contradiction: how to fail the class educationally while at the same time convincing it of the validity of its own failure. How is it possible to attack a class without it realising that it is being attacked as a class? Newsom begins to identify a new approach to this contradiction. Instead of schools behaving as oases of bourgeois culture under attack from the working class hordes of their catchment areas, they are to begin to seek to convert the hordes, not simply by educating the children when they come into school, but by educating and influencing the hordes in their own homes, in their

148

very communities. The home-schooler will act as the first missionary as education seeks out its new enemy on its very own territory. Not surprisingly, for Newsom, the situation is not regarded like this: in Newsom, industrial relations conflicts and trades disputes are held to come about because of problems in communication, and many of education's problems can be remedied by better communications. Do working class people really understand education and what it is the schools are trying to do for their children? Has not education neglected its duty to educate the parents into a sense of what education is? Time then, to remedy this situation. Education must involve parents in the school so that areas of conflict between school and home can be removed. "Education needs a better communication service".20

Newsom does not map out a community education service but he does begin the debate which receives a great deal more attention from Plowden and so his Report is important for its place in the explanation of the aetiology of a community education service. Newsom's brief was to investigate with reference to the average and less than average pupils and this was a major factor in driving him to search for a form of compensatory education; and to this end he focused his community ideas towards those areas which he felt to be most in need of such an education; that is, the inner city slums and the suburban council estates where "the school may have an important socially educative role in the community".21 Newsom is not suggesting any drastic educational change but he is putting forward the need for a drastically improved way for education to communicate with and present itself to those sectors of society hitherto deemed un-interested and uninterestable in it.

The schools cannot do the job alone, and parents cannot delegate their responsibility for guiding their children. Many situations would be helped simply by the schools knowing more of the home circumstances and the parents knowing more of what goes on in school... But there is a percentage of homes - and in some districts a majority - which such arrangements do not touch. In dealing with these problems, the schools, and the parents need special help. There may be a strong case for having additional members of staff who have special responsibilities for home visiting, and who

149

> act as liason officers with all other medical,
> welfare and child care services in the
> district.22

Newsom is concerned with beginning to find new ways
of hopefully involving some of those parents who
have been so little involved in the education of
their children. This approach has, at its heart,
the aim of transforming the way in which such
parents view and relate to schools; and the method
for the achievement of this aim will be one whereby
schools go out into their communities, specifically
by way of home-visiting. That the schools will be
changed by this new practice cannot be denied, but
the extent to which they will be changed is
debatable, given Newsom's emphasis on the need, not
so much to change educational practice, but to
better communicate it. The approach will accept
the school's rules, culture, curriculum, teacher
professionalism, etc., as non-problematic: what it
will seek to do is alter parents' perceptions of
these things. It will struggle to bring into harmony the culture of the home and school, but in a
very one-sided manner, for it will be the home
which must change so as to better correspond with
the school.

This new way forward for home/school relations
has an ideological purpose to it and its own contradictions. There is an implicit assumption that
as a result of better home/school links, working
class pupils will achieve more at school. However,
the Report focuses on the working class, not as a
class, but as a collection of individuals, and so
the successes which might result from this strategy
are experienced and seen as individual ones, not
class ones. So the strategy deals in success and
failure on individual terms and in so doing, it
seeks to better justify the failure of the majority
of working class pupils, for fail they will. If
this strategy were to succeed in helping a good
number of working class pupils to succeed within
education, would it be much more than raking a few
more geniuses from the rubbish, whilst leaving most
of the rubbish where it lay: thus, could we not see
its primary purpose as one which seeks to convince
the rubbish of the justice of its location and
identity? The strategy will operate by way of a
process of cultural imperialism which will aim to
demolish aspects of parents' working class culture
and replace them with aspects of culture of the
bourgeoisie, to the point that the parents will

150

comprehend the validity of the educational failure
of their own children, seeing it as being, in the
final analysis, their own responsibility. We have,
then, to place this community education/home
visiting strategy in the overall concern of Newsom
for education and its place in his capitalist
society.

> Their greatest service to the community, and
> there is none greater, will be as men and
> women who can be relied upon to make a success
> of their own lives and by the quality of their
> living to bring up their children to do the
> same. This is not something which can be
> taken for granted or left to <u>traditional</u>
> <u>methods of indoctrination</u>... an education
> <u>which is</u> genuinely secondary can equip the
> boys and girls with whom we are concerned to
> <u>make the right choices</u> and to carry them
> <u>out.23</u> (Our emphasis)

Plowden and Community Education

Plowden is not a diatribe against a class
analysis of education, simply because we say it is;
the Report itself proudly boasts of its antipathy
to any such analysis.

> Socio-economic classes are heterogeneous and
> artificial, and it is not so much the family's
> occupation or income that is operative here as
> its attitudes and traditions of child care,
> its child centredness, its whole cultural
> outlook.24

The whole cultural outlook of families which she
identifies as so important, is actually one aspect
which allows us to identify a class as a class.
Instead of seeing it this way, Plowden sees only a
characteristic which families have in common,
regardless of class. The fact that a whole
cultural outlook, closely linked to educational
failure, is an outlook which is common among
working class people, is overlooked or regarded as
insignificant to Plowden. The fact that it is the
working class which predominantly has the wrong
cultural outlook, is almost accidental, as far as
Plowden is concerned. Their being working class
does not explain, for Plowden, their wrong cultural
outlook; it is simply the case that it happens to
be working class people who have the wrong outlook,

151

it is not a working class outlook which is wrong.
How could it be? Classes are, after all, artifi-
cial. In Plowden a class phenomenon is changed
into something else merely by description: thus the
educational problems to be addressed are not class
related but are all about cultural outlook and
attitudes. "Parental attitudes appear as a separate influence because they are not monopolised by
any one class".25
    Plowden's recommendations and suggestions to
future educational practice cannot be ones which
address education as being something related to
class, but must instead be ones which work against
any such class related view of education. Plowden's community education will, consequently, be
concerned with attitudes and how they can be
changed.

> Our argument... is that educational policy
> should explicitly recognise the power of the
> environment upon the school and of the school
> upon the environment. Teachers are linked to
> parents by the children for whom they are both
> responsible. The triangle* should be
> completed and a more direct relationship
> established between teachers and parents.
> They should be partners in more than name.26

In Plowden there is a particular model of how
school is influenced by the environment and how it
should seek to influence that environment. The
school basically is influenced in a negative way by
the inadequacy of the cultural environment and this
should be counteracted by the school influencing
the environment in such a way that the parental
partners to the education of the child will more
fully play their part: and play it according to the
rules laid down by their more senior, knowledgeable
partners. And when schools begin to do this, positive results are held to ensue. Plowden tells us
how this has happened with regard to a particular
school (we assume the Head is being quoted).

> The pattern of home/school relations began to
> change. Instead of only meeting parents who
> had chips on shoulders, my staff found much

* Coventry City Council has, for a number of years,
used this triangle as its Community Education logo.
It is red and along each side is printed: parents,
teachers, children.

smoother and more positive relationships for
us all to work with.27

We would dearly like to know what kinds of 'chips'
were on which parents' shoulders, but unfortunately
we are not told. What is important is a community
education approach which removes 'chips from shoulders' and smooths out relationships. It is a one-
way process in Plowden for it makes demands on
parents so that teachers have a more positive relationship with which to work. What matters in this
new approach to education is "whether parents understand what the schools are doing for their individual children and teachers realise how depend-
ent they are on parental support".28 This one-way
process wishes to make parents understand what the
schools are doing for their children, while
teachers are to understand how necessary it is for
them to get parents to understand.
     Plowden stresses the mutual respect there will
be between parents and teachers in their
educational partnership. The teachers are to seek
to challenge and alter the views which parents have
of schools. What are the parents to do; how are
they to be equal partners, able to seek to
influence and alter the attitude of schools, and
how can this relationship be one of equals, each
respecting the other when the whole culture of the
parents is such that it must be changed? It is
not, of course, a relationship of equals and it is
made abundantly clear by Plowden - parents are to
have no influence on educational matters. "Complete control" over professional matters will rest
with the Head and the teachers. Parents will benefit by being allowed to come into School and help
out in the library and they can be invited into
school "to learn about its ways and to make things
that will be useful for the school". These partners in the education of their own children are, in
effect, to be treated as little more than 'grown-up
children'* themselves. Partners in more than name
- hardly!
     The Plowden Report is an important one in
terms of its relationship with what has come to be
known as community education; and for three
reasons. First, community education comes out of
the Report as a specific way of responding to and

* This expression was used by a Deputy Head of a
Coventry Community College when talking of parents
who came into College to pursue their studies.

challenging a working class culture that is held to pose problems for education; second, this community education is the vehicle which seeks to guarantee the reproduction and development of the individual model of intelligence with its claims to cultural neutrality and value-freedom; and thirdly, this community education response is articulated in a certain way and so will consist of certain things. It will insist that professionals remain firmly in control of all things academic, whilst allowing parents to help out in school, to participate in certain areas of the school's life, and these will grow in number as parts of community education, and of course to 'rub shoulders' with teachers.

The ways in which community education is regarded and practiced have changed since Plowden and descriptions of it have become a great deal more sophisticated. These changes do not negate the relevance of Plowden, for it was within the Plowden Report that the trends towards a community education were identified and propagated. It was there that community education was 'cranked' into being and it was from Plowden that much of what is called 'community education' came, bringing with it many of Plowden's ideological assumptions about the world. These assumptions have become part and parcel of the everyday practice of community education, whether many of the practitioners realise it or not.

Plowden's community education can be seen to be very much a part of mainstream educational change and not some form of radical break with the normal pattern of change. It has sought to widen the arena of education, by seeking to involve more parents of the children being educated; but it has done this in a particular way and with a particular long term aim. 'Provided education' has been concerned with ending the self-education of the working class and changing utterly its culture. Plowden's originality here lies in the belief that the drive to end the cultural reproduction of the working class can best be achieved by focusing, not only on the children, but on the whole family, thereby aiming to secure its co-operation to the ending of its own distinct form of existence and to do this under a banner which proclaims respect for that existence.

Concluding Remarks

Can it be shown that reformism, which is a

strategy designed to change and modify prevailing conditions, in fact serves to perpetuate them?30

This question of Stuart Hall's has been ever present, and in the main it has been answered positively: Newsom and Plowden have been concerned to help in the reforming process but their ideologies have been such that they could only conceive of educational intervention in a specific direction and aimed at a specific class, despite their desire to emphasise the un-importance of class and the crucial centrality of parental and cultural attitudes. Consequently they were led to prescribing reforms which would aid the continuation and reproduction of the structure of society as a whole, which Hall and ourselves would hold, at the end of the day, to be responsible for the problems which Newsom and Plowden locate, and indeed for such problems being defined as problems.

The Reports of Newsom and Plowden are most important because they do not simply sit on library shelves. They have served and do serve as guides to educational action and thereby their ideologies implicitly present in their practical suggestions and theoretical assertions, do become part of educational provision. They become non-problematic, taken-for-granted educational facts in the practical world of educational work. For example, Cave, a Senior Inspector for Schools in Cambridgeshire writes:

> In emotional development it would seem that the ability to deal successfully with stress and frustration depends to a considerable extent on innate factors. Some children seem to be constitutionally more able to tolerate frustration and adversity than others.31

This notion Cave has, without doubt and it seems with little or no thought, simply taken from Plowden. It cannot fail to impact on the way he carries out his work as Senior Inspector. Our analysis is not simply made for a sense of academic satisfaction; it is to draw attention to the way in which educational ideologies become guides to educational practice in the real world and so assist in the reproduction of it.

From The Times of the mid-nineteenth century, to H.M.S.O. published reports of the mid-twentieth, the culture of the working class has been one of education's major problems. For the same period, the culture of the bourgeoisie has been seen as problem free. Can we not see The Times and the Reports of Newsom and Plowden then, as examples of bourgeois culture itself, looking at what poses a problem for itself; for surely if this were not the case, then at some time in a hundred years, education would have found the culture of the bourgeoisie problematic? It never did. Nor did it find the continued educational success of the bourgeoisie problematic: no explanation for it was needed, its existence was its explanation. In the sense of educational reform resulting from the bourgeoisie examining what constitutes problems for it, how can Newsom and Plowden be seen? They have to be identified as advocating a community education which will continue the struggle of 'provided education' to alter the problematic working class culture to the point where it ceases to be problematic. And community education hopes to achieve this goal with the consent and participation of those whom it seeks to negate, in the cultural sense. And it hopes to do this by home/school contact and the creation of community schools. Its long term aim is for the culture of the working class to be indistinguishable to that of the bourgeoisie. That we regard such an aim as an impossible one, does not lessen the impact such educational work will have, nor the fact that community education will have a part to play in educational change for a considerable future, nor does it mean that its ideologies will not become taken-for-granted beliefs of educational practitioners.

Community education then, will have to struggle towards achieving its goal. What it will be struggling against we can now see as we look to our Sheffield fieldwork.

REFERENCES

1. G. Grace, Theorising the Urban: Some Approaches for Students of Education. From G. Grace (ed.) Education and the City. RKP. 1984. p. 94.
2. D. H. Hargreaves quoting a Salford schoolteacher in Hargreaves, The Challenge for the Comprehensive School: Culture, Curriculum, and Community. RKP. 1983. pp. 34-35.
3. The Newsom Report: Half our Future. HMSO 1963. Children and their Primary Schools: The Plowden Report. HMSO 1967.

4. The Newsom Report (N.R.), para. 15.
5. N.R. para. 16.
6. N.R. para. 306.
7. N.R. para. 279.
8. See particularly an article by Tim Brighouse
   in Network April 1982, CEDC Publications.
   Brighouse writes on the relationship between
   education and unemployment:

   Should we not acknowledge that we should
   never have led them to expect that they
   would all have full-time paid employment in
   the first place.

9. The Plowden Report (P.R.), para. 11.
10. P.R. para. 16.
11. P. S. Wilson, Plowden Children, from R. Dale,
    G. Esland and M. Macdonald (eds) School-
    ing and Capitalism. RKP. 1976, p. 160.
12. P.R. para. 15.
13. P.R. para. 16.
14. P.R. para. 29.
15. P.R. para. 31.
16. P. S. Wilson. op. cit. p. 159.
17. P.R. para. 422.
18. P.R. para. 212.
19. N.R. para. 329.
20. N.R. para. 43.
21. N.R. para. 134.
22. N.R. para. 204.
23. N.R. para. 315.
24. P.R. para. 37.
25. P.R. para. 101.
26. P.R. para. 80.
27. P.R. para. 110.
28. P.R. para. 111.
29. P.R. para. 126.
30. S. Hall, Schooling, State and Society. From
    R. Dale, G. Esland, R. Fergusson and M.
    Macdonald (eds) Schooling and the National
    Interest. Falmer Press 1981, p. 5.
31. R. G. Cave, Partnership for Change: Parents in
    Schools. Ward Lock Educational 1970, p. 27.

Chapter Six

WOMEN WEREN'T SUPPOSED TO....

"But I don't have to accept a stone wall just
because it's there and I don't have the strength to
breach it." (Dostoyevsky, Notes from Underground)

In the main we have been concerned with the
struggle in which 'provided education' is engaged
in order to have its definition of education accepted by all. Though it struggles against the
whole culture of the working class, part of its
struggle is specifically against any processes of
working class self-education. We briefly located
and discussed some historical examples of this
self-education in our fourth Chapter: time then to
bring our educational struggle up-to-date. In this
chapter, we will be concerned with the facilitation
of a process of working class self-education within
the City of Sheffield. Our Sheffield fieldwork was
a study of a number of 'projects', funded in the
main by the City Council. We will not describe
each particular scheme (Appendices 1-4 serve this
purpose), but will explore themes common to all.
It was our wish to discover to what extent these
projects facilitated working class self-education.
Such a self-education would be one containing some
of those traditions encountered in Chapter Four;
but what it might be in practice would be discovered by looking at its practice. Thus, a working class self-education will come to define itself
as we discuss our projects.
    When we approached our Derbyshire fieldwork,
we did so with an appropriate methodology: in
Derbyshire this consisted of a survey of Derbyshire's literature, a questionnaire and follow-up
interviews. This method would have been totally
inappropriate to our work in Sheffield. Here, a
time commitment was essential for 'getting to know
people' was the methodological foundation stone
upon which a necessary friendly social intercourse
could be built. To find out whether and to what
extent a working class self-education process was

in operation, it was necessary to get to know the projects and the people involved in the setting of the projects. Our research was done by surveying Sheffield's literature and by dropping-in to projects; by attending some management committee meetings of projects; by sitting-in on educational sessions and by talking to people involved in the projects.

Sheffield and Community Education

Until 1968, adult education in Sheffield was organised by way of Evening Institutes, which normally shared school premises. They were often managed by teachers from the schools where they were based and these teachers were paid as part-time Centre Heads. A re-organisation of education within the City resulted in the creation of 'Campuses'. These were community schools/colleges in everything but name. They represented an attempt to integrate adult education and youth provision into a coherent system based on the school site. Our comments can be neither exhaustive nor definitive, but it does seem to have been the case, that within a short period of time, these campuses were being regarded as incapable of achieving the aims which had been envisaged for them. They might well have been called campuses, but they were essentially schools doing some things which hitherto they had not done. In addition to this problem of the aims of the campus, was one which came about as a result of a growing professionalism within adult education. This produced a situation where the Centre Head was less and less likely to be a full-time school-teacher engaged in a part-time job, and more likely to be a full-time adult education worker, and often trained as such. This change to a new breed of Centre Head, brought to the surface considerable conflict between adult education and the statutory education of the school, for the Head of School was also the Head of Campus and thus the de facto Head of Adult Education, regardless of the job description of the Centre Head. The Divisional Principal we spoke to concerning this matter, believed that by 1974/75, the Campus concept had virtually ground to a halt, primarily because adult education could not thrive in such a setting, nor could it have any realistic hope of influencing its setting; that is, it could not change school.

Having largely failed to live up to the ideals

> of community education - either as an inte-
> grated internal community or in their re-
> lationships to the outside community - the
> campuses are undergoing some changes. Adult
> education has been progressively moving its
> limited resources away from the large institu-
> tions and the traditional evening class pro-
> gramme into more accessible and convivial
> neighbourhood centres. This has been in an
> attempt to relate to working class communities
> largely alienated from the big educational
> institutions.... Furthermore it is a recog-
> nition that much valuable educational work can
> be carried out in the community in the course
> of daily lives and not just in formal courses
> in classrooms.1

We found a Local Education Authority actually
admitting its recent errors most refreshing: too
often we encounter a refusal to recognise errors
and an unwillingness to see that ideals are not
being lived up to; and instead of this recognition,
we find an increase in Local Educational Authority
propaganda as to its educational ideals; a more
fluent explanation of the ideals which aims to
convince us that they are being lived up to. All
too often rhetoric takes over from reality. This
did not seem to be the case in Sheffield. Here, a
community education service, tied to schools, began
to break loose and to move towards trying to
recognise and facilitate working class self-
education in working class areas of the City. Much
of the traditional evening class style of work was
abandoned and a more radical stance adopted. This
change of style and emphasis can be seen easily in
class attendance figures:

    1974/75   23,780 enrolments
    1983/84   15,834 enrolments2

and the radical new stance which would stress co-
operative learning and would pay particular
attention to the position of women and the
unemployed. With regard to women, "The curriculum
had been firmly rooted in women's domesticated
role. This is now being challenged by much of the
recent work with women."3 And with regard to
unemployment, "In general the strategy has been to
develop new centres for the unemployed to use
casually (drop-in) for social and recreational
purposes and to attempt to build an educational

ployment and other subjects of concern and interest. It indicates an acceptance of the essential validity of working class experiential knowledge, and the potential of the working class to develop that knowledge.

Helen Gould the Community Tutor at Huntingdon School, we remember, was slowly working to persuade her teacher colleagues of the potential among working class non-professionals, of the knowledge which such people had, and of their right to contribute to the educational debate. All our projects in Sheffield treat the validity of the experiential knowledge of the working class as self-evident and the questions revolve around adding to and sharpening that knowledge. This adding to and sharpening takes place in two ways: first, there is the learning by doing - the skills and knowledge gained in actually running the centres; and second, there is the rigorous and more disciplined learning which takes place in week-end or week long residential courses. As we discuss our projects we will see how this self-education is one which does not aim for the isolated fulfilment of the individual but rather aims at the fulfilment of individual members of the working class. It aims at enabling working class individuals to better understand the world and so struggle within it as members of their class, not escapees from it. And as such it has much in common with the self-education processes of nineteenth century Britain: the Chairman of the Central Board of the Co-operative Union in 1883 writes:

> In the first place, the object of education of this kind is not to make us rise out of our surroundings. We may and ought to try to rise above our worst selves; but if we get above our friends and neighbours, above the old home which reared us and helped to make us what we are, or wish to move, as it is called, in a 'higher circle', it does not at all follow that we thereby move in the right direction. It has sometimes been urged against our universities that this is the result of their education. All I can say is that if young men come to us and go back in any sense ashamed of that from which they came, we in the universities ought to be ashamed of ourselves.[8]

Women at Open Door

Traditional adult education in Sheffield, as in many other Local Education Authorites, had very much revolved around a curriculum for women which rarely departed from teaching those skills associated with woman as mother, wife and home manager: women could join all manner of cookery, dressmaking and soft furnishing classes. Such classes carry a thinly hidden curriculum which discourages any questioning of woman's role in society. Is there a different kind of education happening for women at Open Door; how is it experienced; does it encourage questioning; and does it carry any liberating potential? Important questions.

One day of each week is 'Women's Day' at Open Door when the centre allows admission only to women. The main purpose of this day and the drive behind much of the work with women, is to facilitate reflection on the problems specific to women. One of the fruits of C. Wright Mills' sociological imagination

> ... is the idea that the individual can under-
> stand his own experience and gauge his own
> fate only by locating himself within his
> period, that he can know his own chances in
> life by becoming aware of those of all indiv-
> iduals in his circumstances.9

Apart from Mills writing in the masculine gender, his comments are most relevant to the purpose of Women's Day and the work which takes place with women at Open Door.

> It is by means of the sociological imagination
> that men now hope to grasp what is going on in
> the world, and to understand what is happening
> in themselves as minute points of the
> intersection of biography and history in
> society.10

Many of the working class women who use and run Open Door are in the process of developing some sort of sociological imagination to make sense of their lives as women. This is not taking place without some pain and some difficulties with regard to relationships with partners, nor without some objections being raised by some men using Open Door. When the Women's Day first began some men had argued that the problems of women would not exist without Women's Days being set aside for them. However, these objections did not have a great deal of support and even that has diminished drastically, for as the Women's Work has progressed, the ideas of the objecting men have changed. And it has been the reality of women's self-education which has been the major causal factor behind the change of ideas of the men.

Tom Eddison, a centre worker, talked with us on the issues connected to women at Open Door and his comments are valuable for they tell us about the work, but more importantly, they give us a real indication of how people's ideas are changed and particularly men's ideas. Tom is 29 years old and has spent ten years of his working life in the Liverpool Ambulance Service where he was a shop steward and a branch secretary with NUPE (National Union of Public Employees). He and his wife moved from Liverpool to Shropshire where his wife was to follow a Polytechnic course as a full-time student. At this time, Tom explained, he was very much a traditional working class man and he began to resent his wife studying, feeling her place should be at home with the children. He issued his wife an ultimatum that she choose between studying and being his wife, according to his definition of what a wife should be. She chose to leave him. Until his divorce was absolute, Tom looked after the two children of the marriage. For Tom this was the factor which forced him to change his ideas. He talked of the never-ending work which was needed in order to hold down a full-time job and look after two children. He told us of the tremendous support he received from women neighbours who told him how marvellous he was to be doing what he was doing. He began to realise how women did what he was doing, and often much more, all the time as a matter of course; and what was more, such never-ending work was expected of them.

Tom believes men change their ideas because of experiences such as his own, though not necessarily so drastic and not because of any theoretical analysis of the issues. He believes men who have the theoretical grasp of the issues still behave very much as traditional men unless a 'something' forces them to change their ideas to the extent that their practice is changed. Changing ideas in the abstract, unrelated to practice means little. This 'something' could very well be a change in the ideas of their partner eventually confronting their

165

own ideas in the arena of practice. Tom outlined how attending courses is often a very everyday experience for active male trades unionists; to go on a course is normal. When on such courses a male trades unionist might well question aspects of capitalist society - the role of the State, the function of the police, etc., but "it is not automatic that a man ends up challenging his role as a man". For Tom, the challenging of one's role is much more likely for women attending courses because, in order to attend a course, a woman will have to overcome obstacles which tell her she is a wife, a mother and how dare she abandon her family in order to go away and study.

Tom, like many people at Open Door, was very aware of the difficulties involved in women's work and was highly critical of any radical feminist approach which failed to work with working class women on such issues as nurseries, equal pay and opportunities and instead tried to focus on issues such as the right of lesbians to adopt children. Tom was opposed to any approach which sought to negate class and focus exclusively on gender. He was concerned to see Open Door working on a whole series of issues of concern to working class men and women; to see it helping working class men and women to educate themselves. Within Open Door it seemed, most users accepted the idea of a partnership between men and women. Though the work with women was carried out separately, it did not seem to be separatist. Tom explained how working class men must not be treated as the enemy of working class women. Lady Olga Maitland has more in common with Norman Tebbitt than she does with May Hobbs. "Working class men who've been trod on and walked all over are pissed off; they're not morons beyond redemption." Thus we have to see the work with women at Open Door as very much a part of an overall approach towards facilitating a working class self-education which must include men and women, but one in which there is room for a special approach to women owing to the special ways in which they are oppressed within capitalist society.

The Women's Weekend

The first weekend course for Open Door women took place in 1981. The reasons for the weekend were primarily social as opposed to educational: it simply seemed a good idea to give women using the centre a chance to get away for a weekend. One of the women adult education workers associated with Open Door contacted other workers in the Adult Education Service with a view to running a joint weekend course. She received a negative response and felt this was because of an unwillingness to recognise how support for such a weekend might well exist among working class women. Not only was there support among working class women, but it was such that two weekends had to be arranged as sixty women wanted to participate. The weekend was to be first and foremost, a break from routine for those attending; if the educational aspect to it worked, then that would be seen as something as a bonus. It was hoped that coming together over a weekend would help to increase the general confidence of the women. As a consequence, the course itself had to begin with the world as the women knew it; their lives had to be their educational resource.

The weekend course is now something of a tradition at Open Door and for those women attending their first course the content is historical.

> On the weekend we will be looking at women's history - but not the history of queens, princesses and ladies. It's our history, the history of our mums, grannies, aunts, ourselves, etc., how they lived in their families, how they worked, how they coped with child bearing and rearing, etc.11

In November 1984, a group of Open Door women attended a weekend course. Like its predecessors it was held at Northern College, near Barnsley, and was tutored by women adult education staff associated with Open Door. We talked to the tutors and some of the women who would attend, both before the course took place and when it was over, and we asked the students to complete a short questionnaire. Fifteen women attended the course, all of whom except one were mothers. Their ages we list in Table 6.1

Table 6.1. Ages of Women on Weekend Course.

```
Aged 20 - 30,  5.
 "   31 - 40,  5.
 "   41 - 50,  2.
 "   51 - 60,  2.
 "   60 Plus,  1.
```

Ages were not obtained for any sexist reason; rather we wanted to know whether Open Door was only
dealing with a particular age group and we were
pleased to find a spread of ages which suggests
that a wide range of experiential knowledge will be
available to be shared. None of the women had had
any full-time education beyond 'O' Level, though
many had experience of day-release courses or evening classes. Four of the fifteen had stayed at
school beyond the age of sixteen, but had not taken
'A' Levels, nor thought of further education. Education had not been particularly important to any
of the women for it had not really connected to
their own lives. All of them, however, enjoyed the
educational aspect of the weekend and stated a
willingness and interest in attending a similar
weekend course. The benefits to the women of the
Weekend were of three kinds: the course itself,
the company of the other women and the change of
routine. All of the women enjoyed the weekend and
some regretted that it was only a weekend and no
longer.

Particularly important is the existence of a
facility such as Northern College, which can allow
working class women not only to benefit from the
educational elements of such weekends, but also to
have a weekend free from the everyday routine of
washing, cooking and cleaning, and for a change, to
'enjoy being waited on'. One of the women told us
the weekend had made her "more aware" and another
explained that she had never previously realised
"how interesting education could be". Talking of a
course for men and women which had been held at
Northern College, concerning unemployment, one
woman with no experience of education in the pre-
ceeding twenty-five years of her life told us, "It
showed me I'd got potential. I didn't know I had.
It just opened me up... I surprised myself." After
coming back to Open Door after the Unemployment
Course, this woman became involved in drafting the
constitution of the centre. When we talked to her
she was considering making a start of the study of
sociology. She had no particular interest in sitting an examination in the subject but felt that
its study would be interesting in itself and would
help her in her continuing efforts to make sense of
the world. Her experience of Northern College she
looked forward to repeating. Its teaching staff
she had experienced as understanding and sympathetic. "If you didn't know everything, you didn't
feel inadequate." To her the student body of the

college was essentially a group of ordinary working
class people who happened to be at college. "They
talk like you" instead of university students "who
are all la di da". Northern College students
"didn't talk above my head".

The more people we talked to at Open Door, and
for that matter at other projects, the more important Northern College began to appear. We will try
to allow this importance to emerge as it emerged in
our fieldwork. When we describe the facilitation
of working class self-education we are forced to do
it in an apparently contradictory manner: we have
to illustrate what it means in practice by reference to the individual as opposed to what it means
to the class itself. However, by showing what it
does mean to the individual member of the working
class, we suggest what it could begin to mean for
the class, or rather a large proportion of it.
Here we will write briefly about two women users of
Open Door who are also members of the Management
Committee. And here we will see how Sheffield City
Council's funding of such schemes does actually
facilitate the kind of self-education which is our
concern.

Carol Baker

Carol is aged twenty-eight, married with two
young children. She became associated with Open
Door as a result of her husband's involvement.
Before Open Door was actually able to open its
doors Carol's husband, along with a number of men
and women, had spent a considerable amount of time
and energy getting the premises into reasonable
shape. They effected repairs, constructed parti-
tions and decorated the premises throughout. Carol
did not begin to use Open Door until her youngest
child was aged twelve months (she is now three).
Gradually she became more and more involved until
she was eventually elected to the Management Committee, of which she is now a very active member.
As a member of the Management Committee she has
been involved in liaising with local schools for
access to facilities for the unemployed, has helped
organise trips to Derbyshire and London and along
with many members of Open Door, was actively involved in organising support for the families of
miners on strike during the industrial action of
1984/85. Along with many others she spoke of this
strike as being "an education". The education here
is a better understanding of the world and it came

about as a result of engaging in practice in the world. Being an active member of Open Door means engaging in practice not as dramatic as a national strike, but nevertheless, practice which has educational value.

Carol and her husband Mike, have different attitudes towards the weekend courses which Open Door takes to Northern College. Mike is unemployed but when working had experience of work-related college courses. He is not enthusiastic about Open Door or Northern College courses, for his interest in courses only exists if they relate to work or its possibility in some direct way. Carol on the other hand, is very much in favour of weekend courses dealing with issues such as unemployment and community organisation. She feels it possible that at some time in the future she might well consider some form of serious full-time study. She believes her husband's stated dislike for the kinds of courses associated with Open Door and Northern College results, not so much from their failure to relate to work, but more from her relationship to the courses. 'It's more to do with little wife at home who's started doing these things.' Carol had a clear understanding of why this was so, but her optimism about the long-term outcome was obvious. She felt sure Mike would eventually agree with what she was doing as long as what she was doing made sense - "I'm working on him". Her optimism seemed well-founded, for in January 1985 we met her and Mike at an Open Door Management Course held at Northern College and being part tutored by Northern College staff. Both were enjoying what they were doing and were making worthwhile contributions to the course, as indeed were all who participated in it.

Mary Hanlon

Mary started using Open Door when she attended an English class there, primarily to keep a friend company. She had originally lived in the area, but had only recently returned to it having spent six months in another part of the City living in a Refuge for Battered Women. The physical violence she had experienced at the hands of her husband (now ex-husband) and the way in which her complaints about this violence were treated by the police, had forced her into questioning her attitudes towards marriage and the role of men and women within it; and the role of the police in present day society.

In 1984 when we first met her, Mary was attending a woodwork class at a local school which she found to be of some benefit being a single mother with three children. She was also attending a maths class and a sociology class. She was considering sitting Sociology 'O' Level, but told us that she wasn't interested in the qualification for its own sake, but that it provided a way of being able "to see something at the end of it". When talking of her days at school, Mary told us she had some regret for not having taken it more seriously, but she was also critical of school and the way it educated her and the rest of her sex. "Women weren't supposed to need to know about Maths and English." She and most of her friends were subjected to a curriculum which revolved around having babies and looking after them. In 1983, Mary attended a weekend course at Northern College along with people from centres throughout Sheffield with similar aims to that of Open Door. The course centred on ways of communicating and campaigning on issues such as unemployment and was tutored by Northern College staff. "Some of it were a bit above my head, but some of it were fun." Mary was aware that at that time her confidence was pretty low. This was hardly surprising, for she was a woman in her early thirties with three children and still carrying the scars, psychological if not physical, of violence from her once husband. Her first weekend course experience highlighted certain problems. "I felt really inferior being asked to talk about things I didn't know."

However, by late 1984, when we first met her, her confidence, she felt, had increased considerably. We found her looking for new experience, not fearing it. "Now I want to do everything I've missed out on before." In late 1984, Mary was about to go on a Women's Weekend course at Northern College and was looking forward to it. She felt that her first experience, though at the wrong time in her life, had at least allowed her to have a taste, so that she now knew what to expect.

Mary was well aware of what she regarded as the important issues in her life and was in the process of exploring her life and reflecting upon it so as to better understand and deal with it. "Its about confidence and I'd lost it. I'm only just trying to get it back." Though having been beaten by her husband and having spent time in a refuge for battered women, Mary was a long way from

171

seeing herself as a tragic figure. She was a gutsy, capable woman dealing with life as much on her own terms as can anyone (from the working class). She was beginning to make those kinds of connections described by Mills, where biography and history can be seen to intersect. She was examining her life with the assistance of friends and was also using literature as a resource to do the same. Happy as a Dead Cat, a novel by Gill Miller, had helped her to make a number of connections. She thought she would get a great deal out of the Women's Weekend, for it was for and about women. For herself she felt at present she was trying to sort out her own identity. "If I just get involved in lots of things then there must be something I really want. I just want to be more than a mother." Mary talked about the difficulties and pressures involved in being a mother, and particularly being a mother without a partner: just to go to the cinema to see a film or to the local pub for a drink with friends, necessitated making arrangements for baby sitters and of course involved financial cost - two halves of lager could end up costing £4 or £5. She is not yet sure what she wants out of life, but is sure that she wants more than is at present on offer, more than "watching one day disappear like the one before".

It seemed to us she was heading in a direction where she would create and discover that which she wanted. There seemed to be two aspects to her life working in her favour. First, literature was becoming a resource in her efforts to make sense of her life: when Mary talked of Gill Miller's novel, she told us how she recognised her own life, not simply in the novel's plot, but in its language. The language of this novel to some extent reflected Mary's own use of language, but it also showed her a need to go beyond such language, for in many ways the language of this novel is the language of protest and much needed destruction; it is not a language of construction. And of course, a language of construction is needed if one hopes to engage in construction. Second, in using Open Door, Mary was able to reflect more on her own life, not simply as an individual woman, but more as a woman 'among sisters'. She was interested and concerned with the overall position of women in society; how they were placed with regard to housing, jobs, wages and how they would be able to develop solidarity between themselves.

In January 1985, Mary and approximately

twenty-five others, attended Northern College for a
weekend course focusing particularly on the management of Open Door. The course was one which drew
out from those attending it what they knew and then
re-presented this knowledge to them in such a way
that they could begin systematically to organise
what it was they knew. The teaching method sought
to allow people to learn from themselves and each
other, as opposed to teaching them that which the
teacher knew. However, the tutor did not abdicate
his responsibilities as a tutor by only allowing
students to use as a resource those things which
they already knew. He gave the students the 'hard'
information which they needed to deal with their
subject and when necessary acted as a guide to
them. Much of the hard information passed over was
concerned with local government organisation and
issues surrounding rate-capping, for all those
attending the course were either members of Open
Door's Management Committee, or active centre members and so needed such information in order to
understand what possibilities existed for the immediate future and to help them develop strategies
accordingly. Mary's reaction to this course
'fitted' our notion of a working class aim for
knowledge in order to act in the world, and a
notion of knowledge as something to be shared. "I
want to know more so that I can go out into the
community and let a lot of other people know." She
wanted to know more about rate-capping and the
local/central government struggle taking place at
this time so that she could inform others and with
them find ways of organising to play a part in this
struggle.

People use Open Door for a variety of reasons
and it is often the case that dropping in for a
coffee can lead to participation in things educational. With regard to women at Open Door, the
educational things have, as a major aim, an increase in confidence for the women; such an increase in confidence as to their own abilities
leads to a better understanding of the world for
women. It also brings the possibility for individual women to join together in order to make an
impact on that world. Women at Open Door have
become involved in education within their communities and as working class women have instigated
and taken part in various actions, campaigns and
struggles in those communities. As members of the
Management Committee they are learning how to run
and develop a resource for their area, and in the

173

courses they attend either as women or as Management Committee members, they are developing and taking further those skills and abilities learned by doing what they are doing.

In Open Door and in our other projects we find a learning by doing, a reflection on that doing through specific courses, a recognition of working class experiential knowledge and use of it as a resource and an understanding of the potential as yet largely untapped, of working class people. In each project there is also present the dialectic of individual/class concerning how people learn and what it is they do learn. Also important to all our projects is the notion of an education 'in order to' and it is in order to act in the world. This action aspect to education is very much a part of the traditional way in which the organised working class regarded education. In the early and mid-nineteeth century, this way of viewing education was common among working class people: education would help to provide guides to action in the world and this action would have as its goal the liberation of the class. Though this goal of education for the class disappeared from view and education came to be seen as a way of escaping from the class, the goal did not cease to exist. It was obscured and forgotten, but it never died, for it related to the real world which confronts the working class and as such it is a part of the working class struggle against that world. It takes as a central tenet "experience-based learning in which real problems are tackled in real settings".12

Chapel Green Community Project

The objectives of the project are:-

1. To provide a central base for community groups such as tenants associations, the unemployed, handicapped, for outreach work and to give the community a focal point for all related activities.
2. To integrate differing community groups into an environment of shared leisure, training, job opportunities, recreation and community services.
3. To create jobs in relation to the project itself, and create opportunities through meaningful training/education for jobs in the future.
4. To provide resources, e.g. a printing

workshop, horticultural facilities, knitting
workshop, D.I.Y. and building workshops for
potential worker co-operatives.13

The people involved in this project, particularly
the members of the management committee are faced
with a massive and difficult task which will con-
sume a great deal of time and effort. All involved
will need to learn a certain amount about local and
central government and how they work in practice,
so that they can better pursue the objectives of
their project. During the three months we sat in
on management committee meetings, the committee was
involved in negotiations and discussions with six
departments of Sheffield's City Council; South
Yorkshire County Council; the Department of Employment and the Manpower Services Commission (MSC).
To negotiate with such bodies requires a certain
level of knowledge as to how such bodies operate
and what are their responsibilities. During some
of the time we spent with the management committee,
it was involved in: drawing up job specifications
for the key workers it would recruit to the project
(they would be appointed under a community programme and their salaries paid by MSC); was engaged
in discussions with accountants and solicitors
about wage-payment systems and building insurance
and was also exploring the benefits to be had by
seeking charitable status. Learning cannot be
avoided if one is dealing with such bodies and
individuals on such a range of issues. To carry
out this project work to any level of competence,
necessitates an understanding of how such organisations work, and crucially, how they can be made to
work for the benefit of the people of the Chapel
Green area.
    The project's difficulties are compounded in
many ways, though lessened in others, by the project's insistence that "self-management is an integral part in such a community based project".14
The project wished to manage itself, to have people
of the area running it and accountable to the
people of the area; the self-management process was
to be as open and democratic as possible. Not
surprisingly this style of operating brings considerable problems associated with the relationship
between democratic management and day to day decision making. Minutes of meetings, copies of
letters, logs of telephone conversations - all
become crucial. A commitment to democratic management can result in people being reluctant to set

175

tasks for themselves and others, and less than keen to check that work is followed through; it can mean decisions being avoided as no-one wishes to appear pushy or look as if they're trying to behave like a boss. These problems exist within the project but the management committee members are aware of them and are constantly working on them. Against the problems of democratic self-management must be considered the benefits and these revolve around a wider participation in discussion and decision making and hence an educational advance for a larger number of people, for if all are partici- pating in the work, all should be learning from it.

Just as Open Door takes its users and managers to Northern College for courses dealing specific- ally with community organisation, so too does Cha- pel Green. Thus the education resulting from doing, is backed up and sharpened by Northern Col- lege: an education born of practice is honed by the opportunity to be assisted to reflect upon that practice. As with Open Door, we will focus on two individuals, to show how a process of self-educa- tion is taking place. This will bring again to the fore the role of Northern College in the area.

Jimmy Dawes

Jimmy worked as a maintenance fitter until being made redundant in 1980. The company he work- ed for had been a large one and its workforce had been fully unionised. After four months on the Dole, Jimmy began another job working for a small non-union company; he worked long hours and re- ceived lower wages. In 1983 he was again made redundant and has not worked since. In 1983 he saw a computer course advertised at Chapel Green and he attended it. Whilst on the course he became in- volved with the unemployed group which met at the centre. "It was somewhere to come... not stuck in the house... it breaks down the isolation, similar to a work situation in that you're meeting people." With members of the unemployed group Jimmy attended a course on understanding unemployment at Northern College. His attendance was due to two factors. First, his involvement with the unemployed group and secondly, he explained, how two members of the project's management committee were instrumental in persuading him that he would get something out of attending. (These persuaders, Jenny and Bob, we will encounter shortly.) Jimmy explained the per- suading as "influences which rub off on you". When

176

he first encountered Northern College, he saw it as
"a big, impersonal place - a bit daunting for
people who have been out of work and education for
some time". He believed that for people like himself, depression was often an initial reaction when
they realised how little they knew, but most over-
came this reaction and instead of mourning the
little they knew, became determined to know more.

His growing involvement with Chapel Green he
sees as something of a result of attending Northern
College. He explained how, when working as a maintenance fitter, although a union member, he was not
an active one. "I were in a union, I made the
numbers up." He was concerned with wages and working conditions but "had no real understanding of
the economic set-up". Even when made redundant he
didn't bother to question the existence of mass
unemployment. "Having been to Northern College, I
now know why... I question things a hell of a lot
more and I'm more confident." Northern College had
made him more aware of his own potential and he was
now beginning to explore that potential. "I'm more
interested in what's happening, interested in politics and power, power to do things." Jimmy intended to apply for one of the community programme
posts, soon to be advertised at the centre. "I
want a job but I particularly want a job here. I
want to help it develop. I feel, I suppose, some
sort of sense of ownership." (He was later successful and was appointed as a community worker at
the project. Had he been unsuccessful he would
have given thought to applying to be a full-time
student at Northern College.)

As a result of his involvement in the Chapel
Green community project and his attending courses
at Northern College, Jimmy had changed from being a
politically apathetic working class man to being
a politically concerned one. He had become
interested in the working of the world in which he
lived and was keen to develop his understanding of
it. Northern College and Chapel Green have played
crucial roles in facilitating Jimmy's self-education and it seems very likely both will continue to
do so. In March 1985, Jimmy and other members of
the project were attending a Northern College day
course on the training which the project was to
provide for its thirty plus MSC paid workers then
in post.

Bob McAdam

Unlike Jimmy, Bob had been an active trades
unionist for many years, and had spent a considerable part of his life engaged in political and
economic struggle, conscious of his engagement. He
is a Scot who has lived and worked in the Sheffield
area for twenty-two years, many of them spent in
the employ of Firth Browns. For thirteen years Bob
was a shop steward; he has also been a delegate to
the Sheffield Trades Council and to the Confedera-
tion of Shipbuilding and Engineering Unions. He
has extensive experience of trades union education,
and out of desire to increase his education, he
applied whilst at Firth Browns to become a full-
time student at Northern College. When he applied
he was hoping it might help him towards working in
a full-time capacity for his Union. As his application was being considered, he was made redundant.
His Northern College application successful, he
began his full-time course in 1983.

In Sheffield, as in most other towns and cities from Pittsburg, to Sidney, active trades unionists tend to know each other, regardless of whether
or not they work for the same employer. Bob knew
Jenny and her husband by way of involvement in
trade union and community issues and, as a result,
became involved in the Chapel Green project. At
this time, Jenny was a community work apprentice on
long-term placement at the project. In March 1984,
Bob was elected to the project's management committee and in July of that year when the chairman
resigned, Bob was elected to the chair.

Bob is somewhat sceptical towards community
centres, seeing them as places which provide activities, but do little else. For him the project is
of the type he would like to see in many other
areas and cities because, when compared to community centres, it can be seen to have "a completely
different approach" in that it aims to create a
small number of jobs itself and aims to be a centre
from which groups of people organised around issues
can work. Unlike community centres which tend to
set up their activities and then carry on running
them, the project aims to move. "There's a lot of
scope for it to develop." Bob was concerned that
the style of management embraced by the project,
though important and worthwhile, did create problems. The democratic approach could too easily
result in an excess of time being spent 'trying to
get things right' at the expense of actually carry-

ing out the work. If too much time was spent trying to ensure management was democratic, then results could be produced which would be opposite to those desired. That is, people in the area could come to see the management committee as being divorced from them, spending all its time debating with itself, instead of working with the people. It would be working on its approach to work instead of doing work. Bob saw no simple answer to this problem, nor to the one concerning just how a project does involve itself with the people of the area to the point where the project can really be seen as the property of the people of the area. A management committee comprising people from the area did not necessarily make the project itself the people's property. Though aware of no neat answers to these problems, Bob felt it most important that they be recognised as problems. This recognition was forthcoming from the management committee.

In seeing how Jimmy and Bob became involved in the project, we can locate networks and their development to aid the self-education of the working class. Centres such as Open Door and Chapel Green have contacts with each other and this takes in more and more people to the network and increases the rub-off effect, mentioned by Jimmy, as so important to explaining his involvement. When such a network is also keyed into the brick-work of an educational institution such as Northern College, then we begin to see the increasing possibilities for a real working class self-education. In the operation of such networks, we see the continuation of the working class tradition of the neighbourhood scholar, the self-taught man or woman who is an educational influence on friends and neighbours. These 'organic intellectuals'[15] were once numerous in working class areas of cities, particularly heavily industrialised cities such as Glasgow, Sheffield and Liverpool; but in present-day Britain, they are much thinner on the ground; fewer and fewer workers lend their mates copies of the Ragged Trousered Philanthropists.[16] Time cannot be turned backwards and the conditions, which gave rise to such people and practices, cannot be re-created, but it is possible a different set of conditions can produce similar results and possible that policies can be created which assist in the production of such organic intellectuals and re-kindle such practices. Open Door and Chapel Green, with their learning by doing and further

179

learning by reflection upon doing, facilitated by Northern College, can and do play a valuable role here. In our next chapter we will be concerned how such organic intellectuals can play a part in a strategy which would seek to exploit the contradictions inherent in a provided community education: for if education is again to become an arena in which the working class can seek to challenge bourgeois hegemony, then the role of working class organic intellectuals will be crucial. To what extent do the policies of Sheffield City Council, as reflected in the funding of Open Door and Chapel Green and similar projects, allow for and facilitate the development of such people? It has become apparent to us that local authority policies can have real effects here, are capable of encouraging this organic education within the working class. Sheffield's Community Work Apprenticeship Scheme (CWAS) is an important example of such a policy in action.

CWAS and Jenny McCardle

> The CWAS aims:
> 1. To provide socially useful, full-time, paid employment for local persons who wish to utilise their experience, ability and commitment in the service of the people in Sheffield.
> 2. To provide a new model of employment for the utilisation and development of the skills and abilities of mature working people who have not had the opportunity to develop their work potential through lack of professional 'qualifications'.[17]

Jenny left school at fifteen with no formal educational qualifications. Before getting married she worked as a winder at G.E.C. Since marriage she has worked part-time as a shop assistant and as a school and hospital cleaner. Her family background is Sheffield working class, though political and trades union activity are absent from it. In the early 1970's, Jenny felt unable to become involved in the growing Women's Movement: though sympathetic to many of its aims, she felt it was "up in the air" and somewhat obsessed with theorising. "They weren't talking about me, a woman with kids, a rent book and all that." Thus she had nothing to do with the Women's Movement. She was, however, very much involved with issues concerning women. Jenny

sees the beginning of her community involvement and
her political awareness arising directly from her
experience as a woman with kids. This first community and political action consisted of a struggle
which she and other women of her area waged to gain
a playscheme. They wanted a playscheme, not simply
to be provided, but for the mothers whose children
would use it to be involved in its planning and
operation. She explained how this initial community involvement slowly led her to other forms of
action: she became involved in struggles for repairs to council housing, in debates and campaigns
for the provision of facilities for young people,
and for four years was active in a tenants association concerned with the modernisation of the
city's housing stock. This work on housing modernisation brought her into contact, for the first
time, with Northern College when she attended a
course for tenants organisations at the college.
"The first time I went I was shit scared." After
years of having written nothing, apart from shop-
ping lists, she was scared of having to take notes
and possibly even write an essay; she was also
scared of going away from her home and into a
strange environment. She is now convinced of how
valuable that first course was, though she did not
feel so at the time. She attended further weekend
and week long courses at Northern College, as well
as one for community activists which, on a part-
time basis, lasted for a year.

For Jenny, increased confidence has been one
of the major results of her attending Northern
College courses. She has also begun to question
seriously State provided education, whether it be
schooling or university education. She sees much
of schooling as totally unrelated to the real world
and is suspicious that much of university/poly-
technic education is more concerned with class than
it is with education. Her Northern College experience she says, "made me know that I want more
education - but a different education". The different education, she explained, would be different
to that which is normally provided by the State in
its universities and polys. She wanted very much
to further her own education, but was unsure
whether she ever would, and if she were to do so,
just how would she do it.

If CWAS had not existed, it is almost certain
Jenny would not have begun community work. Access
to it would have been denied her because of her
lack of qualifications; and her antipathy towards

universities and polytechnics would have probably stopped her gaining the relevant qualifications. She is more interested in a practical approach to community work than a theoretical one, which she sees as being the concern of the universities and polytechnics. She backed this up by referring to community work students she had encountered on placement. "They didn't have an idea of what to do. They could give you all the answers of what to do on paper, but as for actually doing anything!" Against being a student on a theoretical community course, as she saw it, she preferred being a community work apprentice on a wage, albeit a small one. We discussed the issue of accreditation with regard to the CWAS and she saw this as posing a difficult problem for anyone on the scheme wishing to leave Sheffield to do similar work in another city. However, she did not feel its importance should be over-emphasised for the CWAS had had as its aim the recruitment of working class community activists from Sheffield to work in Sheffield.

Jenny's entry into community work came about as a result of the conditions of her own existence as a mother: playschemes for children proved to be her starting point. The self-education process which accompanied her participation in community action has been considerably assisted by the courses she has attended at Northern College. In her life as a working class mother, influences have rubbed off on her and her influence has rubbed off on others, Jimmy Dawes, for example. Circumstances, from accidental social contact through to deliberate educational intervention, can get together to change people as they have changed Jenny. If these circumstances cannot be created by local authorities, their chances of occurring can be increased. A local authority which is committed to its working class residents and believes in their potential, can make an impact by helping to facilitate the making real of such working class potential. It can concretely attempt to aid the process of working class self-education.

Sheffield Pensioners Action Group and Joan Forrester

Community education continually stresses how education has to be regarded as part of a learning for life, how community education should be involved in helping to educate the retired, as well as the working, unemployed and school children. It is all too often the case, however, that the educational provision for the retired is designed in terms of ways to use their newfound 'leisure' time, by taking up new hobbies, or by trying to pass an 'O' Level or two. Our Sheffield fieldwork shows us a very real educational alternative to much of community education's offerings in this area. We close our discussion with a description of how one retired woman in Sheffield has begun a process of self-education, as a member of the Sheffield Pensioners Action Group (SPAG). SPAG is assisted by the City Council insofar as it has been the provider of premises and support. SPAG, like Open Door and Chapel Green, also keys into Northern College's educational brickwork.

"I've always been an ordinary working class girl", Joan tells us. Her life began in Sheffield and thus far she has spent all of it in the city. As a schoolgirl, Joan was a member of the Brownies and later the Girl Guides. She left school at fourteen with no educational qualifications and spent the next three years of her life earning a living as a 'day girl'. A day girl was a domestic servant, who did not live on the premises where she worked, doing the major part of the necessary housework for her social superiors. At the end of each working day she went home. As a day girl, Joan did no cooking, but she did clean, wash dishes and clothes, lay and light fires and look after the children of the house when their parents were not present. Joan's working week was a seven day one with the occasional Sunday afternoon free, and for this, she was paid five shillings a week. In the three years she spent earning her living this way, she had 'three places'. A day girl did not have a job, she had a place.

Joan's next employment was with a photographic company in the city. She helped in the darkroom and dealt with customers. As the company was the most prestigious photographers in the city, her employer insisted she lose her Sheffield accent and he accordingly 'corrected' her speech until all trace of accent had disappeared. He believed this to be necessary if she were to deal successfully with his respectable customers. (In 1985, Joan is a Sheffield working class woman who speaks without trace of a Sheffield accent.) In the early 1930's, Joan's father was unemployed and as a result she was visited at her place of work by "the means test people". Her employer dismissed her at once for he wanted "nothing so common as the means test

associated with his business". From then until her
marriage in 1936, Joan worked in factories in the
City which were engaged in various aspects of the
steel industry. By the time she married, her
involvement in church-based organisations had come
to an end and she was not to re-join an
organisation of any kind until the late 1960's.

In the late 1960's, her husband was found to
be suffering from Parkinson's Disease and because
of this, Joan joined the Sheffield branch of the
Parkinson's Disease Society. She helped the
society in many small ways and after some time
became a member of its organising committee. She
told us she felt somewhat out of place due to her
working class background and identity, for the
majority of the committee and active society
members, were middle class.

By 1981 her husband had died and Joan was re-
married. She was also past the age of sixty and so
was 'retired'. In this year, she entered the SPAG
caravan, which was parked in the City centre, and
bought a copy of SPAG's newspaper. At this time,
SPAG had no premises of its own and so used to meet
and conduct its business at Transport House (the
offices of the Transport and General Workers
Union). Such an accommodation situation did not
encourage a growth in membership. From dropping in
to buy a newspaper, Joan became increasingly
involved with SPAG, especially after SPAG was able
to move into its City centre premises in February
1984. These premises have been most significant in
enabling SPAG to grow and increase its activities
and membership. They are provided by the City
Council at a peppercorn rent and there is a 50%
rates reduction, for SPAG is a non-profit making
charitable body.

When we first talked to Joan, she was about to
attend, along with other SPAG members, a course at
Northern College. She was slightly apprehensive,
as she thought it might be "high fallutin". She
told us that when she first knew she was going on
the course, she was "scared stiff". Once she was
at the college however, her fears soon disappeared,
for she and her fellow SPAG members were made to
feel most welcome by the full-time students at the
college. "After that I had no problem at all."

Joan feels that SPAG has given her a real
interest in life, and that never having been a
joiner of organisations, SPAG is the first one she
has really joined. She seemed to fit into SPAG in
a way she had never managed with the Parkinson's

Disease Society. For Joan, as for the other activists we have encountered, Northern College proved
to be a tremendous confidence booster. "My husband
says I've gotten to be very cheeky since I got
back. I never used to answer back before." Not
only has the college boosted her confidence, but it
has made her capable of being a better member of
her organisation. She believes the college showed
her how the work of SPAG was important; it helped
to give the work of SPAG its context, and for Joan,
"It's made me feel important." Joan feels that for
most of her life she has done her living for
others, and that she "wasn't the slightest bit
important to anyone except my son and husband".
Now, as a SPAG member who is learning all the time
to be a more useful member, she feels she is more
useful to more people than immediate family. It is
not the simple fact of having joined an organisation; rather it is the particular organisation that
she has joined which is important. SPAG is an
organisation which acts in the real world towards
achieving aims, which Joan believes to be worthwhile.

> In this 68th year of mine I'm doing more and
> more, am more involved with people than I've
> ever been in all my life. And if a year ago
> someone had told me I'd go to college, even
> for a few days, you could have knocked me down
> with a feather.

Joan's enthusiasm towards Northern College and her
appreciation of its relevance to organisations like
SPAG, was shared by many SPAG members on the
course. They spoke to us about how different was
education at the college, to that which they had
previously experienced as education; of how the
course was helping them to discover skills and
abilities they had either forgotten they had or
never realised they possessed; and of how the
course would be of value to their SPAG work in the
real world. Some of SPAG's members had, when working, been active trades unionists, and one seemed
to speak for all, when he told us, "Northern College helped us to remove the rust and polish our
own abilities". Northern College students had
played their part in making the SPAG members' experience an enjoyable one for they were "free from
hostile or condescending attitudes". The type of
education practiced by the college showed for one
member, how the following did not have to be the

reality of colleges. "The rich are educated; the poor are trained."

SPAG is primarily concerned with increasing the efficiency of its campaigning work and when it pursues education it does so in order to benefit its work. Alice Sergeant its Secretary, who is also a County Councillor, explained, "We want to learn communication skills. We want to know how we can be more effective in putting our views over." That members are learning communication skills was made abundantly clear at the National Pensioners Conference, organised by SPAG and held in the City Hall of Sheffield, in October 1984, for the video which was used to open the conference was made by SPAG members, with some assistance from Shirecliffe College in Sheffield.

Sheffield City Council, we can say, realised by the mid 1970's that the community education approach of the campuses was one which had failed and would continue to fail to involve educationally the working class of the city. It therefore began to devolve its adult education out from the campuses and into neighbourhood venues. As well as changing venue, it began to change its content and method of delivery. Whether it was formulated in the way we phrase it is not important at this moment; but we can say that these decisions meant a working class education could be pursued away from the influences of school; the working class of the City would have a chance to develop a self-education process, with the City Council playing the role of the facilitator. In effect, Sheffield City Council dropped out of the community education strategy. Positively this meant that a democratic socialist strategy could be pursued with regard to working class adults and education , for the pressures to continually reproduce traditional adult education courses were no longer so strong; school would stop dictating to adult education. Negatively, this meant schools were removed from what could be the influence of the developing working class organic intellectuals. The strength of Sheffield's approach was also its weakness; by separating the education of the adult working class from school, it removed the influence of school but also removed the school from the influence of the adult working class. It is probable that this split was essential, for without it, it is doubtful whether a self-education could have been facilitated which would help to produce working class organic intellectuals with the potential to influence schools.

Sheffield now has an infant working class self-education process in operation and this can offer a very real possibilty for change in the area of schooling. A straightforward community education approach has little chance of effecting change within schools; but if such an approach were to be linked to one aiming to facilitate working class self-education, then, we believe, the chance for meaningful and worthwhile change within school ceases to be small. This notion will be explored and a strategy put forward in our next chapter.

REFERENCES

1. A. Baldwin, An Overview. From **Perspectives on Adult Education: Articles on New Developments in Sheffield.** Sheffield City Council Adult Education Department. November 1982.
2. Education Statistics 1984. Sheffield City Council.
3. Baldwin op. cit.
4. Ibid.
5. Adult Education Budget Working Party Report on the Budget Requirements for Adult Education 1984/85. Sheffield City Council.
6. Services in Sheffield: A Guide to Policy. 1983/84.
7. A. Baldwin, Styles and Methods of Neighbourhood Adult Education Work. From **Perspectives on Adult Education.** op. cit.
8. A. H. D. Acland, The Education of Citizens. From D. A. Reeder. **Educating Our Masters.** Leicester University Press 1980.p. 208.
9. C. Wright Mills, **The Sociological Imagination.** Pelican 1981. p. 12.
10. Ibid. p. 14.
11. A letter sent to all women due to attend the Open Door Women's Course at Northern College. Dated 1/2/84 and written by the Course Tutors.
12. D. Hargreaves, **Network** February 1982. CEDC.
13. The Chapel Green Community Project. p. 2.
14. The Chapel Green Feasibility Study. August 1983.
15. For a discussion on the notion on organic intellectuals see particularly A. Gramsci On Education. In A. Gramsci, **Selections from Prison Notebooks.** Lawrence and Wishart 1982.

References

16. The Ragged Trousered Philanthropists, a novel
      by R. Tressell, is the novel regularly cred-
      ited by many socialists in Britain, specif-
      ically those aged 50 plus, as having been a
      key factor in their becoming socialist.
17. From the Chief Education Officer's Report to
      Sheffield City Council Education Committee.
      Post 16 Sub-Committee. April 5th 1982.

Chapter Seven

OF SELF AND COLLECTIVE EMANCIPATION

"When I think back on all the crap I learned in
High School it's a wonder I can think at all".
(Paul Simon, 'Kodachrome')

Community education has two distinct strands to it:
one concerns home/school relations and aims to
better educate children by way of parental
involvement; the other concerns the school and its
place in the community and here we find a plethora
of additions to the school - evening classes,
luncheon clubs, playgroups, youth clubs, mums and
toddlers and adult students in classes alongside
children; the aim here is to make the school a more
open and attractive institution. Neither strand
treats the school as problematic nor challenges the
bourgeois nature of education, nor the professional's right to define and control the situation.
Both strands are referred to , however, to justify
community education's claim to be involved in
changing schools. Community education does represent change, but a very specific form of change;
one which alters the appearance but leaves the
basics intact. The fundamentals of education remain intact for the key role of community education
is the protection of these fundamentals. Changes
are thus made in order to avoid making changes.
       Contradiction is present in all phenomena.
The bourgeoisie has had to struggle constantly to
attempt to educate the working class as it would
wish it to be educated, for a cast-iron guarantee
cannot be obtained concerning the uses to which
literacy and numeracy will be put. The Education
Act of 1870, was a definite victory for the bourgeoisie, but the contradiction within it which
resulted in the School Boards, actually produced a
base from which an attack upon the education established by the Act could be launched. The working
class of the time did not simply accept the Act;
rather they took its provisions and its contradictions and used them against the purposes for which

189

the Act had been placed on the Statute Book. The working class of 1870 had wanted compulsory State provided education, but a very different form of education to that which the Act provided. Faced with the education which the Act provided, certain members of the working class set about trying to change and use this education for purposes opposite to those for which it was provided. In effect they continued the educational struggle, but on new grounds.

Like those men and women of 1870, we are concerned with the education of the working class; an education in which as little ideological wrapping is involved as possible, in which the subject matter is cleansed of its ideological components.1 We are concerned with the contradictions which always exist within education, whereby it can be used in a manner different to that for which it was provided. We are concerned with the location and exploitation of such contradictions. And it is because of this we must welcome community education; not in any sense for what it is, but for the contradictions within it and the opportunities they present.

Community education consciously seeks to involve the working class in schooling, by way of home-school links and attractive school-based activities. The involvement, of course, aims that the working class will more readily appreciate what schools are doing. For the first time, in many decades, a way is offered for a working class involvement in schools. From our view it may be offered for all the wrong reasons, but nevertheless, it is offered; and the offer must be taken up and exploited if a way is to be found whereby schools can begin to benefit educationally the working class, even within the context of capitalist society. A way of exploiting this involvement, a way of challenging education in schools has to be found, for it is most unlikely that a challenge will come about simply as a result of community education welcoming parental involvement. For a challenge to be made with any hope of it being effective, it will have to be made by 'educated' working class parents, but they will need to be educated in a different way to which provided education would wish them to be. This challenge would have to be made by capable, educated members of the working class, who refuse to accept, and struggle against the 'one world' view of Midwinter and most community educators. Our concern is with the self-production of such educated members of the working class, for it is they, who by their involvement in community schools, will make the issue of control of schools and rights to educational definition, more controversial, and they, who will determine the relative success of the outcome of such a challenge with regard to the working class as a whole and its education.

Our first step towards 'mapping out' some sort of strategy for challenge, is to examine the educational role and philosophy of Northern college, for as our last chapter illustrated, the college is central to the facilitation of self-education among the working class of Sheffield.

Northern College: Its Role and Educational Philosophy

Northern College is a residential adult college located between Barnsley and Sheffield, South Yorkshire. Its creation was brought about, to a certain degree, by the recommendations of the Russell Report of 1973.2 The college, however, was to be more than just an adult residential college, more than 'a Ruskin of the North'.

A new provision, compared with other long-term Colleges, was that half the places should be reserved for students on short courses so that the College could become a resource for more than those who wished to make the major change in their lives implied in undertaking two years' full-time study.3

The college first opened its doors to students in 1978. Our fieldwork took place during 1984/85, by which time the college had had six years of developing and working with its short course strategy. The college learned its methodology in the process of work. Though it was still learning whilst we were engaged in our fieldwork, it had, by 1984, arrived at a coherent educational philosophy and way of working with students on both short and long courses. Long course students tend to go on from the college into further full-time educational study, either at a Polytechnical College, or at a University. We will not be discussing the 'class transfer' aspect of this, nor will we be concerned with the long-term courses and their students: our concern is with the college's short-course students, those who are not deemed to be making major changes in their lives by coming to college. These are the students who, without doubt, will be going back to their working class communities after their educational experience at the college.

When we began our fieldwork with various groups in Sheffield, we hoped to discover whether and how the projects in which they were involved, facilitated a self-education process. Though we knew of Northern College, we did not expect it to be particularly significant with regard to our projects: we did not expect it to be that which we found it to be. In our fieldwork we met and spoke to a great many people at Open Door, Chapel Green, SPAG and at other centres throughout the City and all those we spoke to had had, or were about to have, some form of educational contact and experience at the college. This varied from people who had been on the two year full-time course, to those who had been on weekend courses, or week long courses. We began to discover how the college fitted into the facilitation of working class self-education in the Sheffield area. Northern College began to appear to us as less the long-term residential college of which we had heard, and more the provider of short courses of educational benefit to specific groups engaged in some form of community action. It began to appear as an educational institution, playing a crucial role in this facilitation of self-education, by way of its working with groups to reflect consciously upon their practice. As such, it is a very important institution, for a learning by doing has to be backed up by a reflection upon the doing and what has been learned in it. David Browning, a college tutor, explained the relationship between the tutors and the short course students.

> We start from where people are; it is a problem-centred as well as a client-centred approach. The work we do together must grow from people's own ideas of where they are and where they want to go. But it must, at the same time, be skilfully joined with our own ideas and understandings, as people intervening in the community and inevitably bringing our own influences to bear. There must be conceptual work to stand alongside the practical activities, to deepen understanding as well as skill.

Northern College provides this back up: it helps

practice to be made sense of both practically and conceptually.

Individual working class people in the Sheffield area become involved in local community action and projects; they learn and educationally benefit from this involvement; that learning is then made more coherent and taken further by their participation in Northern College courses, with the aim of adding to the value of their contribution to their community action and projects. There is no doubt about Northern College making a contribution, and a valuable one at that, to the self-education of the working class in the Sheffield area by way of its short course programme. There are a number of points of importance regarding the way in which the college goes about its educational work, and all of them stand as contradistinctions to the way in which provided education operates. No short course students are admitted to the college as individuals; they enter only as members of groups. And these groups enter the college in order to gain a better understanding of a particular thing so that they may act on, or with that thing. They do not come to the college to acquire knowledge in some abstract sense, but to discover the knowledge they already have and to sharpen and develop it with a view to using it in their struggle to comprehend the world and act on it. Individuals do not come to compete with each other, very much the tradition within education, but to learn from each other and themselves. The college then, seeks to practice a form of co-operative learning.

> Even today, this most common and effective way by which man has developed from his forbears, corporately identifying problems, devising strategies for resolving them and carrying those strategies out, is not only neglected in school, but actively stamped out. Outside schools, men and women have known that only united can they thrive, whilst inside the order of the day is still cut-throat competition and individual attainment. (Just imagine, for instance, the establishment's reaction to a proposal for an 'O' Level to be awarded only to groups of not fewer than six candidates.)[4]

A co-operative learning approach breaks all the rules of provided education where each individual is encouraged to learn as an individual and to regard what he has learned as very much his own private property. Northern College's educational practice aims to release knowledge in the sense that it strives to help people to know what it is they know; it is to release the knowledge of the world which practice in the world has given people, even though they might not realise it.

In our fieldwork we began to identify these aspects to the college's educational practice as we talked to those community activists who had experienced the college. The aspects we felt, must surely be parts of an overall educational philosophy with which the college operates. It was necessary then to add to the reactions and comments of Jenny, Bob, John, Joan and others, as well as our own perceptions, the perceptions of the college itself regarding its educational philosophy. To this end we met and talked with the principal, Bob Fryer.

Fryer explained, as had Browning, how the college sought to commence its educational work with the material the students brought to the college; the content, in effect, of their own lives and their work in their communities. The college would use this material as the base upon which it would build. There is a recognition here, that the practice of living is not separate to learning and indeed has to be seen as the base from which and upon which learning is built. This approach accords well with what Gouldner describes as "knowledge as awareness".

> In a knowing conceived as awareness, the concern is not with 'discovering' the truth about a social world regarded as external to the knower, but with seeing truth as growing out of the knower's encounter with the world and his effort to order his experiences with it. The knower's knowing of himself - of who, what and where he is - on the one hand, and of others and their social worlds, on the other, are two sides of a single process.[5]

Both Gouldner and Fryer would appear to have an image of man making himself in the world by his practice in it; and a philosophy of education where education has to be understood as the conscious unravelling of the knowing of the world gained from practice in it, the ordering of the experience of it.

Northern College treats the student's life and

practice of living as the key material for educational work. The culture and belief system of the working class student is not attacked and its negation sought, as is frequently the result when education interfaces with the working class. Indeed, to a large extent as we have shown, the purpose of such interfacing is to bring about such change to the culture of the working class as to make it no longer recognisable. But equally important, Northern College does not romanticise and treat as sacred the culture of the working class. There is no Wilmott and Young near anthropological bliss when encountering the culture; a reaction frequently found within community education, when it seeks to present itself as the champion of the class and respector of its way of life. For the college all experiential knowledge is valued, but it is not at all treated as equally valid; not regarded as being without need of critical reflection and examination. The college's educational philosophy insists upon walking the tightrope here, insists that the experiential knowledge of the working class be valued and respected, but also insists that a critical examination of it is necessary and that such a critical examination is evidence of respect for it.

Where Gouldner talks of truth growing out of the knower's encounter with the world, Fryer talks of understanding coming about as a result of the student critically reflecting upon his experience.

> In other words, not to think that knowledge and understanding and study reside in a series of articles and books and even more importantly in the tutor's head: but to understand that through a critical reflection upon their own experience and through an ability to bring into articulation their own experience with concepts and ideas and approaches which have been adopted by other people; by writers, by authors, indeed by other members of their group, by the tutor - they can enhance their own understanding of their own experience. They can qualify it, they can sophisticate it, they can understand its nuances and its complexity.

Neither Gouldner's nor Fryer's education is a soft option; indeed it is more sophisticated and demanding than the model offered by provided education, for it aims at an understanding of the world and one's place in it, by utilising the

concepts and ideas of others gone before and those
still present, as facilitators to critical reflection upon practical experience. Knowledge then is
not something residing in the individual and hence
the role of education cannot be delineated in individual terms; knowledge is not private property.
Fryer explained that the role of the college,
therefore, is different to that of the traditional
educational institution, in that students are not
meant to leave with the benefits of their educational experience locked within them, to be used as
a form of currency to acquire job or status. Their
educational experience is intended to assist them
in their role as community activist/organiser, to
the benefit of the action or organisation in which
they, and others, are involved. "If the knowledge
has any virtue it's got to be spread around."
     Here we see a connecting thread between
Northern College's educational philosophy and
perception of its role and the way in which working
class radicals of the nineteenth century conceived
of education. To them education was invariably 'in
order to' and this in order to was related to the
collective improvement and eventual liberation of
the class; it was an education which would be
utilised in the world, would guide one's practice
in it with a view to changing it. Of the college's
short course students and their education, Fryer
tells us:

> While it might be interesting in itself what
> they've been doing while they've been here, we
> hope they get value from it for the
> educational experience itself, but in addition
> to it having been valued in itself, we would
> hope that people can go back and utilise the
> self-understanding, the critical awareness,
> the development of skills within their own
> community activities. Now that's a very
> important feature because that feature of the
> college means that the college's life doesn't
> only exist within the walls of the college or
> within the heads of the persons that come to
> the college.

Fryer hopes that the effects and benefits of the
college will be radiated out from those who attend
it to others in their communities; a multiplier
effect occurring because the college refuses to see
education as private property.
     Traditional bourgeois provided education, when

successfully consumed by a minority of the working class, is as much about class transfer as it is about anything else; indeed, adult education itself, even Northern College long-course variety, has an element of this transference to it.6 The short courses of Northern College, however, do not have this element present. They are concerned with an education which will enable working class men and women to act more efficiently as members of their class, in the interests of their class, not primarily provide them with an escape from it.

The short course education gives many people their first real taste of education as something relevant to them and not as something in which they fail. They are able to build upon their own strengths and abilities.

> So for them it's a re-awakening or an awakening for the first time to the idea that education has a part to play in their own development as humans and for the purposes ultimately of self and collective emancipation.

Like Rennie, Fryer does not believe that education, of itself, will bring about radical societal change, but he does see it very much as having a role to play in any such change. It can be seen as an aid to the liberation of the class. For Fryer, education is not a cultural manifestation for a few individuals whereby they might eventually be allowed to share an elite culture.

> If you don't have that elite notion then you must think that education is somehow about control; that knowledge is about how people control their environment, their social, their material, their intellectual, their physical, their economic, their political environment...

For Fryer, education can help the working class to mount challenges to control in these crucial areas of life. His belief is valid and the college's work has shown it to be so. In our fieldwork, we were led to Northern College by the impact it had had upon the people associated with our projects. These individuals were working class men and women lacking formal educational qualifications, who had obviously benefited and were continuing to benefit from their college educational experience, and that experience was being put to use in their communities and to the benefit of those communities. It

was not weakening the culture of their working
class communities, the aim of education from Bernard to Midwinter, but was sharpening it by acting
with it in its interest. People who had begun to
be active in their communities attended courses at
the college, and returned to their communities to
re-engage in action with heightened consciousness
of the ways and purposes of their action. They
were involved in running devolved adult education
centres in their neighbourhoods, community projects, participating in pensioners' struggles and
various campaigns on issues from transport to
creches and nurseries.

When we finished our fieldwork in the Sheffield area, Northern College was beginning to turn
its attention to possible contributions it could
make with regard to community education as expressed in community schools, etc. And it is this
possibility which is crucial to exploiting community education's contradictions. Fryer talked of
how progressive veneers can be put on to phenomena,
to persuade us that change has taken place; how
community education can be seen as a way of legiti-
mising the everyday practice of schools.

> Now we've been wanting to say, 'how can the
> experience of Northern College be given to
> people so that their children or the children
> of their community don't, as it were, suffer
> the disadvantages of initial education that
> the people that come to us suffered'. We've
> been talking about it, about organising a
> special course precisely for those people.
> Now if we do get those off the ground, it'll
> be quite exciting, because partly, it'll be
> our own educational authorities who will be
> sponsoring those people, who eventually will
> see the consequences in terms of a much more
> critical, a much more sceptical, a much more
> active population, often against the local
> authority's initiatives.

Northern College has helped, and still is helping,
to facilitate a self-education process among the
working class of the Sheffield area, and this has
led to the self-production of working class organic
intellectuals, capable of challenging taken-for-
granted processes and institutions in society.

If education and schools are to be challenged
with the long-term aim of changing their practices
so that it is of educational benefit to the working

class, then the educational philosophy and practice of Northern College have to be taken up by educational authorities, so as to facilitate working class self-education in their own areas.

Our discussion of Northern College's educational philosophy brings us to our suggested strategy for real and significant educational change.

A Strategy for Change

If our ideas of educational change were concerned, for example, with changes to examinations and the day-to-day management of schools, then we would possibly be offering, simply, suggestions as to a new form of in-service training for teachers. However, this is not the case; we agree with Mr Rollings, the Head of Huntingdon School - there is no magic method of training, and especially so, when we are concerned with a form of educational change which challenges so much of that which is taken for granted, by teachers and educationalists. 'Provided education' does not operate with a model of a dichotomous struggle between the two major classes of capitalist society as an explanatory factor to its own becoming. When it enquires at all as to its origins, it posits an uncomplicated quasi-evolutionary process of change whereby changes take place naturally as if according to an externally provided plan; one made not by man which specifies adjustments and alterations until the unequal society becomes the society of equality. It is as if time, left to its own devices, will guarantee a better world. It sees educational change brought about, not as the result of any class struggle, but more the result of a natural drive to improvement, manifested in an increase in goodwill, on behalf of the members of the ruling class in a position to allow change to take place. 'Provided education' not only ignores class and class conflict as explanatory factors in educational change, but it equally ignores the importance of class in the way in which education operates. It never finds the culture and value system of the bourgeoisie at all problematic, whilst the culture and value system of the working class is a constant problem for it: yet, despite this situation, education itself is somehow regarded as being free of class bias. Education is never addressed as being problematic in the class sense; the working class always is so addressed.

Being unconcerned with class on any level

other than the epiphenomenal, it is not surprising
that 'provided education' sees its only valid subject as the individual, with his or her individual
capability and intelligence. Indeed, seeing its
valid subject in this light, is an example of the
ideology with which education operates. It is one
which consistently denies class and insists the
individual against class, and it has been the case,
that in order to continue to insist the individual
against class, educational ideology has helped give
birth to community education.

Not all individual teachers see education in
this light of course, but education, as a system,
sees itself in this light. No form of in-service
training on its own could begin to hope to deal
with and change radically this situation. The
situation is however, where no near as hopeless as
it might seem from our brief resume°: teachers
might well believe they are engaged in an educational practice very different to the one in which
they are engaged, and that belief and the practice
it relates to, can give cause for optimism. Harry
Rée, for example, tells us:

> We must refuse to accept a system or a society
> where in-built subservience is induced through
> its institutions. Community education is
> pledged to destroy such slavery.7

As long as Rée believes this, we must believe it
possible to convince him that his community education is doing little in terms of its pledge and may
actually be obstructing it. We must view, then,
the Rée's within education as very much potential
allies to a cause of radical change. Nevertheless,
in-service training alone is not enough. Community
educators often say that education is too important
to leave to teachers: so it is. The School Boards
of 1870 would not have become the radical bodies
they did become, had not the articulate, educationally concerned sections of the working class struggled over them. Schools and community schools
similarly have little chance of changing, unless
similar sections of today's working class are involved in a struggle over them. The schools need
to be influenced by the working class if they are
to educationally be of benefit to the class.

Over a period of time, as we have seen, the
language of educational debate abandoned its stri-
dent denunciation of the working class as educable, and, instead, utilised a language of liberal-

ism with a progressive reformist veneer; in so
doing it succeeded in persuading many educationalists and lay people that this language was a reflection of a corresponding change within education
to such a degree that class was no longer an issue
within it. The rhetoric of a progressive and equal
opportunity education came to be accepted as a
description of reality. Within this liberal language there was, and indeed had to be, a recognition
of the potential of the working class and an acknowledgement of its experiential knowledge. Though
not the outcome of any conspiracy, the recognition
and acknowledgement were primarily parts of a strategy to involve the working class in an education,
which had as part of its goal, the invalidation of
the class' experiential knowledge and the careful
direction of its potential. In order to continue a
class based education system a rhetoric described
it in a very different manner, and still so describes it. This can allow people to sieze upon the
contradiction here and demand that some of the
ideas encapsulated in the new rhetoric be pursued
at the expense of the reality such rhetoric serves
to obscure. If education boasts of its progressive, liberal nature, then why not demand that its
practice begin to reflect its boasting?

Our suggested strategy is concerned with facilitating an exploitation of such contradictions
within education generally, and community education
specifically, in order to offer long term hope of
education serving the class, which it has for so
long judged so harshly. And this strategy is the
result of our theoretical analysis of education,
educational change and ideology, and the relationship of these things to the working class in capitalist Britain, combined with the lessons we have
learned from our Derbyshire and Sheffield fieldwork. The strategy has three aspects to it. In
putting it forward, we take account of an economic
and political climate in which public spending is
regarded as something to be curtailed and
restricted, not expanded. Thus we make the
strategy as cost-effective as possible. For it is,
after all, being put forward in all seriousness as
a way in which local education authorites can seek
to bring about much needed educational change.

Aspect One: Facilitating a Working Class Self-Education Through Practice

Local Education Authorities would have to

discover ways of facilitating a working class self-
education, through doing. The specific way in
which this would take place would depend, to an
extent, on the nature of the authority and the
social and political history of the area; there
would, however, be themes common whatever the area.
Without doubt most authorities would have to change
the emphasis of their adult education service.
They would need to begin to move away from the
traditional evening class approach, for in some
ways we have been generous to even describe this
service as an educational one, revolving as it does
around cake decorating and keep-fit. Committed to
an adult education approach aimed at benefiting
their working class residents, some authorities
might decide to begin to devolve their adult education out from the schools and into some form of
neighbourhood centre. Such a move would not be
made for its own sake, but would be made in order
to locate a form of educational activity in a venue
not solely concerned with education: thus, this
education would have the potential of being seen as
a part of ordinary life. It would not simply be
placed in this new setting; its management would
also be devolved to the management of the neighbourhood centre, so that the people themselves
would come to run and develop their own adult
education in this setting. The school's adult
education worker would assist and advise the centre
management. If authorities contemplated such a
move, it would be essential for them to give considerable thought to the centres to which they
would devolve adult education. Most authorities
already run community centres and many run centres
making some form of provision for the unemployed.
Such a situation where an authority runs two types
of centres might well have to be brought to an end,
for it is very difficult to justify having a separate centre for the unemployed, because they cannot
be seen as an homogenous group and it does not make
sense to treat them as one. Thus, authorities
might need to review, in a comprehensive manner,
the centres for for which they are responsible.
Many community centres are valuable centres for
their communities, but it must be said that there
are probably an equal number which are community
centres in nothing but name; are centres which are
of little service or value to their local working
class residents. With regard to all centres within
an authority, a co-operative way of working with
local people would have to be found be found so

that the authority and the people would be able to explore the possible shape the centres should take. This could well mean that an authority would have to challenge vested interests associated with certain centres by closing such centres, negotiating a new purpose and organisation for them and then reopening them. centres which were already of value might be re-organised with little difficulty. The aim of the re-organising, whether small scale or massive, would be to create centres which could be described as community centres/unemployed centres /devolved adult education centres.

Some authorities would not wish to devolve any of their adult education out from their schools. In their case the centres would be an amalgam of community and unemployed, but they would have to be allowed to develop their own style of adult education if they so wished. And like the 'three in one' centres they would need to be centres in working class areas, managed by local people, wherein working class people would be able to take on roles which carried a process of learning by doing.

As this learning by doing would be part of a long-term strategy, authorities would need to ensure that these centres 'keyed into' the authorities' schools. This would not present too much of a problem; once an authority had begun to move away from the traditional evening class programme approach to adult education, it would free its adult education worker, who could then work part of his/her week with these centres, acting as an educational partner/guide.

Authorities would not, of course, need to embark upon this restructuring of their community education service in a vacuum. They would be able to seek advice from authorities such as Sheffield and from centres such as Open Door: and, no doubt, from other centres and authorities pursuing this type of approach to educational/centre work with the working class.

If the centres were successful, and Open Door in Sheffield shows, in many ways, that they can be, then they would be responsible for providing a useful service to the people of their area, and for playing a significant part in the self-production of working class organic intellectuals, capable of entering fully into education's debate. The other partner to this self-production process will be the 'short course college'; our third strategy aspect. Before we discuss the third aspect, we must examine the position of the schools themselves and the community school in particular.

Aspect Two: The Community School

The community school does, without doubt, offer a way for working class people to get involved in schools and the education which they provide. Accordingly, authorities pursuing our strategy would need to begin to metamorphose all their schools into community schools. However they would have to ensure that they did not simply follow the practices hitherto pursued when carrying out this metamorphosis. Community education has tended to try to create community schools by purchasing the teaching staff's co-operation, as opposed to educating the staff into support for a community education philosophy. It has done this by making salary arrangements for those members of staff deemed to have community commitments - an extra scale point may be given to a physical education teacher, in return for looking after community sport. This approach produces a section of a school's teaching staff in receipt of salary additions for its community work: it leaves many of the school's teaching staff untouched financially. Another approach has been to allocate a community commitment to all the staff in the school, whereby they are deemed to have a 10% community workload and a 90% teaching load. This arrangement does not result in some teachers being paid more than colleagues. Such arrangements should no longer be made: in paying some teachers and not others, a message is given to all teachers that community education is something for which one is paid, and hence, if one is not in receipt of a community addition to salary, one need not get involved in community education. Similarly, giving all staff a community workload suggests to staff that community education is an addition to the normal work of teaching; it is something which can be quantified - 10% - and as such, it can be seen to be separate to the rest of the work involved in being a teacher.

The community education in our strategy would be much more a philosophy of education to which the staff must be won over, than a method for school management to allocate community tasks among staff. One of the central beliefs of this community education would concern the rights of parents to become involved in it and not simply as consumers of the school's definition of it. A long term goal would be to involve people of the area in the school with no areas being regarded as inviolate, with a view to the people and the staff becoming equal partners to an educational dialogue geared to significant change. These community schools would follow the present practice of making their facilities available to the people of the area, but they would need to keep to an absolute minimum the procedures of access for the people. The community schools would not be under any pressure to follow community school traditions by seeking to establish a whole range of evening classes, for this practice would no longer be regarded as something of a definition of community education.

These community schools would not need to appoint community tutors, for their community education would aim to become a new approach to education, in which all staff would be involved. Crucial to this style of community education would be the changing of staff attitudes and beliefs; staff in-service training. It is probable that a 'community tutor' of some kind would be seconded to the school for a period of time to assist here; but not until such a community tutor had also undergone appropriate re-training. Some of the school's in-service training would have to include local community activists; those who would be running the neighbourhood centres, for example. This would benefit such people but it would also benefit the school's teachers, for it would be a concrete statement that community education was about the right of the community to be involved in that education. A real involving of the local community would be a definite aim for the community education to be practiced by these community schools: but it would be an aim, and we must remember that aims relate to targets, and the long term target, and it would be long term, would be the transformation of the school so that it ceased to practice a pedagogy and teach a curriculum destined to fail educationally its working class students.

We do not believe that education left to educationalists, is at all capable of bringing about such a transformation of the school: indeed, the whole history of 'provided education' shows us this to be so. A challenge from organic working class intellectuals will have to be made if such a transformation is to become a real possibility. The third aspect of our strategy is central to the production of such intellectuals.

Aspect Three: The Working Class Short Course College

Our first two aspects required no real extra resources, more a re-arrangement of existing resources: that is not so here, for some extra resources would be needed, but expenditure on them need not be large, for reasons which will become clear as we discuss the notion of the short course college. If we are to aim to facilitate the self-production from within working class communities, of working class organic intellectuals, then it is not enough to create self-managing neighbourhood centres where these people can learn by doing, nor is it enough to seek to involve them in educational debates and training within community schools: in addition, it is essential that we enable them to critically reflect upon the new practice in which they are engaged. In brief, we need Northern College-type facilities throughout the country. This is not utopian; even within a situation of financial stringency, something approaching this is achievable.

Individual local authorities would not attempt to establish their own short course colleges: they would join with other authorities to form consortia so that such colleges could be established. A consortium would consist of three or four geographically-close authorities. After considerable planning, it would locate and utilise one secondary school deemed surplus to requirements, as a short course adult college. The college would be residential, for it would aim to provide weekend and week-long courses and so the building would have to be altered to allow for its new usage. This would involve expenditure, but as a consortium would be the parent body to the college, the expenditure of each member of the consortium would not be excessive. The college's short-course programme would be determined in a similar manner to the way in which Northern College determines its programme: that is, it would be the result of negotiation with community groups and organisations requiring short courses. A curriculum would not simply be offered; it would be negotiated and all curricula would aim to facilitate a critical reflection on the practice in which the students had been engaged. The college would probably come to run courses related to tenants associations, community centres, welfare rights and community education. It is also likely that the college would begin to explore an educational relationship with local Labour Movement as well as with the Workers' Educational Association. With regard to this area of its work, the college would be most valuable for it could begin to place on the agenda once more, the organisation of education in Britain. The Labour Movement, in general, has been supportive of comprehensive and community education; but it has been a fairly uncritical support. The college could help to remedy this situation.

The college would be the significant weld between the first two aspects of our strategy. Many of its students would come to it via their participation in their neighbourhood centres and they would go away from it more capable of entering into an involvement with their local community school.

Given financial restraints, how would the college be staffed? As community schools would aim for all their staff to be community tutors, then these professionals who had worked as community tutors would be freed from that role. Some of these erstwhile community tutors would work with the neighbourhood centres, as already stated, but many would eventually come to be the tutorial staff of the short course college. The consortium then would not be involved in recruiting and paying new staff; it would use its staff in a new capacity. In this staffing area, a consortium would not have to begin its work 'from cold', as it were, with no previous experience upon which to base its work. It would approach a college, such as Northern College, or The People's College of Northern Ireland, for assistance in its own establishment. It would attempt to arrange the secondment of a senior member of staff from one of these established colleges, who would help the new college to begin its work, along correct, tried and trusted lines. There would be some reciprocity here, for the community tutors who would come to staff the college would need to be trained, and to this end they would be seconded to the established colleges to work as tutors undergoing in-service training.

Even within a climate unsympathetic to public spending, this strategy could be pursued, for the majority of the resources required already exist. It is a matter of education authorities changing their educational philosophies and thus re-arranging their resource allocations; a re-structuring with some additional expense is needed, a wholesale commitment to massive new funding is not necessary. Each aspect of the strategy no doubt already exists as an aspect of a local authority's community education policy; neighbourhood centres in Sheffield, community schools in Australia and Folk High Schools in Denmark; our strategy aims to create an approach which welds the three aspects into one, in order to bring about long term educational change. We are concerned with changing an education which constantly and consistently reproduces educational failure among the working class and in order to bring about such change, there has to be an articulate working class challenge to bourgeois hegemony within education. The strategy aims to create the conditions for such a challenge to be made.

REFERENCES

1. For a discussion of the need for the ideological cleansing, see 'Marx and the Crisis in Education', Chap. 8. of B. Simon, Does Education Matter. Lawrence and Wishart 1985.
2. Adult Education: A Plan for Development. The Russell Report 1973. HMSO.
3. A New Approach to Adult Education. A Paper presented by the Academic Board to the Council of Management of the Northern College. July 7th 1983. p. 2.
4. J. Watts, Preface to G. Holmes, The Idiot Teacher. Russell Press 1977. pp. X/XI.
5. A. W. Gouldner, The Coming Crisis of Western Sociology. Heinemann 1971. p. 493.
6. For a brief but interesting discussion of the cultural aspects of class transfer associated with adult education, see J. O'Shea and P. Corrigan, Surviving Adult Education. In Vol. 52. No. 4. Adult Education, November 1979.
7. H. Rée. Network June 1984. CEDC.

Chapter Eight

INDIFFERENT TO THESE RIGHTS

"What's wrong with being patronising as long as it
makes money." (A B.B.C. Producer on '40 Minutes',
24/1/85)

Radical approaches to the education of adult members of the British working class have shown time
and time again that those whom education has judged
to be educational failures are, indeed, no such
thing. A radical approach to education consistently shows to working class people that they do have
brains capable of thinking on an abstract as well
as a practical level. Colleges specifically working with working class people stand as testimonies
to this educable capacity of the working class and
the educational practice of such colleges is valuable. It is, however, not enough for good educational work to be done with groups of working class
adults in different parts of Britain: not enough
for radical adult education to illustrate over and
over again how compulsory education 'has got it
wrong': not enough for radical adult education to
continue to carry out an educational salvage job on
the adult working class: it is time to seek to put
an end to the education system which makes Northern
Colleges necessary. Radical adult education must
have as its long term aim changing, and changing
utterly, the schooling system which systematically
fails the working class as a class. The lessons
learned in radical adult education, with regard to
curriculum and pedagogy, are of great relevance to
the compulsory education of children and their
relevance has to be made to impact on that education. Radical adult education has to influence
mainstream child education: the reproduction of an
education system, massively at odds with the interest of the working class, has to be brought to a
halt.
     This task cannot be carried out by radical
adult education acting alone; allies must be found
if the necessary struggle is to have a chance of

success. The natural ally is, of course, the working class itself, and specifically those sections of it who have benefited as students in a radical educational environment. There will be local education authorities which will welcome the possibility of better understanding the education system they operate, and they too can be potential allies. And community education has its use for it provides the access to education and school so essential if the working class is to enter an educational struggle/dialogue.

The strategy of Chapter Seven does offer us a way forward. We will end our discussion by pointing to a different educational future should our strategy not be adopted, but before sketching out that scenario, we must describe where we are now, for within our present can be seen the two strands which could be the keys to our future.

The Way We Are

The staff of our community school in Derbyshire was not particularly fluent in its explanation of community education, and consequently it was no difficult task to reveal the lack of impact community education was making, even on its own terms, in that school. This lack of fluency, however, is not so readily encountered when dealing with the more established community schools; those in Coventry and Leicestershire, for example; and we are in no doubt that in a few years, were we to visit Huntingdon once more, we would find a much more fluent argument and explanation of community education. The fluency of explanation, however, must always be seen as that, and in the first instance nothing more than that. We must not assume any necessary correspondence between the descriptive words being used and that which is being described. Midwinter, we remember, told us how important it was for education to advertise itself well, so that it could sell itself to people not usually interested in it, and much of his community education was about this selling of education by way of image presentation. And indeed, a decade later, much of community education can be seen in this light; an innovative packaging and advertising of a not very much altered product. The advertising has two aspects to it: first, it aims to enable education to be sold to its disinterested working class consumers, and second, it aims to sell community education as an advertising device

210

to those teachers and educationalists as yet not
constituent parts of community education. Community education is, as yet, only an educational
change undertaken by a minority of education authorities, and as such, it is engaged in a continuous
drive to sell itself to the majority and it attempts to do this by presenting fluent and sophisticated explanations of itself and its activities.
Within 'provided education', then, community education is engaged in a struggle so as to become a
taken for granted aspect of education. Whether its
practitioners realise it or not, they are attempting to make community education the way of working
educationally on the working class, so that it will
not oppose the way in which it is to be educated,
and in order to succeed they need to present community education in such a manner that they can win
over the noncommitted and unconvinced.

The relationship between products and their
advertising copy has always been a tenuous one and
we must bear this in mind when we encounter the
writings of community educationalists. Much of
what has been written about community education
comes from the pens of those who work as community
educators. One of the major difficulties associated with the old sociology of education, was its
location within colleges of education responsible
for training teachers and educationalists, for this
location tied the sociology of education too closely to the practice of education and this resulted
in a stifling of research and a narrowing of
critiques. A similar, and in many ways, more
critical state of affairs, now exists with regard
to community education, for most of its written
material comes from its practitioners. This means
that its authors have excellent day-to-day knowledge of what community education does, but they
cannot discuss or discover any 'why' of the doing
which would bring into question the value of the
doing. As a consequence, they generally make no
real enquiry as to the aetiological 'why' of community education, and instead, they tend to accept
the simplistic explanations which they and other
practitioners put forward. They confuse what an
education system is with how it is ideologically
presented. Thus they see the failure of working
class children in schools as a failure of the
education system, for schools should be about educating all, regardless of class: their concern
then is to remedy this fault within education's
system by making a strategy of home-schooling/

community education a part of education's system. They do not consider it a possibility that schools have, as one of their purposes, the failing of working class children: by not considering this they render themselves unable to assess critically their own strategies for dealing with this failing and they remain unable to see how their own strategies may relate to validating, in the eyes of the working class, the continued educational failure of its own children; they remain incapable of seeing how community education might well be part of an overall class and cultural struggle, aiming to negate in the class and cultural sense those whom they think they are serving. By far the vast majority of those writing about community education are unable to treat it as anything other than a good idea whose time has come.

The analysis of education, as offered by many community education writers, attempts to operate in a political vacuum with no sense of the historical. For example, a situation where schools once denied access to parents is contrasted with one where parental access is encouraged and the contrast is seen as an example of straightforward progress. No consideration is given to the possibility that both ways of dealing with parental access to school might serve the same ultimate end; and that such an end might be the assurance of education remaining firmly in the hands and control of the bourgeoisie. It is not considered likely that contradictory approaches to a subject may be appropriate according to conjuncture. Most community education writers take no cognisance of the political implications of education and community education and they fail to do so because they have little or no theoretical understanding of education.

> Community education development is likely to be tolerated only when it does not significantly affect élite control over knowledge accreditation and distribution.1

To this comment we must add that community education has to be seen as a way of ensuring the continuation of élite control over knowledge, etc., for its avowed purpose is to present to the working class a fluent explanation of education as it is, not as the class might wish it to be: it is to get parents to support schools, not to change them.

Taking the educational world for granted and being tied into and committed to community education, are aspects common to many who write on community education. Just as the old sociology of education experienced a caesura producing a new radical and more rewarding sociology of education, so too community education literature is in need of such a breaking. This work is part of such a process. Community educators have to learn that an understanding of the world does not come about as a result of accepting the explanations which phenomena offer for themselves; nor by believing the rhetoric which they, as advertisers for community education, themselves create.

Community education then is not an approach to education which pays any significant attention to its own origins and this restricts considerably the kinds of debate in which community educators engage. Community educators fail, as do their mainstream colleagues, to appreciate the contradictory nature of reform. They do not understand where reforms such as community education come from; nor what their purposes are and subsequently they confuse their hopes for a thing with the thing's purpose. This failure to appreciate the complex contradictory nature of reform is not merely a theoretical failing; it is one which has real effects in terms of the practice of education and community education. Within community education we give an example of this failing with reference to adults joining school classes as students. One of the major benefits held to accrue from this practice is the expectation that schoolchildren will regard the presence of adult students in their classes as evidence of the real value of what the school offers. The adult presence will help to alleviate "the critical state and the crisis of control" produced by the children "having to be there at all".2 The adult presence is to illustrate to the children the real value of the education offered to them. Such an illustration will help to lessen the disciplinary problems held to result from the children's failure to value the education which school offers to them. The community educator does not ask why children see school as they do, nor why they accord so little value to the education offered therein, nor is the question posed as to whether an education could be offered to the children which would be seen as worthwhile having from their point of view. The community educator looks only at the child's rejection of education and fails to question that which is being rejected. If that which is being rejected is not to be examined, then it is apparent that the adult presence can be seen as a way of helping to justify the refusal to examine the rejected education, for the adult presence physically states such an education is worth having. Thus a community educational reform can have the effect of diverting attention away from the real issue - in this case the curriculum, in the broadest sense of the term, offered in the school.

As well as failing to appreciate the contradictory nature of its own becoming, community education also fails to have a philosophy of education relating to its own present and practice. There are two important explanatory factors to this failing. First, community education operates with a model of the world which is essentially pluralist, a model which has groups and individuals aiming to pursue certain goals. The groups and individuals all have rights to define themselves and their goals, and none of their goals, nor definitions, are any more valid than those of their neighbours. In this model of the world there is no objective 'truth' other than the plurality of truths central to the model. Community education treats education in a similar manner: it refuses to accept that there can be such a thing as an objective analysis as to the purposes of community education (though any such objective analysis, for us, would not be without contradictions), and so sees no need for a philosophy for itself, because community education is not one thing: it can vary from city to city, school to school, and from one individual community educator to the next. The second explanatory factor relates to the nature of community education as advertising. Any advertiser for as long as the product to be advertised exists, must be engaged in a never-ending search for a more effective advertisement. Community education, as both the advertisement and advertising agency, is engaged in such a quest. In such a situation there is no philosophical guide to practice; the only guide in operation is concerned with the effectiveness of the image presentation. In Midwinter's language, is a spanking image of school and education offered?

Community education, if it has no real educational philosophy behind its practice, will engage in practice in a somewhat random manner. It will be seeking constantly to find new ways of presenting education and this will be its only real coherence. Even the limited aims of Midwinter, with regard to parental involvement, will come to

be forgotten as unlimited possibilities open up for
new advertising strategies to be pursued. What is
being advertised will become virtually irrelevant
as the advertising itself becomes all important.
This is, to a great extent, the current state of
play with regard to community education. Classes
are taken out of schools and into city centre
stores, colourful caravans are hired to tour council estates, bars are opened on community college
sites, community festivals are held in inner city
streets, and more and more schools 'go community'.
And as these things are happening, there are few
people asking, to what purpose? Why are such
things being done; how do they relate to an overall
aim; or are they aims in themselves, things to be
done for their own sake? Community education is
able to offer a superficially attractive explanation here; one that talks of blurring the distinc-
tions between school and community, of demonstrat-
ing that education is continuous and for life, that
learning can be fun and that schools are most
definitely changing. Under the surface, however,
little has changed in any significant manner. Community education is a gullible consumer of its own
P.R. material; it believes its own propaganda and
as long as it has no educational analysis or meaningful philosophy, it will continue to do so. One
retired citizen in a pottery class can become an
example of cross-generational learning and a steel
band playing in the school hall whilst curry is
consumed, an example of multi-cultural education in
practice.

Community education then can be seen as something of an approach which piles innovation on top
of innovation in order to persuade its community
that change has taken place within schools and
education: The visible innovations are presented
as the results of this change, its obvious mani-
festations. The question has to be asked, of
course, whether such innovations are genuine testimonies to change, or mechanisms to obscure the fact
that little change has taken place.

We would suggest that community education, in
practice, is an endless drive to engage in and
publicise examples of 'good practice'. It is well
on the way to being seen, by mainstream educationalists, as a good thing in itself. Being seen in
such a light is, to an extent, the result of the
hard work of community educators who have been
tireless in putting forward their case. They have
convinced mainstream colleagues and policy makers,

of various political persuasions, that community
education is the way forward for education. In
doing this they have re-presented the justifications and ideologies to be found in the mainstream
educational theories, vis-a-vis education and the
working class. They have posited community
education as a way of altering the culture of the
class, so as to make its existence less problematic
to the bourgeoisie, and they have sought to show to
the bourgeoisie how community education may be
seen, not only as posing no threat to it, but as a
possible saviour of it. They have offered
community education as a way of halting a rush to
violence, which they see as an ever-present threat.
In this they have a great deal in common with the
educationalists of the late eighteenth and early
nineteenth centuries, who offered the bourgeoisie
of their day education as the social penicillin to
ward off the sickness which had afflicted their
class cousins in France in 1789.

> In our day, the Educationalists are still what
> they were in Cobbett's time - the pretended
> friends, but real enemies of the people... You
> would educate us, not, as you sometimes
> pretend, to fit us for the exercise of politi-
> cal rights, but to make us indifferent to
> these rights.[3]

Though this comment comes from an edition of the
Northern Star in 1848, it has its relevance to
community education in the late twentieth century.
Having been formulated as something of an antidote
to any tendency towards insurrection, it is not
surprising that community education, in its practice, seeks to pose no threat to the order of
capitalist society. Its practice in the main,
takes no real account of the capitalist nature of
society with its fundamental conflict between capital and labour power. It is true that community
education would wish to remedy some of the most
glaringly obvious inequalities of capitalist society, but it wishes to do so in order to ensure
the reproduction of the type of society which can
give rise to these inequalities, and it believes
first and foremost in asking the permission of the
powerful so that remedial action may be undertaken.
When it does this, as Midwinter makes most clear,
it carefully explains to the powerful how their
power might be guaranteed continued existence by
its new servant. It asks the powerful to feel

sorry for those who are oppressed by the exercise of power and seeks to explain to the oppressed how they are part and parcel of the same community as those who oppress them. Community education in this arena is absurdly naive, for it believes that appeals to the better nature or compassion of the bourgeoisie will result in serious attempts being made to better the lot of the have-nots of capitalist society. As Lovett tells us:

> We do not inhabit a world in which spontaneous fellow-feeling can resolve our social problems. In a world of massive economic scarcity and brutal conflicts of interest, the politics of goodwill amount to a straightforward deception: their adherents are not confronting our problems in a new and more wholesome way; they are running away from them and taking their followers with them, leaving in the driving seat others, already in power, who have no intention whatsoever of wandering off in search of gentler pastures.[4]

Whether seeking to persuade the powerful to address the problems of the powerless, or presenting us with a brand spanking new image of education; community education stresses continually how schools have to be seen as integral parts of their communities and communities as resources for schools and partners to the dialogue concerning education. As has been one of our themes, we have to welcome community education for the contradictions it brings to the fore with the attendant possibility of their exploitation to the benefit of the working class. The first strand which could be a key to our future is this community presentation of education. We have to act as if we believe the advertiser's copy and take up the offer of involvement in schools and education. If they are to be changed, the working class has to be a party to, and to an extent initiator of, change.

As we have shown, there is a tradition within the working class for radical sections of it to be involved in education and educational struggle. The tradition has for some considerable time been dormant: the bourgeois struggle for the right to define education was, to a degree, a victorious one. Community education brings to us the possibility that this struggle over rights to definition can once again be a major item on the agenda for educational debate. Community education in its

aim to secure the compliance of the working class
with an educational system of little benefit to it,
places on the agenda the whole issue of control of
education and schools. It seeks to involve the
working class in education on education's own
terms, but the terms of involvement cannot be
rigidly guaranteed. As community education is a
liberal advertising of education, its liberalism
can be used for purposes opposed to those for which
it was adopted as a strategy. With Simon, we agree
that the task is no less a one than the transformation of the ethos and content of the education
given by the State's education system.

> The aim must be to define a content of
> education which both provides access to
> knowledge... and which systematically
> encourages mental development through
> promoting an understanding of both nature and
> society as they really are.5

Simon is strong in his insistence that all fatalistic notions concerning the impossibility of the
task should be abandoned. Though serious Marxist
critiques of education in capitalist society stress
its role as an agent for the reproduction of that
form of society, some of them are very 'non-Marx-
ist' in their analysis, for they ignore contradiction and seem to posit a bourgeoisie that can do
nothing but win, and often without having even
engaged in any form of struggle. Absolutely
central to our analysis is the concept of struggle,
for it is the engine which produces change which
resolves contradictions and in the very process of
their resolution gives rise to new ones. Community
education then seeks to resolve many of the cultural contradictions of education in capitalist
society and in so doing it brings to the fore the
contradictions of control of that education. This
most important contradiction must be seized upon:

> Every means must be found to strengthen local
> democratic control of the schools and school
> systems, and to provide scope for teachers,
> parents and school students to participate
> effectively in the government and control of
> schools.6

The Way We May Be

With Simon, we would hope very much to go

forward towards bringing about educational change
with all possible allies, but we part company with
him over the relatively simplistic way in which he
treats the key workers in this matter; that is, the
teachers. That teachers need to be allies is not
in question; the difficulty surrounds the way in
which they may be enlisted to the cause. Fictional
teachers like Ursula Brangwen and real teachers do
not, as stated in our first chapter, simply teach
as they would wish: they operate within an education system with its own rationale, its own views
of the world and its own ideologies. As operators
within this system, and having been trained to
operate within it, they internalise many of its
ideologies and beliefs concerning the education the
system operates. It is also the case that teachers
are workers who have to negotiate salaries and
conditions of service and, in order to do this,
they have to be able to claim specialist expertise
and knowledge: they claim, in effect, to be professionals. Whether they are to be paid the salaries they believe they need and to which they claim
to be justified is not an issue here: the issue is
the claim to professionalism. This claim is one
which fits very well into our analysis of education
within capitalist society where neither miner nor
mechanic is to be allowed to have any right over
education's definition. The rights to definition
will be allowed only to professionals. A claim to
professionalism for the purpose of salary increases
is one thing; it is quite another matter to make
claims to professional status in order to exclude
non-professionals from the debate. This form of
professionalism is a barrier to educational progress, for it denies a right to working class 'non-
professionals' to engage in the educational debate.
     Community education offers little hope as a
breaker of barriers here, for, despite its rhetoric, it is engaged in constructing its own claim
to expertise, to professionalism within the profession of teaching. It is community education which
aims to secure the support of the working class for
education as it is, professionalism and all.
     When we wrote of the two strands as keys to
our future, we had in mind the specific contradiction to which we now turn. The aim to secure
working class support, or community support as it
is usually described, can result in a working class
involvement which seeks to change school and education: on the other hand, it can result in a form
of community involvement which seeks to ensure that

no changes are made to education, that, if anything, the 'progressive' changes which have been made are reversed. To illustrate our argument here, we draw attention to two major educational disputes which occurred in Britain in 1985.

In Bradford, the Local Education Authority sought to discipline one of its Headteachers for writing an article in a right wing journal without having sought to discuss it prior to its publication. The article was strongly critical of the type of multi-cultural educational policy Bradford attempted to operate. The issue received considerable attention from the national media in Britain and was the subject of court cases. The union to which the Headteacher belonged supported his right to act as he had and regarded the local authority's claim to a right to disciplinary action as one which was at odds with, and a challenge to, the Head's professional judgement on matters educational. The Board of Governors of the particular school supported the Head against the Local Education Authority.

In Manchester, a school sought to expel a group of pupils for allegedly carrying out acts of vandalism on school property. They were alleged to have daubed obscene and racist graffiti on the walls of the school. The Local Education Authority opposed the expulsion of the pupils and a dispute came into being between the authority and many of the teachers at the school. The school's wish to expel the pupils was supported by its governing body and, as in Bradford, the relevant teaching union backed its members against the local education authority on the issue of professional expertise with regard to education. A member of the National Union of Teachers Executive for Greater Manchester summarised the issue thus: "It is a question of professional judgement. The judgement of the teachers is being challenged by people who do not work in schools and don't know schools."7

Our concern with both cases, lies not in the correctness or otherwise of the positions taken by the relevant unions, but in their positions being based upon the right of the professional to expect to have their professionalism unchallenged. In both cases, the teacher unions ask us to take for granted that with regards to things educational, teacher knows best. Not only do we disagree with such a notion but we see within these two cases cause for considerable concern. In both cases the governing bodies supported the professionalism of teachers. They wanted to ensure that the professionals remained in control; that local authorities did not alter the practice of allowing the professionals to decide school policy. We do not need to be possessed of particularly vivid imaginations to envisage a scenario wherein progressive local authorities and teachers might wish to bring about educational change only to be halted by governing bodies committed to a notion of education and professionalism intolerant of change. Community education, as part of education believing itself to be progressive, may actually hasten a situation where further progress is halted. In striving to bring about community involvement, it is possible that community education will succeed in involving only those who wish things to remain as they are, or indeed to 'turn the clock back'. A community say in education which results in strong support for traditional educational methods may well be seen as the device to put a stop to any meaningful progress. Thus, community education as the advocate of further community involvement in schools, could well become the agent responsible for reversing the limited progress made in the last decade or so. Community educators who believe in the liberal progressive nature of community education could well find themselves having helped to create an educational situation far from their liking. A community say in penal policy in Britain could well take us back a century, with people once again being hanged for a host of offences: so too, with education, a community say might well result in attempts to re-introduce corporal punishment on a large scale, to concentrate more on the supposed basics of education at the expense of the frills, one of which might well be community education itself.

Liberation and social control, with us two centuries past, have not disappeared: they are present still and exist as possible futures each capable of being struggled for by the classes with an interest in each approach to education to be provided by the State for the working class. If the working class is not able to make effective challenges, is not able to achieve some degree of control over the system which educates it, then the control which the bourgeoisie already has, will, without doubt, be strengthened and this cannot fail to be anything other than at odds with the interest of the working class. Local Education Authorities, groups of educators, and the Labour Movement have to come together to facilitate a self-education process capable of rising to this most crucial challenge. As community education frequently tells us in its advertisements, education is too important to be left to educators. So it is.

REFERENCES

1. E. Batten, Community Education and Ideology: A Case for Radicalism. In C. Fletcher and N. Thompson (eds) Issues in Community Education. Falmer Press 1980, p. 30.
2. R. Moore, Schooling and the World of Work. In I. Bates, J. Clarke, P. Cohen, D. Finn, R. Moore and P. Willis Schooling for the Dole: The New Vocationalism. Macmillan 1984, p. 72.
3. The Northern Star 29/1/1848. From B. Simon, Studies in the History of Education 1780-1870. Lawrence and Wishart 1960, p. 223.
4. T. Lovett, C. Clarke and A. Kilmurray, Adult Education and Community Action. Croom Helm 1983, pp. 154-155.
5. B. Simon, Does Education Matter. Lawrence and Wishart 1985, p. 186.
6. Ibid. p. 195.
7. Quoted in The Teacher (Newspaper of the National Union of Teachers) Vol. 42. No. 9. 25/10/1985.

Appendices

APPENDIX ONE: OPEN DOOR

Open Door is a neighbourhood centre located in Birley Moor Road, Sheffield. Its premises were once used regularly by Brightside & Carbrook Co-operative Society as a Dance Hall. When no longer used for dancing the premises stood empty for a considerable time and so fell into a state of disrepair. Consequently, between the City Council's leasing of the premises and the opening of Open Door, a large amount of cleaning, painting and decorating had to be carried out. This was done by those people in the area, who from the start, had been involved in what would become Open Door.

Open Door consists of one very large room, two small ones and a coffee bar. The large room is partitioned to allow for economical use of space. As a neighbourhood centre, Open Door is very well placed as it is directly above the Co-operative Supermarket, and as such, right in the middle of Birley Moor Road shops, which are used extensively by the people of the area.

Open Door's funding comes from the Departments of Adult Education and Employment. From its early days the centre wished to develop a neighbourhood approach to adult education, one which was not simply concerned with traditional evening classes and class numbers. With regards to unemployment:

> The aims of the centre were not 'tea and sympathy', not just to take people's minds off being unemployed, but to get people together to start asking questions.*

* From 'What is Open Door' by Estelle Clayton. (Estelle worked as a coffee bar assistant at Open Door. In 1985, she was a mature student at Sheffield Polytechnical College.)

Appendix One: Open Door

A range of activities takes place at, and is organised from, Open Door; from camping weekends in Derbyshire, to Women's Weekend courses at Northern College. The centre operates a crèche, a toy library, provides reprographic resources for the area, offers welfare rights advice and provides good, cheap snacks and lunches. The coffee/lunch bar is in many ways the heart of the centre, for many people do 'drop in' for a coffee or meal and this often proves to be the start of what becomes an involvement in the centre. The centre also acts as a base from which political campaigns can be run. Centre users have been active in campaigns concerning playgroups, eye clinics at the local Health Centre, housing, and during 1984/85, the Miners' Strike.

There is a staffing input from the Adult Education and Employment Departments, but it is accurate to say that these departments do not 'run' the centre: their staff assist the Management Committee in the running of the centre and the Management Committee is very much composed of local people who are active in their area. Open Door is a neighbourhood centre which allows the possibility of a working class self-education through participation; a self-education through coming together to engage in a practice of importance to all.

APPENDIX TWO: CHAPEL GREEN COMMUNITY PROJECT

The project was launched formally in March 1984, the culmination of two years hard work by a group of local people supported by several departments of Sheffield City Council. Among its aims, the project is concerned to provide a central base for local community groups in the Chapel Green area of the City and to provide job opportunities. The central base, a large building which once served as a Children's Home, now accommodates a variety of local groups. Meeting there regularly are groups of young people, pensioners, women and the unemployed. An advice centre operates in the building and a new branch of the Workers' Education Association has been formed within the project; a crèche operates as does a catering facility and the project is also well equipped with computers. With regards to the creation of job opportunities the project has had a measure of real success here.

The Management Committee has secured funding from Sheffield City Council, South Yorkshire County Council, the Department of the Environment, the Manpower Services Commission and the European Economic Community's Social Fund. This funding has been made available to renovate completely the building, to provide for adult tutorial salaries and to operate an horticultural project, in which able-bodied workers and physically and mentally handicapped workers will construct and run nurseries.

The project is committed strongly to the principles of self-management and accountability, and this commitment has, not surprisingly, driven the engine of self-education. The members of the Management Committee have had to learn a great deal in order that their day to day contact with departments of local and central government might be fruitful.   The engine of self-education, once started, is not easily stopped.   At Chapel Green this has been the case.

APPENDIX THREE: THE COMMUNITY WORK APPRENTICESHIP
SCHEME (CWAS)

The details concerning the scheme are taken from a
Sheffield City Council Paper, 'A Brief History of
Community Work Apprenticeship Scheme'.

The Sheffield City Council's Community Work
Apprenticeship Scheme (CWAS) originated in
proposals developed in 1980 within the
Employment Forum (which preceded the setting-
up of the Employment Committee), and then
approved in principle by the Policy Committee
on 25th November 1980. Initially the Scheme
was funded under section 137 of the 1972 Local
Government Act.

The Scheme was seen as part of an attempt
by the City Council to pioneer new forms of
employment which better match (a) the needs of
unqualified unemployed people and (b) the
demands being put on local government to
respond to the urgent needs of working class
communities.

The aims of the Scheme were summarised as:

1. to provide socially useful, full-time,
paid employment for local working class activists who wish to utilise their experience,
ability and political commitment in the service of working class people in Sheffield,

2. to provide a new model of employment for
the utilisation and development of the skills
and abilities of mature working people who
have not had the opportunity to develop their
work potential through lack of professional
"qualifications".

          *   *

Traditionally, recipients of Local Authority
services are depicted as passive, on the re-

227

cieving end of autonomous professional
"expertise". The Community Work Apprenticeship Scheme is part of a movement towards
replacing this notion of autonomy with the
concept of accountability to both users of
services and our City Council Management Committee who are answerable to "representative"
forms of democracy. The Scheme is committed
to working in the interests of services and so
accepts its responsibility to working people
in communities to provide them with competent,
skilful workers who have an understanding of
the needs of the community.

*   *

Sheffield City Council believes it should be
part of its employment strategy to open up
such jobs to working class men and women who
have the ability and some relevant skills but
not formal educational qualifications or specific skills and confidence which are often
assumed to be the result of further and higher
education. This is largely due to the inadequacy of the existing education and training
system.

Community and youth work related jobs
concerned with improving and democratising
services provide a clear opportunity to use
the experience and skills gained by working
class activists in the community and industry.
Through them the needs and demands of the
working class can be more clearly expressed.

A policy of recruiting working class
activists brings an opportunity to implement
specific Local Authority policies of positive
action in favour of black people (men and
women) and white women.

If working class men and women are to be
successful in taking on jobs in the public
service in community work and similar fields,
they require a programme of adult education
and training which will:-

a. validate and build on existing skills,
competence and understanding;
b. increase confidence and lead to the acqui-
sition of new and necessary skills, competen-
ces and understanding;
c. provide a framework of political and social
analysis which can both be the basis for reflection and practice in this area of work
within the State and also enable people to

work out the implications of their move from
unpaid activism to a paid worker, in a positive and creative fashion.

The City Council has committed itself to provide permanent jobs for the apprentices upon
their successful completion of the Community
Work Apprenticeship Scheme, but the Scheme's
training programme aims to equip apprentices
to work in a variety of employment situations
throughout the country.
        *   *
The CWAS provides training for mature, working
class adults who do not have formal qualifications.   This goes beyond a commitment to
'second chance' education for those who were
failed by or who were never given a 'first
chance' at school.   There is a clear role for
this sort of education and CWAS sees as important the fact that it provides socially useful
paid employment for local working class people
without formal qualifications.
        In addition, the skills, abilities and
experiences of working class adults who have
had experience of working collectively with
others can and should be used in organising
with other working class people.
        The working class is not seen as passive,
waiting for things to be done to and for them.
The experience and knowledge which trained
apprentices can bring to their work can add to
rather than substitute for the aims of local
people.
        The skills which the apprentice brings to
the Scheme are valid and the Scheme provides
an opportunity to build on rather than replace
them through the on-the-job and day-release
training.   The Scheme is aware, and values
highly, the different sorts of experience
which apprentices can bring into the Authority.
        A model of training and work that relies
upon the "transfer" of experiences, ability
and commitment of local activists into being
employed by the local state depends for its
success on the existence of substantial skills
and experience and understanding of collective
organisation.   Given that such skills are not
susceptible to 'traditional' measurement, i.e.
by academic qualifications, we have to apply

qualitively different yardsticks for selection
criteria that also take account of a variety
of cultural backgrounds and experience.
       One of the starting points of CWAS is
that, though essential, a working class background in itself is insufficient to provide
apprentices with the tools with which to assist other working class people to organise
for and defend their interests.

       Apprentices on the Scheme are workers
with the responsibilities of full-time workers. At the same time these workers are on
an apprenticeship and are receiving training
with the demands and responsibilities of workers in training.

APPENDIX FOUR: SHEFFIELD PENSIONERS ACTION GROUP
(SPAG)

SPAG is one of more than 220 individual branches of
pensioners organised throughout Britain, affiliated
to the British Pensioners and Trades Unionists
Action Association and subscribing to the National
Pensioners Convention's Declaration of Intent. SPAG
operates from attractive premises in the North
Gallery in the centre of Sheffield. Its offices
are open five days a week. SPAG's main aim is to
campaign for the improvement in rights and entitle-
ments of pensioners in Sheffield. Its Education
Officer told us the aim was to "co-ordinate pensioners in order to fight to improve their lot".

SPAG has close links with other pensioner
organisations as well as with Trades Unions.
SPAG's Secretary, Alice Sargent, stressed the need
for a constant process of education in order to
operate more efficiently. Not only do SPAG members
attend Northern College as 'students', but some
contribute as 'teachers' to the first year of the
Social Studies course at Sheffield Polytechnical
College, by discussing SPAG's work with the students following the course.

SPAG, then, is very much involved in education
and it relates this education to its work. What
its work is can best be seen in the article from
the Sheffield Morning Telegraph newspaper of February 23rd 1985, which we reproduce in full.

Elderly Fear The Worst

Pensioners in Sheffield feel that the Government is pulling services from under their
feet. A survey by the Sheffield Pensioners
Action Group asked pensioners what they
thought of existing services such as meals on
wheels, chiropody, day centres and hospital

aftercare. Almost 1000 people replied and
most felt that these services were inadequate.
Pensioners also feared the Conservative
Government was destroying the National Health
Service and Social Security system.

Seven out of every ten felt they were
worse off than five years ago. 'Local pensioners have never been so insecure and
angry', said spokeswoman Alice Sargent.
'We've worked all our lives to build up a
system, which is now being torn apart by this
Government. They seem to think that
pensioners are morons who don't matter. We
support the Council totally in their stand
against the Conservatives.'

Mrs Sargent added that most of the people
who answered the survey felt that their old
age pensions were inadequate and that they
feared that it would soon be cut even more.
'They are already trying to stop the £10
Christmas bonus, so I don't know where they're
going to stop, but we're going to fight them
all the way.'

The Group has 1200 members plus more than
10,000 affiliated through unions and other
organisations. Several members serve on
council committees and have been distributing
leaflets against the Government's policies for
the last month.

Mrs Sargent, herself aged 70, is on South
Yorkshire County Council. 'It is not the
local council's fault that pensioners are
badly treated', she said.

SPAG will have its fourth annual meeting
this Tuesday at 1.30pm, at Transport House, on
Harshead, Sheffield.

INDEX

Index

For Product Safety Concerns and Information please contact our EU
representative GPSR@taylorandfrancis.com
Taylor & Francis Verlag GmbH, Kaufingerstraße 24, 80331 München, Germany

* 9 7 8 1 1 3 8 2 2 5 2 9 9 *